RELIGION, BELIEF, AND SPIRITUALITY IN LATE LIFE

L. Eugene Thomas, PhD, (1932–1998) taught Human Development and Family Relations at the University of Connecticut since 1968. He was engaged in cross-cultural study of successful aging for the past two decades, conducting field work in the United States, India, England, and Turkey.

Susan A. Eisenhandler, PhD, graduated with highest honors from the University of Connecticut where she majored in sociology and was elected to Phi Beta Kappa. Professor Eisenhandler holds an MS (University of Wisconsin) and a PhD (University of Massachusetts) in sociology and has been a faculty member at the University of Connecticut at Waterbury since 1986. She teaches a variety of traditional sociology classes and has created new courses including: Women, Aging and Identity; The Literature of Aging, co-created with Glen MacLeod; and most recently, The Idea of Community: Communitas to Cyberspace. Her qualitative research on identity in old age has included work on the meaning of identity documents in late life, the management of stigma, and the meaning of relationships between older parents and their adult children. Her ongoing research explores the ways in which community-dwelling older adults define and experience religion and spirituality.

RELIGION, BELIEF, AND SPIRITUALITY IN LATE LIFE

L. EUGENE THOMAS
SUSAN A. EISENHANDLER
EDITORS

MaryAlice,

It seems that we
have been on this aging
journey awhile though one
we've only moved one
state from since our
UMASS days. Continued wishes for
aging well.

Best wishes!
Susan
22 September 1999

SP SPRINGER PUBLISHING COMPANY

Copyright © 1999 by Springer Publishing Company, Inc.

Springer Publishing Company, Inc.
536 Broadway
New York, NY 10012–3955

Cover design by Janet Joachim
Acquisitions Editor: Helvi Gold
Production Editor: Pamela Lankas

99   00   01   02   03/5   4   3   2   1

Library of Congress Cataloging-in-Publication Data

Religion, belief, and spirituality in late life / edited by L. Eugene
  Thomas and Susan Eisenhandler.
      p.   cm.
  Includes bibliographical references and index.
  ISBN 0-8261-1235-8
    1. Aged—Religious life.   2. Aging—Religious aspects.
I. Thomas, L. Eugene. 1932–1998.   II. Eisenhandler, Susan A.
BL625.4.R45   1998
200'.84'6—dc21   98-42897
                                                              CIP

Printed in the United States of America

This book is dedicated to the memory of L. Eugene Thomas. Gene was a pioneer in the qualitative study of aging and religion—he was an imaginative scholar whose research and writing opened new pathways in the domain of human science. His commitment and concern for students and colleagues will be recalled by many. His love for learning inspired others and added depth and richness to the study of aging and human development. Godspeed.

Contents

Contents

Contributors

W. Andrew Achenbaum, PhD, is a Professor of History at the University of Michigan, Ann Arbor, and Deputy Director of its Institute of Gerontology. He received his BA from Amherst College, an MA from the University of Pennsylvania, and his PhD from the University of Michigan.

Stephen Bertman, PhD, is Professor of Classical Studies at the University of Windsor in Windsor, Ontario. His books include *The Conflict of Generations in Ancient Greece and Rome, Doorways Through Time, Hyperculture: The Human Cost of Speed, and Cultural Amnesia: America's Future and the Crisis of Memory* (forthcoming).

Patricia C. Burke, PhD, is an adjunct professor at Cambridge College in Springfield, MA, and works as a training and writing consultant for corporate and non-profit clients. She has also taught human development and women's studies courses at the University of Connecticut. Her research focuses on the female identity-development process with special emphasis on changes in identity throughout the life span and the role of work in the identity-development process.

James J. Dillon, PhD, is Professor of Psychology at the State University of West Georgia. A life-span developmentalist by training, his research focuses on transitional periods across the life span.

Andrew Futterman, PhD, is Associate Professor of Psychology at Holy Cross College in Worcester, MA. His research focuses on religion and depression in later life.

François Garand III, is a graduate of Holy Cross College in Worcester, MA and is currently Supervisor of Student Technology Resources at Holy Cross College.

Joshua Haugh, a graduate of Holy Cross College in Worcester, MA is a Research Assistant at Massachusetts General Hospital and Harvard Medical School.

E. Olcay Imamoğlu, PhD, is Professor of Social Psychology in the Departments of Psychology and Gender and Women's Studies at Middle East Technical University, Ankara, Turkey. She has received her Master's degree from the University of Iowa and her doctorate from the University of Strathclyde, Scotland. Her research and writing have focused on exploring the interplay between the social-cognitive and environmental factors over the life span, with a special interest in gender issues.

Robert C. Kastenbaum, PhD, is Professor of Gerontology in the Department of Communication, Arizona State University, Tempe, AZ. He is editor of *The International Journal of Aging & Human Development and Omega: Journal of Death and Dying*. His books include *Defining Moments: Aging as Drama; Dorian, Graying: Is Youth the Only Thing Worth Having? The Psychology of Death*, and *Death, Society, & Human Experience*.

Susan H. McFadden, PhD, is Professor of Psychology at the University of Wisconsin Oshkosh. She is also an Associate Director of the Center on Aging, Religion, and Spirituality, St. Paul, MN.

Melvin E. Miller, PhD, has been interested in philosophy, narrative, and the creation of meaning for most of his life. His longitudinal research on the development of world views and religious perspectives naturally evolved from such interests. He received the PhD from the University of Pittsburgh. Since then, in addition to postdoctoral clinical and psychotherapy studies, he has twice been a Visiting Scholar at Harvard Divinity School. He is presently Professor of Psychology and Director of Psychological Services at Norwich University.

Stephen M. Modell, MD, earned his MD from the Medical College of Ohio in 1984 and received an MS in Clinical Research Design and Statistical Analysis from the University of Michigan in 1991. He was awarded Honorable Mention in the 1995 Nellie Westerman Prize Competition in Clinical Research Ethics of the American Federation for Clinical Research. Dr. Modell holds a research position in genetic ethics with the Department of Health Management and Policy at the University of Michigan's School of Public Health, where he is currently studying religious perspectives on aging and the human genome.

Robert L. Rubinstein, PhD, is Professor, Department of Sociology & Anthropology, at the University of Maryland, Baltimore County. A cultural anthropologist, he has conducted research in the United States and in Vanuatu (South Pacific). His areas of interest include death and dying, older men, and health and aging.

Lars Tornstam, PhD, is Professor of Sociology at the University of Uppsala Sweden. He has been the leader of the Swedish nationwide, cross-faculty, research program: *Elderly in Society: Past, Present and in the Future*. He holds the first Swedish chair in social gerontology and is the leader of The Social Gerontology Group at Uppsala University. The home page of the group informs about the wide range of research activities and publications: www.soc.uu.se/research/gerontology.

Foreword

The editors have collected a wonderful set of chapters with great significance for an understanding of aging and old age. These chapters attest to the vitality and creativity of people in later life and the continued drive of humans to make meaning of and to confront, at all ages, questions concerning the person and the spirit.

Several themes commend this book.

First, the editors and authors are working to push the study of religion, spirituality, and later life out of a "dark ages" of nescience. Although a simple stereotype might suggest that older people should be more interested in spirituality or religion than those of other ages, such an observation hides a complexity of experiences under an assertion of simple patterning.

Second, the editors and authors use the spectrum of qualitative research methods to describe the spiritual and religious experiences of the persons in their samples. Even in those chapters that present quantitative data, there is a recognition that qualitative methods are essential for understanding the personal experience and subjectivity inherent in each person's view of his or her life. Thus the editors and authors clearly emphasize the role of qualitative or ethnographic interviewing as key in terms of gaining access to the subjective world of religious belief and spirituality.

Chapters emphasize one or another kind of research interviewing to be sure, but under the umbrella of qualitative research, methods are varied. These include literary analysis (Bertman), intellectual biography (Achenbaum and Modell), illustrative biographical case studies (Miller), analysis of group interactions (Eisenhandler), dialogic approaches (Thomas), life narrative (Burke), analysis of letters (McFadden), as well as larger sample research (Imamoğlu) or research with supplementary qualitative interviews (Futterman, Dillon, Garand, and Haugh). This variability attests to the flexibility of qualitative research methods, as well as to the inherent difficulty in "getting at," comprehending, and expressing the subjective.

In this context, these methodological traditions also share another important attribute. They rely on an interaction between a person's subjectivity (his or her personal meaning system or personal accounting of life experiences) and some other vehicle to spring subjective experiences loose and to shape them into communicable form. This "other vehicle" can include another person such as an interviewer or a group member; a culturally sanctioned task, such as producing biography or narrative; or other, similarly reflective media such as writing letters or diaries.

A further important contribution of these chapters is that they take the emerging study of religion, spirituality, and aging into profound new directions. For example, work by Imamoğlu, including the chapter in this book, represents one of the very few sustained set of sources in English (with which I am familiar) to examine religion and aging in an Islamic context. Most of the chapters here present bright, newly articulated approaches to the study of subjectivity and community. They fulfill a promise in and of themselves and suggest pathways to continued exploration of spirituality and aging.

In these chapters, one cannot help but notice the overarching presence of Erik Erikson and his work on life-span development. He figures in some way in the chapters by Miller, Imamoğlu, McFadden, Futterman and colleagues, and Tornstam and, along with his wife Joan, forms the subject matter of the chapter by Achenbaum and Modell. The profound impact of his work on understanding culturally patterned life-span development and personhood in later life continues to be both influential and useful as an organizing framework for religious experience over the life span. The focus of so many of these chapters is thus around issues of personal growth and development and about the role of spiritual life and evolution in them. This focus suggests an important role of spirituality in development in the last part of life, and the chapters point in exciting directions concerning the specifics of how this might work out.

Interestingly, much of what is written in this book is poised between transcendental goals in a developmental sense (as, for example, in the important notion of gerotranscendence developed by Tornstam) and the more pragmatic domain of problems and activities of everyday life, for example, the use of spiritual techniques to face health problems, dissipating energies, and difficulties with undertaking some everyday activities (McFadden). Indeed, it may be that the essence of spirituality in later life is found in the close linking of daily tasks and activities, physical health and bodily conditions, with an evaluative stance of transcendence that permits a reconsideration and reevaluation of everyday life.

Some chapters focus on informants who might be labeled as spiritual masters or spiritual elite, for example, those who spent long periods in reflection on the spiritual or developmental component of one's own or humanity's life course. These include sages (Bertman), the Eriksons (Achenbaum and Modell), "especially spirited research participants" (Miller), a very special, lifelong thinker about religion (McFadden), and a small sample culled from a larger sample of persons experiencing gerotranscendence (Tornstam). In contrast, other chapters speak to more ordinary persons and their spiritual searches and experiences.

This is an important book on an important subject. When reading and writing about "the elderly" we must always remember that this is a false "otherness," as those of us who are not elderly are likely to become so. Given this perspective, the active focus on spiritual life by so many who are old and the particular ways in which spirituality and religion become subjectively meaningful are critically important, because they are maps of the territory through which all of us have passed or are likely to pass.

—ROBERT L. RUBINSTEIN
University of Maryland, Baltimore County

Research on Religion and Aging— Mapping an Uncharted Territory

L. Eugene Thomas
Susan A. Eisenhandler

G Stanley Hall (1922), in his seminal book on "senescence," denigrated the place of religion in old age, characterizing it as a necessary fiction for weak souls who lacked the courage to confront aging without delusions. Carl Jung, on the other hand, writing a decade later, observed, "Among all my patients in the second half of life . . . there has not been one whose problem in the last resort was not that of finding a religious outlook on life" (1934). It would seem that Hall's point of view has prevailed in the field of gerontology from its inception until recent years. The situation has begun to change in rather dramatic ways, however, with a burgeoning of research and interest in religion and aging in just the past decade.

This growing interest in religion by gerontologists and others working with the elderly has been widely noted. Moberg (1996), in a review essay of recent books on religion and aging, subtitled his article "From benign neglect to belated respect" (p. 264). This growth in interest in religion and aging seems to be especially concentrated on the area of health, both physical and mental. It is significant that of the seven books that Moberg analyzed in his review essay, four were devoted to the topic of health.

Another sign of the growing awareness of the importance of religion by gerontologists is suggested by a special symposium devoted to aging and mysticism at a recent meeting of Gerontological Society of America (GSA) (Atchley, 1997). The fact that such a topic would be given serious attention at the annual scientific meeting of the GSA is itself an indication of changes in attitude toward religion among gerontologists—at least—public statements they are willing to make on the topic, as opposed to the private interest they may have held, that had heretofore remained "in the closet." At this particular symposium, several presenters, as well as responses by members of the audience, stressed the point that we can't fully understand development in the later years without taking into consideration the religious and spiritual dimension. In particular, they stressed the importance of religion in helping prevent the increasing inwardness of aging from degenerating to narcissism.

CONCEPTUAL IMPLICATIONS

These two outwardly dissimilar concerns—that is, seeking to understand the relation of religion and important issues related to aging (such as health), and making use of religious insights to understand the normal personality development in old age—are not—unrelated. The truth of the matter is that in order to understand the place that religion plays in health, or any other issue related to aging, we must have a fuller understanding of the existential meaning that religion holds for the individual. To be sure, there can be empirical studies in which various religious variables (institutional beliefs, religious participation, etc.) are correlated with health, or other variables of interest. Yet limits of this "black box" approach (i.e., in which grossly defined religious belief and participation variables are given as input, with various health characteristics, for example, are examined as the outcome) are apparent. Even if we had high and consistent correlates between religion and these other variables, we still would not be helped to understand why these correlations hold, or what they really mean.

For this we need to know much more about the ways in which religious beliefs and behavior impact on personality, and how this maps onto life satisfaction, health, or whatever other areas of aging that are of concern. In order to tease out these processes, we need to know far more about religion than what institutional beliefs an individual does or does not subscribe to, and more than how frequently they attend corporate worship and engage in private prayer.

First, we obviously need to know more about the content of the religious beliefs themselves. For example, we need to know more about a person's beliefs about the existence of God or belief in life after death than a check mark of "yes" or "no" on a questionnaire, which can tell us little. The reluctance of most social scientists to grapple with the theological intricacies of religious beliefs is understandable, in view of their lack of philosophical or theological training. To throw all religious beliefs into a few convenient hampers is not poor theology, however, but it is poor social science as well. The finer the distinctions that we can make, the more robust and meaningful the findings we are likely to uncover. For instance, if a person's belief in life after death carries with it the specter of eternal damnation, this is likely to have considerably different psychological consequences for the individual than if he or she holds a more benign view of life after death. To lump these varied beliefs together in some omnibus variable labeled "belief in immortality" obscures what, for the individual, might be crucially important distinctions. The same problem no doubt holds when religious behavior is indiscriminately assigned a numerical value ("attends religious services X number of times a month," etc.) without giving attention to the content and religious significance of the behavior.

In addition to the content of religious beliefs, we also need to know what these beliefs and behavior mean to particular individuals. From the content of a person's belief in life after death, for example, we might make an informed guess as to whether assent would give an individual comfort or raise more anxiety about death. But even knowing the theological content of a belief, there are nuances and idiosyncrasies of individual cognitive worlds that make it hazardous for us to impute the meaning or importance that an individual might place upon a particular belief, without having more information from the individual. For instance, one person might believe in a benign afterlife, and take comfort from the fact that they anticipate meeting loved ones when they die, while another person might hold a similar belief about the afterlife but find the prospect of confronting individuals there with whom they have unresolved conflict, to be anything but pleasant to anticipate. Belief in an immortality and a "benign" afterlife, given these individual circumstances, might well have positive or negative valence for an individual, depending upon the idiosyncratic associations they might hold.

RESEARCH IMPLICATIONS

These examples border on the obvious and trivial. They point out, however, the fact that the content of religious beliefs and the meaning that these particular beliefs hold for an individual are far from insignificant. This, in turn, has important implications for research on the relationship between religion and aging. It obviously means that social scientists need to be more sophisticated in the way we define religious beliefs and practices, and spirituality. Despite the fact that most social scientists aren't theologically trained, it is necessary that we at least be aware of the complexities of religious beliefs that we study, and the meaning that various religious practices hold for individuals, and seek to do justice to this complexity in our research designs.

Further, the fact that we need far more information about the nature of beliefs and practices, and the personal meaning that they hold for an individual, has far-reaching methodological implications. It seems clear that what is required is a more sophisticated research methodology than that typically used in quantitative social science research, which in turn points to the need for a more inclusive research paradigm. We have suggested elsewhere (Thomas, 1989) that the Human Science paradigm offers a more expansive framework for theory and research in gerontology, which is needed if we are to do justice to the complexity of meaning and purpose in our study of aging. This would seem to be especially important in the study of aging and religion, for which meaning and purpose is the quintessential focus. The Human Science paradigm, which draws upon the humanities as well as the social sciences, allows for qualitative as well as quantitative methodology. This approach offers an expanded palette for theoretical and methodological approaches that are needed to work on a canvas, which does justice to the contents and meanings attached to religious beliefs and practices.

CHARTING AN UNKNOWN TERRITORY

Having stated the issue in abstract theoretical terms, the situation might be characterized metaphorically with reference to geographic exploration and early attempts at map construction. It might be said that researchers in the field of religion and aging are in many ways like the members of the Lewis and Clark expedition, when they set out to chart the Louisiana Purchase at the beginning of the 19th century. It will be remembered that President Jefferson gave the explorers the charge to determine if there existed a navigable passage to the Pacific Ocean, and along the way to make general maps of the vast new territory and bring back specimens of the flora and fauna of the different regions. Given the vastness of the territory, there was no possibility that Lewis and Clark and their small crew could make detailed maps of the area. If they had tried to make detailed maps as they went along, they would have been mired in a task that would take decades to complete. What they, and the young Republic first needed to know was the overall dimensions and characteristics of the new territory, in order to determine what further detailed information might be needed (e.g., if they had found a navigable Northwest passage, there would have been more demand for information about river depths and the direction of tributaries, than in the types of plants and the extent of mineral deposits to be found in the territory).

It isn't stretching the analogy to suggest that, like the huge Louisiana Territory, the field of religion and aging is a vast and relatively uncharted area. We are just beginning to get field reports on narrow areas of the territory, particularly in the areas of religion and health. At the present time, the field of religion and aging might well be characterized by James Birren's description of the field of psychology and aging in general, which he described as "one of scattered islands of more or less densely packed information" (1988, p. 155). Our "islands" of knowledge in the field of religion and aging aren't as densely packed as other areas of information in the field of psychology and aging (e.g., cognition and memory), but like the larger field, we need charts and maps to see how the individual pieces of information fit together, and, perhaps more importantly, to determine significant areas that have been neglected.

A further instructive comparison with the Lewis and Clark Expedition concerns the potential sources of information about the new territory. The explorers started their trip with only rudimentary maps. As they moved beyond their jump-off point of St. Louis they were keenly aware that they were going where no White man had gone before. But what they tended to forget was that although White men had not passed there before, the territory was far from unexplored—Native Americans had made these plains and hills their homes for centuries. On occasion the explorers, as a last resort, did seek information from friendly Indian tribes as they desperately sought to find connecting rivers and passable mountain passages. But on the whole they went about their work as if they were the first humans to pass through these lands. One wonders how the expedition might have been helped to avoid unnecessary hardships, and the scope of its findings enriched if the explorers had engaged interpreters who could systematically draw on the knowledge and understanding of those indigenous inhabitants who had long lived on the land.

We don't want to push this analogy too far, but there are striking similarities to the present field of religion and aging. Researchers entering this field are keenly aware of the absence of previous social science research, rendering the field for them virgin and uncharted. But what they, like Lewis and Clark, tend to forget is that the field is far from uncharted. There have been indigenous inhabitants in this territory, so to speak, who have grappled with issues of meaning and purpose, and religion and spirituality from time immemorial. To be sure they were not social scientists (analogously, not "White men"), but the religious and sacred traditions they have mapped—deposited in sacred texts, philosophy, literature, theology, folklore, myths and legends—provide a rich source of information and understanding. To undertake to survey the vast territory of religion and aging without consulting the work of these indigenous experts would seem to be foolhardy, indeed.

Of course, we have not only the writings that they left us from the past, but we have in our midst today philosophers and theologians, along with literary analysts and historians, and a whole range of scholars, who are far more conversant with the issues relating to religion and the existential human condition, than are most social scientists. It would seem only logical that social scientists interested in religion and aging should draw upon the expertise of these "natives" who now inhabit the land of our "uncharted territory. And for this, the human science paradigm provides a broader grid that can use methods and approaches developed in areas other than traditional social science, while drawing on the skills of the social sciences to add precision to the maps when needed. We would fully agree with Birren, that "aging is too important to leave to the scientists, but also, it is too important to leave to the theologians and humanists" (1988, p. 172).

INTEGRITY, REFLEXIVITY, AND RELIGION

As Rubinstein notes in the Foreword to this volume, Erikson's theory of life-span ego development is used by a number of the authors. This is due, no doubt, to the fact that Erikson's theory is really the only comprehensive life-span model we have in the current social science literature. His concept of Ego Integrity, the final stage of development in the life cycle, has received wide attention not only within the social sciences, but in the popular culture as well. In one of his earliest formulations of the concept of Integrity, Erikson notes, "It is a post-narcissistic love of the human ego—not the self—as an experience which conveys some world order and spiritual sense, no matter how dearly paid for" (1950, p. 268). Likewise, his concept of wisdom, as the accompanying "virtue" of this stage of life, has had major impact on both professional and lay thought. Concerning wisdom, Erikson notes that it is "detached concern with life itself, in the face of death itself" (1964, p. 133).

The twin concepts of postnarcissistic love and the facing of death itself point out the reflexive nature of the aging process, and the reflexive nature of the subject matter of those who would study this process. That is, the researcher, who him/herself faces the same human situation of overcoming narcissistic self-concern in the face of eventual death, cannot remain indifferent to these issues—they are a matter of life and death. Indeed, Birren and Renner have noted that "Aging is a major aspect of life onto which our metaphors project our uncertainties, fantasies, fears, and unresolved ambitions" (quoted by Birren, 1988, p. 172), the chief of these fear, no doubt, being the awareness of our own finitude and impending death.

When we come to such existential issues as these, we are clearly dealing with religious questions, or what theologian Paul Tillich (1951) termed "ultimate concern." In defining what he means by the term, Tillich notes that it is "the abstract translation of the great commandment: 'The Lord, our God, the Lord is one; and you shall love the Lord your God with all your heart'" (1951, p. 11). And he notes that he uses the term "concern" to point to the existential character of the religious experience.

Jung places even more emphasis on the place that religion plays in addressing the chief existential question that many (such as Martin Heidegger) consider the defining reality of our human condition, namely the questions raised by the prospect of our own death. And, of course, this brings us immediately into the area that has traditionally been the concern of religion. Carl Jung, in his essay on "The Soul and Death," observes that the great majority of the world's religions might be seen as "complicated systems of preparation for death" (1934/1969, p. 408).

We suspect that one of the reasons that Erikson is looked on as arguably the major theorist of the human life cycle lies in the fact that he seeks to grapple with these reflexive "existential" issues. It isn't by chance that his concept of "integrity" has come to hold so pivotal a position for those who seek to understand the last stage of personality development. Although Erikson didn't spell out explicitly the full religious implications of his theory, there can be little doubt that his formulations leave room for the importance of religion in the last stage of life. Stated differently, his theory would probably not have received the continuing attention from social gerontologists and others if it did not deal with the reflexive existential questions of postnarcissistic love, and the reality of death.

ENLARGING THE MAP

We have used the metaphor of physical territory and map-making to suggest the task faced by those who undertake the study of religion and aging. The very concreteness of this metaphor—charting mountains and rivers and physical distances—misses the self referential heart of religious concerns, however. What is missing, and is too often missing in social science research on religious beliefs and practices, is the dimension of religion caught up in terms like "purpose," "meaning-making," and "spirituality."

E.F. Schumacher (1977) concludes his seminal book, *A Guide for the Perplexed*, with the observation: "The modern experiment to live without religion has failed" (1977, p. 139). By "living without religion," he explains that he does not mean living without churches, but rather without serious grappling with the larger issues of meaning and purpose. And Jung, writing over half a century ago, reminds us that failure to grapple with these issues leads to meaninglessness, adding prophetically, "The lack of meaning in life is a soul-sickness whose full extent and full import our age has not yet begun to comprehend" (1934/69 p. 415).

The impact of the loss of meaning in modern life would seem to fall especially heavily upon the elderly. Robbed of the illusion of endless future expansion and development, indeed, faced with the inevitability of decline and eventual death, the elderly bear the brunt of this modern "condition." The truth of the mater, however, is that the religious dimension has not disappeared from the lives of the elderly, any more than it has disappeared from society. The fact that until recently religion has not appeared on the radar screens of social gerontologists does not mean that it has not bee present and influential in the lives of older individuals. On the contrary, as the chapters in this volume indicate, and as the burgeoning of research on religion and aging testifies, religion has played, and continues to play an important role in the lives of the elderly over the centuries.

The question that remains for social gerontologists, and for others concerned with understanding and serving the elderly, is to determine what, exactly, is the role that religion, and particularly spirituality, plays in the life of the elderly. The authors of the chapters in this book seek to identify some of the dimensions and approaches needed to map this uncharted territory.

To refer to the field of religion and aging as "uncharted territory" is to return to the geographical metaphor utilized earlier. There is a danger of allowing a physical metaphor to define a field as broad and multifaceted as religion and spirituality. Rather than changing metaphors, it might be useful to remind ourselves that maps can be more than representations of cut and dried physical dimensions. We only have to remember that in addition to geographical maps, maps can be used to portray everything from weather to population to radioactive emissions. No one map represents "reality"—rather each map presents a selected aspect of reality as conceptualized and defined by the cartographer. In the present situation, the Human Science researcher can use dimensions to map those levels of reality, often beyond the physical dimensions of denominational affiliation and religious attendance, which appear to be of relevance to individuals as they grapple with aging, and their inevitable decline.

Taking this analogy, it might be said that this book is a beginning work in developing such varied maps. Utilizing the varied textures provided by the humanities and the social sciences, the chapters in this book offer suggestions for delineating the field of religion and aging, and various methods that might be used in studying this elusive field. Unlike the physical map of the geographer, with exact reference to physical dimensions of the topography, at this point the dimensions of the field of religion and spirituality, and even the relevant variables that need to be studied, must be painstakingly identified. But we do need overviews of the field that can help us see where the various parts might fit together. We hope the emerging maps that different investigators develop can help us better to understand the scope of the field and provide some guidance as we proceed with more focused studies of areas of particular relevance. Or to put it another way, such cartographic overviews, as limited as they are, may help us not to lose sight of the larger existential questions that make the field religion and spirituality exciting for us jointly to explore.

REFERENCES

Atchley, R. C. (1997, November). *Mysticism: The experience of spirituality.* Symposium presented at the 50th Annual Scientific Meeting of the Gerontological Society of America, Cincinnati, OH.

Birren, J.E. (1988). A contribution to the theory of psychology of aging: As a counterpart of development. In J. E. Birren & V. L. Bengtson (Eds.), *Emergent theories of aging* (pp. 153–176). New York: Springer Publishing Co.

Hall, G. (1922). *Senescence: The last half of life.* New York: Appleton.

Jung, C. J. (1969). The soul and death. In *The collected works of C. G. Jung*. (Vol. 8, 2nd ed.). Princeton, NJ: Princeton University Press. (Original work published 1934)

Moberg, D. O. (1996). Religion in gerontology: From benign neglect to belated respect. *Gerontologist, 32*, 264–267.

Schumacher, E.F. (1977). *A guide for the perplexed*. New York: Harper & Row.

Thomas L. E. (1989). The human science approach to understanding adulthood and aging. In L. E. Thomas (Ed.), *Research on adulthood and aging: The human science approach* (pp. 1–10). Albany, NY: State University of New York Press.

Tillich, P. (1951). *Systematic theology* (Vol. 1). Chicago: University of Chicago Press.

Creating and Understanding the Text of Late-Life Spirituality

A Handful of Quietness: Measuring the Meaning of Our Years

Stephen Bertman

> *Better is a handful of quietness,*
> *Than both the hands full of labour*
> *And striving after wind.*
> —*Ecclesiastes 4:6*

T
he process of aging offers us a progressively wider perspective on the to-tality of our lives. In effect, the higher we climb the mountain, the farther we can see.

From such a perspective we can make out the path our life has followed and the failures and successes we have had along the way.[1] To our sadness, we may realize that we will never fulfill the dreams of our youth. Yet to our joy, we may discover another standard to more truly measure the meaning of our years.

Such philosophical insights have been voiced from civilization's earliest days and are recorded in masterpieces of literature that date from antiquity to the modern era.

SMALL THINGS AND HAPPINESS

In his old age, King Solomon marked the futility of pursuing grand designs. Instead, he counseled, we can only find true happiness by recognizing the preciousness of each moment. In effect, it is in the small things of our lives, rather than in the big, that happiness lies.

According to tradition, King Solomon set down his observations in the biblical book of Ecclesiastes. The recurrent theme of his reflections is summed up in his repeated use of the Hebrew word *havel*, a word that means "a transient breath of air" but is often translated in English as "vanity" to convey its sense of emptiness and impermanence. "Vanity of vanities," proclaims Solomon. "All is vanity" (Gottheil, 1917, Eccles. 1:2).

Solomon then proceeds to describe his search for lasting happiness and how futile the search turned out to be. Although he possessed the power of a king to command every pleasure, he found that none endured. He had the vast wealth of a king, but he knew after death his riches would be his no more. Even the search for wisdom caused him only frustration and pain. "I have seen all the works that are done under the sun; and, behold, all is vanity and a striving after wind, a crookedness not to be straightened, a void not to be filled." (Gottheil 1917, Eccles. 1:14; Gordis, 1968, Eccles. 1:15)

Rather than looking for permanence in an impermanent world or justice where there is none, he concluded, we should graciously accept what each new day grants us.

> I know there is no other good in life but to be happy while one lives. Indeed, every man who eats, drinks and enjoys happiness in his work—that is the gift of God. . . . Enjoy life with the woman whom you love, through all the fleeting days of your life, which God has given you under the sun, throughout your brief days, for that is your reward in life for your toil under the sun (adapted by Gordis, 1968, Eccles. 3:12–13, 9:9)

Many centuries before Solomon, a similar conclusion was reached in ancient Babylon. In the *Epic of Gilgamesh*, a hero searched for the secret of eternal life. During the course of his quest, Gilgamesh met a goddess who offered him this advice:

> Gilgamesh, why do you rove?
> The life you pursue you shall not find.
> When the gods created mankind,
> Death for mankind they set aside,
> Life in their own hands retaining.
> Gilgamesh, let your stomach be full,
> Make merry by day and by night.
> From each day make a feast of rejoicing,
> Day and night dance and play.
> Let your garments be sparkling fresh,
> Your head washed, your body bathed.
> Pay heed to the little one that holds on to your hand,
> Let your wife delight in your embrace.
> For this is humanity's portion! (adapted, Speiser, 1958, Tablet X)

To be sure, not everyone in ancient Babylonia abided by this advice. For millennia the fertile valleys of the Tigris and Euphrates were ravaged by war as kingdom vied with kingdom for greater power and glory. Today, their dreams of domination lie in the mud and dust. The Hanging Gardens of Babylon, once counted among the Seven Wonders of the World, are but a ruin.

THE QUEST FOR IMMORTALITY

Of the legendary Seven Wonders, only one survives: the Great Pyramid of Cheops. Egypt's pyramids may ultimately prove the most enduring works of mankind. Should alien archaeologists someday set foot on a desolate and deserted planet Earth, it will be the pyramids that will greet them as humanity's final message to the cosmos. As such, the pyramids will stand as an ironic testament to the vanity of human wishes and the futility of grand designs. Despite their massive and forbidding bulk, each one of Egypt's pyramids was robbed in ancient times, thus denying the pharaohs the blessed eternity they had sought by surrounding themselves in death with their golden treasure.

The futility of such efforts was recognized by an anonymous Egyptian poet, who doubted there was even an afterlife for which to prepare. His words still survive on the wall of a Middle Kingdom tomb:

> Those who built tombs,
> Their walls have crumbled,
> Their places have gone,
> As though they had never been.
> None comes from there
> To tell of their state,
> To tell of their needs,
> To calm our hearts,
> Until we go where they have gone.
>
> Hence follow your heart as long as you live!
> Put myrrh on your head,
> Dress in fine linen.
> Anoint yourself with oils fit for a god.
> Follow your heart and your happiness!
>
> Lo, none is allowed to take his goods with him.
> Lo, none who departs comes back again.
>
> (Lichtheim, 1973, abridged and adapted).

RAMSES II

Of all of Egypt's pharaohs, none was more ego driven than Ramses II, whose monuments far outnumbered his rivals', in part because he ruled the longest of Egypt's kings, dying at the age of 97 after a 66-year reign. Yet even Ramses' bid for immortality was blunted by time. As Shelley later wrote in his poem "Ozymandias,"

... Two vast and trunkless legs of stone
Stand in the desert ... Near them, on the sand
Half sunk, a shattered visage lies ...
Nothing beside remains. Round the decay
Of that colossal wreck, boundless and bare
The lone and level sands stretch far away.

If ancient Near Eastern history teaches us any mortal lesson, it is the frailty of human ambition. It is a humbling lesson every preening dictator of today should, but will not, harken to. Yet there are also lessons for the rest of us as well. In the "late life" of civilization, it is still not too late to learn, as we shall soon see.

When it comes to cultures, it is usually from their monuments that we know them, big monuments that trumpet big ideas. But hidden in the shadows of those monuments are people, individual human beings, whose voices are not so readily heard.

THE MIRACLE OF LOVE

Compared to Homer's epic poems, whose heroic dimensions tower over the Greek literary landscape, the poems of Sappho appear as miniatures. Small and personal (most survive as only a few verses in fragmentary form), they bear poignant witness to the miracle of love.[2] In her poetry, Sappho challenged the entire heroic value system that had assigned the highest place to victory in war and to the deeds of war by which manhood was measured. Instead, she scaled down life's most important ratio from thousands against thousands (army against army; fleet against fleet) to one to one.

There are those who say
an array of horsemen,
and others of marching men,
and others of ships, is
the most beautiful thing on the dark earth.
But I say it is whomever one loves ... (Groden, 1966, Fragment 16)

A century later another Greek poet named Praxilla, contemplating her own death, would write,

Loveliest of what I leave behind is the sunlight,
and loveliest after that the shining stars, and the moon's face,
but also cucumbers that are ripe, and pears, and apples.
(Lattimore, 1960, Diehl 2)

Perhaps such sentiments cannot be described as religious in the strictest sense, but they are religious none the less for they provide "a sense of place in a larger reality" (Thomas, Kraus, & Chambers, 1990). They testify to the existence of a spiritual perspective, a value system stripped of social construct but mystically empowered, a system in which what matters is not rank or power, wealth or privilege,[3] but a vital bond between one human being and another or between one human being and the natural world.

MAN AND NATURE

The theme of nature, and in particular man's relationship to it through agriculture, occurs frequently in the lore and literature of ancient Rome. Although we tend to think of the Romans as affluent city dwellers, the economy of ancient Italy was always fundamentally agrarian, and the simple life of the farmer had enduring appeal for an increasingly harried and urbanized society. Thus, the theme of agriculture appears in the writings of some of Rome's most celebrated authors (Cato the Elder, Cicero, Lucretius, Horace, Virgil, and Ovid) and, significantly for us, in connection with late life.

Indeed, the theme is woven into the most famous ancient commentary on aging, Cicero's essay *De Senectute* (*On Old Age*). After a lifetime of political service to Rome's republic, 62-year-old Cicero looked toward retirement and the peaceful life of a gentleman farmer, "to the pleasures of agriculture, in which," he wrote, "I find incredible delight . . . In them I think a man makes the nearest approach to the life of a sage" (Hadas 1951, Ch. XV).

What few realize is that Cicero wrote those words at a time of great political turmoil and personal grief. His second marriage had recently failed; his favorite child, a daughter, had died. Julius Caesar, whose dictatorship had threatened civil liberties, had just been assassinated, and Cicero, who along with others had opposed the dictatorship, was put on Mark Antony's "enemies list." Within a year he would be unjustly executed.

Within this context Cicero sought the consolation of philosophy. Like Solomon, he had discovered in his late life that "better is a handful of quietness, than both the hands full of labour and striving after wind" (Gottheil, 1917).[4]

Following Cicero's death, Octavius Caesar, later named Augustus, became Rome's first emperor. With the coming of the Augustan Age, new writers arose to celebrate the end of political chaos and the return of order. Among them was a poet named Virgil.

In his early works, Virgil praised the spiritual rewards of agriculture. In one passage, for example, he told the parable of a humble peasant who owned only a few acres of land, yet "he equalled in his contentment of mind the wealth of kings" (Bryce 1908, Georgics, 4:127ff).[5]

GRAND ILLUSIONS

Virgil, however, was soon called on by none other than Augustus' prime minister to compose another sort of poem, a grand epic that renewed pride and patriotism in his countrymen. The result was the *Aeneid*, one of the masterpieces of Western literature.

The *Aeneid* is the saga of a Trojan prince named Aeneas, who sails across the sea and endures great hardship, leading his followers to Italy so they could found a new nation in fulfillment of their god's will, a Roman nation destined to rule an "empire without end" (Aeneid 1:279).

Virgil spent the last 10 years of his life working on this poem and in the end died with some verses still unfinished. Tradition says that before his death he instructed a close friend to burn the manuscript should anything befall him (Hadas, 1954). Most commentators take this story as proof of Virgil's perfectionism, his intent not to release the poem to the public until it met his high standards of literary craftsmanship. There is another possible explanation, however.

If we follow the drama of the *Aeneid*, we see that Aeneas' character becomes increasingly dehumanized as the hero pursues his goal of Roman nationhood. By the end of the story, Aeneas has lost his parents, his wife, his new-found lover, and his inner capacity for mercy. In the end, he has changed from a man with human weaknesses to a robot programmed with a divine, but heartless, mission.

Perhaps in writing the poem over the long course of a decade, Virgil came to see that the mindless pursuit of a goal can transform the personality, indeed that it can betray and destroy the very essence of what it means to be human. Having discovered this truth in late life, Virgil may have wished he had never begun the *Aeneid*. Only his death, his friend's hesitation, and Augustus' own insistence ensured the poem's survival.

It is in the small things of life rather than in the big that happiness lies; human relationships matter more than abstract goals do: these are theses that ancient writers, many of them in late life, acknowledged and passionately advanced. In doing so, they challenged the more prevalent view that personal worth should be gauged by the magnitude of one's possessions and honors rather than by the spiritual quality of one's life.

Their sentiments are matched by the thoughts of other, more modern, writers. In 1726, at the age of 59, Jonathan Swift published *Gulliver's Travels*. Although it purported to narrate the fantastic adventures of an English physician, *Gulliver's Travels* in actuality reported Swift's own encounters with human stupidity, prejudice, and cruelty during a lifetime of frustrating service in politics and the church.

In one of the most well-known episodes, Gulliver is shipwrecked in the land of the 6-inch-tall Lilliputians. By combining their minuscule size with their vaunting ambitions, Swift caricaturized both mankind's pettiness and his propensity for grandiose schemes.

As Gulliver relates, the two mighty empires of Lilliput and (equally tiny) Blefuscu had already been at war for half a century—and all because of eggs! A Lilliputian imperial edict had proclaimed that henceforth all boiled eggs should be cracked at their small end. In protest, recalcitrant "Big Enders" refused to change their ways, igniting a destructive civil war that cost the lives of 11,000 Big Enders and the banning of all their books. Afterward, some Big Endian exiles were granted asylum by the nearby empire of Blefuscu, thus provoking a war between the nations.

After saving Lilliput from an invasion, Gulliver refuses to destroy Blefuscu but instead argues for peace. As a result, the Lilliputians charge him with treason. The episode ends with his timely escape and the pointless perpetuation of war.

Like Solomon, Jonathan Swift learned from a lifetime of heartache that in human affairs "all is vanity." Unlike Solomon, however, Swift never found the "handful of quietness" for which he longed.

Fourteen years after Swift's tragic death in an insane asylum, the French philosopher Voltaire published his satire *Candide*. Voltaire was then 65 years old, living in a chateau near Geneva, where he would spend the last two decades of his life in virtual exile for having offended the powerful.

In *Candide*, Voltaire recounts the travels and misadventures of an amiable young man, whose misfortunes clearly prove that in life everything is decidedly not for the best. By the end of the story, Candide and his friends discover a way of coming to terms with life's cruel inequities. Working together on a small farm far from home, they realize "we must cultivate our garden," applying our talents and expending honest labor to produce some tangible good, however humble it may seem. Nor is this a selfish occupation, for when we send the fruits of our garden to market, others can benefit as well.

Recognizing in late life that we cannot "change the world," Voltaire nevertheless realized that we can positively affect the lives of others and that the satisfaction that comes from such good works can be life's highest reward. Through correspondence from his country home and with the help of friends and the power of literature, Voltaire persisted in battling the institutionalized injustices of his day.

Human fulfillment and the means by which it can be attained were also themes in the late-life writings of the German poet Goethe. In *Faust*, Goethe tells the story of a man dissatisfied by life as an intellectual who makes a pact with the devil to sell his soul for one moment of pure bliss.

Completed by Goethe at the age of 59, Part One of the story tells how sexual conquest failed to provide Faust with the satisfaction he sought. Goethe did not finish the tale until 23 years later. Finally, at the age of 82, he completed Part Two, in which his hero at last discovers the avenue to true fulfillment. Rejecting illusory political honors and empty military triumphs, Faust comes to see that happiness is not a possession but a process, the process of creating meaning where there was none before.[6] In what almost seems an anticlimax, Faust ends his days as a civil engineer, draining coastal lands to make them arable, thereby creating something lasting that can be of service to others. Salvation for him lies in such struggle, for "freedom and life are only earned by those who conquer them each day anew" (*Faust, Part Two*, Act V).

MEASURING SUCCESS

If, in late life, we measure the meaning of our years only by the big things we have accomplished, we risk major disappointment. As we have seen, pursuing grand designs can be an exercise in futility; they lead us on, only to vanish before our eyes.

To abandon grandiose goals, however, does not mean to live a goalless life. Being fully present in each moment of time and being spiritually responsive to the presence of others and to the world around us, its need, and its beauty can also be a goal and, if our authors are to be believed, a most worthy one.

Our sense of failure, after all, is but proportionate to the scale by which we gauge success. If we change the scale, we also change the measure of our self-worth. Recalibrating the standard of success can thus provide those of us in late life, indeed, those of any age, with consolation for the past and inspiration for the future.[7]

Across the long span of years, our eyes may fail to see the small things we have done that have made a difference to others. Like George Bailey in Frank Capra's movie, *It's a Wonderful Life*, we may mistakenly think we have failed. Illumined by another light, however, the small things we have done—and can still do—can show us our lives were, and still are, worth living.

NOTES

1. On the practice and value of reviewing one's life in later years, see Jon Hendricks (1995).

2. For ancient testimonies on the power of love in late life, see Stephen Bertman (1989).

3. A story narrated by the ancient Greek historian Herodotus (*The Persian Wars*, 1:30–33) makes the point that wealth and power do not guarantee happiness. According to the story, Croesus, king of Lydia and then the richest man in the world, took an Athenian guest on a tour of his royal treasury. He then asked his Greek guest to name the most fortunate man on earth. Much to Croesus' consternation, his guest named some simple and obscure Greeks who had led dutiful and pious lives. Later, tragedy befell Croesus and proved the wisdom of his guest's words.

4. Like Cicero, other famous Romans valued the pursuit of farming over the pursuit of political glory. In the 5th century B.C., Cincinnatus stopped ploughing to assume emergency

command of the Roman army; then, after defeating his country's enemies, he returned to his fields. In the 4th century A.D., Diocletian returned to his farm in Dalmatia after serving as emperor, and refused to leave it to serve again. Being emperor, he said, couldn't be compared to raising vegetables with his own hands (*Epitome De Caesaribus*, 39). For this latter story I am grateful to my colleague, Harry Bird.

5. I am grateful to my colleague, Charles Fantazzi, for calling this passage to my attention.

6. On the creation of meaning as a deliberate act of will, see Viktor Frankl (1992).

7. Recent research (Lykken & Tellegen, 1996) suggests that our potential for happiness is genetically predetermined in much the same way that our weight is governed by a metabolic set point. Like dieting, the pursuit of happiness can only lead to frustration until we acknowledge our inherited constitution. According to psychologist Dr. David Lykken of the University of Minnesota (Goleman 1996), "A steady diet of simple pleasures will keep you above your set point. Find the small things that you know give you a little high—a good meal, working in the garden, time with friends—and sprinkle your life with them. In the long run, that will leave you happier than some grand achievement that gives you a big lift [only] for a while." See also Myers and Diener (1995).

REFERENCES

Bertman, S. (1989). The ashes and the flame: Passion and aging in classical poetry. In T.M. Falkner & J. de Luce (Eds.), *Old age in Greek and Latin literature* (pp. 157–171). Albany: State University of New York Press.

Bryce, A.H. (1980). *The works of Virgil*. London: George Bell.

Frankl, V.E. (1992). *Man's search for meaning: An introduction to logotherapy* (4th ed.). Boston: Beacon Press.

Goleman, D. (1996, July 16). Forget money; nothing can buy happiness, some researchers say. *New York Times*, p. B5.

Gordis, R. (1968). *Koheleth, the man and his world: A study of Ecclesiastes* (3rd ed.). New York: Schocken Books.

Gottheil, G. (1917). Ecclesiastes. In *The holy scriptures*. Philadelphia: Jewish Publication Society of America.

Groden, S.Q. (1966). *Sappho: Poems*. Indianapolis: Indiana University Press.

Hadas, M. (1951). *The basic works of Cicero*. New York: Modern Library.

Hadas, M. (1954). *Ancilla to classical reading* (p. 340). New York: Columbia University Press.

Hendricks, J. (Ed.). (1995). *Reminiscence and life review*. Amityville, NY: Baywood Publishing.

Lattimore, R. (1960). *Greek lyrics*. Chicago: University of Chicago Press.

Lichtheim, M. (1973). *Ancient Egyptian literature: Vol. I, old and middle kingdom* (p. 196f). Berkeley: University of California Press.

Lykken, D., & Tellegen, A. (1996). Happiness is a stochastic phenomenon. *Psychological Science*, 7, 186–189.

Myers, D.G., & Diener, E. (1995). Who is happy? *Psychological Science*, 6, 10–19.

Speiser, E.A. (1958). The epic of Gilgamesh. In J.B. Pritchard (Ed.), *The ancient Near East: An anthology of texts and pictures*. Princeton, NJ: Princeton University Press.

Thomas, L.E., Kraus, P.A., & Chambers, K.O. (1990). Metaphoric analysis of meaning in the lives of elderly men: A cross-cultural investigation. *Journal of Aging Studies*, 4, 1–15.

CHAPTER TWO

Joan and Erik Erikson and Sarah and Abraham: Parallel Awakenings in the Long Shadow of Wisdom and Faith

W. Andrew Achenbaum and Stephen M. Modell

O f the various pathways to wisdom, those that begin with an "awakening" are the most deceptively straightforward. Awakenings sometimes are occasioned by things dimly seen or by a faint voice. Occasionally, people are moved to connect more deeply with a source of inspiration within themselves.[1] They thirst for spiritual growth or true intimacy. Others seek the consolation of wisdom to deal with fears, losses, illness, or death; tragedies force them to reconsider where they thought they were heading. There are exceptions, of course. We all know grandmothers, a kid in the neighborhood, or someone like Forrest Gump whom we might call "wise," an attribute these people do not necessarily desire nor think they possess. In general, the pursuit of wisdom is intentional. It affords, even facilitates, greater integration of thoughts, feelings, and actions.

As with other paths to maturity, the search for wisdom can be daunting, full of sorrow, pain, and sacrifice. Awakening to the possibilities of greater enlightenment does not guarantee happiness. Neither self-reflexivity nor integrity can ward off the vicissitudes of life. In any case, not everyone wants to become wiser (nor manages to do so) with age. Hence, the focus here is on those who seek wisdom, however defined. How do such men and women characterize the pursuit? When in the search are awakenings likely to happen? Do interpretations of the experience differ substantively over the life course?

In the book of Genesis there are two archetypal couples who, in the prime of their lives, yearn for a deeper sense of what it means to strive to be fully human. God let Adam and Eve name "every living creative" in Paradise. Responsible for nurturing and maintaining the garden, the couple could do anything except eat the fruit of one tree. Eve blamed the serpent, but it was she who decided that eating the forbidden fruit was a means of attaining wisdom (Gen. 3:6[2]). Sure enough, as soon as they had taken a bite, Adam and Eve perceived things differently. They felt shame and experienced fears so great that they hid when the Lord came into their presence. Questioned about his behavior, Adam admitted that "I was afraid because I was naked" (Gen. 3:10). Despite their excuses, God knew that if Adam and Eve were brash enough to "become one of us" by reaching for the apples, they might also be tempted to take from "the tree of life, and eat, and live forever" (Gen. 3:22). So the pair was expelled from Paradise, their quest for wisdom having begun and apparently ended unhappily with that awakening in the garden.

Abram was 75 when the Lord told him to "go from your country and your kindred and your father's house to the land I will show you." God promised that "I will make of you a great nation, and I will bless you, and make your name great, so that you will be a blessing" (Gen. 12:1–2). Abram took God at His word: "So Abram went," we are told two verses later, with no clue as to what Abram thought or how he felt about the call.[3]

Several theophanies occurred in Canaan and Egypt, but not until Gen. 15 was there a covenant: "After these things the word of the Lord came to Abram in a vision. 'Do not be afraid, Abram, I am your shield; your reward shall be very great . . . Look toward heaven and count the starts . . . so shall your descendants be.' " Abram's awakening truly was an ongoing process. He produced a potential heir with his wife's servant but did not seal the covenant until 13 years later when all of the men of his household were circumcised. Abram was given additional signs at age 99[4]: The aging couple, now called Sarah and Abraham, laughed when promised a son; yet a year later, Isaac was born. "Mature religious faith," observes Harold Koenig, "depends not only on placing God at the center of one's ultimate concern but also on keeping him there."[5] With an awakening, scripture suggests, comes the deepening realization that faith and righteousness point the way to wisdom.

Abraham's ultimate test came when Isaac was a youth. God played for high stakes: "Take your son, your only son Isaac, whom you love" (Gen. 22:2) to be sacrificed at "the place that God had shown." Father Abraham lifted his knife. It was a moment of utter despair, since in obedience to God Abraham was about to murder the son he held dear, who if allowed to live would fulfill his part in a sacred covenant made earlier with God (Gen. 17:2). Other interpretations are plausible, however. "Did the father's hands tremble? We are aware only of a singleness of purpose . . . Abraham is now to actualize heartrending yearnings of a lifetime in one heroic and terrifying act. He will attain absolute perfection and freedom. Nothing will be left undone, all smallness and frustration will be gone."[6] Hence the binding of Isaac (or Akedah) reveals supreme personal integrity in relationship with God. It is also possible that Isaac's "look of terror, fear, shock, betrayal, or was it perhaps a look of trust and faith" awakened in Abraham the conviction that his fundamental belief in God made him free to serve the Lord by acting responsibly in honoring the integrity and potential of other human beings.[7] Both Abraham and

Isaac passed the test of faithfulness; the Lord sent an angel to stay Abraham's hand. A ram was found and duly sacrificed; the place of the offering henceforth was called "The Lord will provide" (Gen. 22:14). Later, the angel of the Lord assured Abraham that his offspring would be numerous and blessed, says the Lord, "because you have obeyed my voice" (Gen. 22:18).

Faith and fear continually awakened Abraham in ripening maturity to new depths of understanding during his search for wisdom. The events of the Akedah, during which the Lord saluted Abraham as a God-fearing man for not withholding Isaac from the altar (Gen. 22:12), are the most powerful, but not the only, example. With increasing age, he learned to hear more acutely and to see with greater discernment.[8] According to Kierkegaard, the story shows how dread, pure and simple, can be transforming. Abraham's was "the furthest possibility of faith which has a presentiment of its object at the extremist limit of the horizon, yet is separated from it by a yawning abyss within which despair carries on its game."[9] Kierkegaard understood that people who are aging, like Abraham, continually have to make choices about the ultimate value of their lives. They can react to their immediate (sometimes recurring) fears, or they can choose to act wholly upon their transcendent, heartfelt commitments. "Faith begins precisely there where thinking leaves off."[10] To envision "awakening" as a pathway to wisdom is to recognize that certain people learn how to come to terms with limitations, pain, and evil as they review their life course.

Abraham stayed the course. Genesis 24:1 affirms that when Isaac married Rebekah, "Abraham was old, well advanced in years; and the Lord had blessed Abraham in all things." Remarrying after Sarah died at the age of 127, he observed other cultic customs. Abraham died "in a good old age" (Gen. 25:7), a century after he had left Harran. Although scripture is sketchy about the patriarch's last days, Jewish legend has it that Abraham wanted to see "all the creatures that the Lord has created in the heaven and on earth." The archangel Michael took him in a chariot and showed him things good and bad. Pitying the sinners, whom he once in "anger, cursed and destroyed," Abraham begged for God's mercy.[11] From this higher perspective in his waning days, Abraham arrived at a new stance toward others even those whom he formerly would have judged harshly.

It would be a leap to try to distill from this folklore the end point of Abraham's search for wisdom. A number of questions about biblical events must remain unanswered. What did Abraham think about his awakening? How did the old man recast events earlier in his life, such as when he represented his wife Sarah as a sister to Pharoah, banished Ishmael, or placed Isaac on the altar? Did the old man conclude that his initial insights were immature, incomplete? What role, precisely, did Sarah play in his journeys? Did she pursue her own heart's counsel? Such questions must remain rhetorical.

As we shall see, biblical stories foreshadow many themes in the careers of Joan and Erik Erikson. In middle age, the couple imagined a way to chart stages of human development. As in the case of Abraham and Sarah, the Eriksons did not much alter their direction, although their interpretation of human growth became richer with each passing decade. Like Adam and Eve, the pair took tremendous risks, testing their image of truth against empirical realities. The Eriksons tried to account for contrapuntal forces that in their mind's eye, animated certain universal experiences. This pair of contemporary observers, however, did not merely recapitulate scriptural patterns; they were not constrained by inequalities in marital roles that existed in biblical times. Joan and Erik nurtured the other's insights while individually exploring the ramifications of their particular awakenings. They attest to the complementarity of gendered differences in the search for wisdom.

ERIK AND JOAN ERIKSON'S AWAKENING

Erik Erikson was 48 when he unveiled an 8-stage model of the life cycle. No single source or experience inspired the model. "An expert," Erikson declared at the time, "in addition to some verifiable fact, consistent theory or technical skill must have some meaningful insight."[12] Erikson based his claim to expertise on his mastery of many ways of seeing. An artist who had studied with both Sigmund and Anna Freud, he modified the Freudian theory of psychoanalysis in the course of acquiring a "knack" for child analysis. Erikson in the 1930s interacted with distinguished social and behavioral scientists at Harvard, Yale, and Berkeley. He observed Sioux and Yurok Indian children at play. At a veterans rehabilitation clinic during World War II, Erikson worked with emotionally disturbed men having difficulties readjusting to civilian life. Becoming interested in "loss of identity" in youth, he tried to bolster the patients' sense of self by applying techniques used with psychoneurotic teenagers, adolescent psychotics, and juvenile delinquents. Such clinical activities prompted Erikson to hypothesize that a healthy adolescent "knows where he is going" because both his past and his future give direction.

Immediately after the war Erikson published two papers that contained ideas that would soon bring him fame. In *Childhood and Tradition in Two American Indian Tribes*, he postulated that "every item of human behavior" could be defined according to three kinds of organization: biological; social, which reflected "geographic-historical units"; and "the ego-principle, reflecting the synthesis of experience and the resulting defensive and creative mastery (ego development)."[13] Erikson stressed the epigenetic quality of psychic development. It mattered greatly, he asserted, when certain values-laden issues arose in the life cycle; how well and fully people resolved specific developmental crises affected their subsequent ability to cope with and move beyond later challenges. (Erikson in a 1940 paper had already posited that growth occurs step by step, beginning at the fetal stage, with each successive step inculcating former lessons and anticipating future experiences.[14]) Then, in 1946, in *Ego Development and Historical Chance*, he argued that such social conditions as racism and joblessness affected the deepest layers of a person's unconscious, thereby weakening the ego.[15]

As with most of his contemporaries, Erikson invoked Freud in analyzing early human growth. He observed in 1931 that "children (like animals) can sniff the real essence through any surface: the cruel or kind, the strong or insecure tendency. If we wish to bring up a child harshly or kindly . . . we must be able to do so inwardly."[16] (Sixty years later, his major collaborator, Joan Mowat Erikson, reaffirmed the couple's belief that "the early stages of life are enormously significant for the foundation of human development . . . We know well that an injured sapling will probably grow into a malformed tree."[17]) In *Life History and the Historical Moment* (1975), Erikson offered an "autobiographic perspective" to illustrate some psychobiological factors that "secure the somatic basis for a coherent sense of vital selfhood." In youth "interminable hiking" nurtured the artist's "deep and trusting relationship . . . to what was still a peasant's Nature." His own experiences convinced Erikson that "a person's idiosyncratic gifts demand a prolonged search for a corresponding ideological and occupational setting . . . or where historical change forces a postponement of adult commitment."[18]

Erikson's attention to generational cycles, societal context, and historical time increasingly set him apart from other "classical" analysts. The analyst did not so much reject Freudian theory as he reframed its orientation.[19] Individuals must come to terms with a sequence of historical conditions that unfold on the basis of earlier life events. So Erikson focused on infantile fixations when appropriate, but he also paid attention to how late life was affected by adolescent identity crises and the moral challenges of youth.[20]

Erikson offered the first full-scale elaborations of his epigenetic model of human development in 1950. He was invited to prepare source material to be used by researchers and practitioners in the field of child health and welfare at the Midcentury White House Conference on Children and Youth. The conference's Fact Finding Committee centered on a single question: "How can we rear an emotionally healthy generation?"[21] Organizers of the White House Conference asked the Macy Foundation to convene a symposium on the healthy personality under the auspices of its multidisciplinary series on problems of infancy and childhood. Erikson's contribution, written in collaboration with his wife, was titled "Growth and Crises of the 'Healthy Personality.'" To this first joint effort, the partners brought complementary strengths and shared insights. Joan Mowat was a dancer, an artist who met Erik while also undergoing analysis in Vienna. For the first 2 decades of their marriage, she worked with her husband in creating new learning milieus as they raised their three children. Everyday experiences counted in their theories. "The laws of physical development become highly important when we speak of the *growth* of personality," the Eriksons wrote, "because such development follows the successive levels of the organism's readiness to interact with the opportunities offered in the environment."[22]

The Eriksons' epigenetic diagram mapped out a sequence of stages with components interacting over the life cycle: "Each item exists in some form before 'its' decisive and critical time normally arrives."[23] Originally the Eriksons formulated a seven-stage model, although they felt that they had moved beyond Shakespeare's description.[24] Just before a speech to a group of psychologists and psychiatrists in Los Angeles, at which Erik intended to test reactions to the framework for the first time, Joan realized that they had omitted their own place on the continuum: "The seven chart stages jumped from 'Intimacy' (stage six) to 'Old Age' . . . we surely need another stage."[25] So, while waiting for Erik's train, the pair added an eighth stage—"Generativity vs. Stagnation"—between the sixth and seventh stages. The addition represented a procreative, productive, and generous stage of life concerned with caring. Their description of the stage recalls Abraham's relations with Ishmael and Isaac, who were a source of both surprise and delight to himself, Hagar, and Sarah. In a sense, the addition of an eighth stage to their model recapitulated for Erik and Joan an act of creativity in which Abraham had also participated during a generative phase of his life.

The last-minute revision in the epigenetic model was a defining moment. The Eriksons anticipated that experts would like the paradigm, and they did. "I strongly agree with Mr. Erikson's emphasis on autonomy between one and three years," opined Benjamin Spock. "There are many parallels between the early (one to three) period of autonomy and the latency period."[26] Yet Erik knew that the precise terms were bound to provoke questions that he could not yet answer: "I merely wish to indicate that I have in mind an eventually exhaustive treatment of the matter."[27] The model needed greater critical scrutiny, not simply empirical verification. Just as the Eriksons appreciated the irony of the fact that Shakespeare omitted "play" from his conception of human development, so too were they prepared to acknowledge that they had slighted some of adulthood's important challenges. The Eriksons had made neither space nor time for themselves, and others, at their stage of life. Owning up to this flaw deterred them from generalizing too broadly across individual, generational, and historical time. Intentional self-reflexivity became part of their ongoing scientific awakening to nuances and continuities inherent in their model.

No wonder, then, Erik Erikson chose to describe the first edition of *Childhood and Society* (1950) as "a subjective book, a conceptual itinerary." Erikson saw himself becoming "maybe a new kind of historian in committing himself to influencing what he observes." Like Abram the nomad he "came to psychology from art," and then worked "face to face" with children in a small American school in Vienna. But Erikson's behavior also resembled Adam's. Aware that multidisciplinarity was a dubious academic objective, Erikson the Adamic scientist offered *Childhood and Society* as a "blueprint of our method" so other analysts could test the cogency of its theory and data for understanding the relationship of the ego to society.[28] "This is a book on childhood . . . Long childhood makes a technical and mental virtuoso out of man, but it also leaves a lifelong residue of emotional immaturity in him."[29] Fittingly, *Childhood and Society* was dedicated to "our children's children."

Writing a foreword to the second edition of *Child and Society* 13 years later, Erikson italicized the phrase "conceptual itinerary"; the phrase "caught my eye." He went on to note that his students at Harvard urged him not to make "drastic changes" in the text, "as if tampering with an itinerary written in younger years was not one of an older man's prerogatives." Erikson gave another reason for limiting his revisions: "I have come to the conclusion that the book's shortcomings are inseparable form its character as a record of the first phase of one worker's itinerary and that like many first voyages it provides impressions which on re-visiting prove resistant to undoing or doing over."[30] Consistent with his own epigenetic model, Erikson wished to return periodically to his original awakening to gauge how much progress he had made on his journey.

The second edition of *Childhood and Society*, the publishers claimed, was "revised and enlarged." Erikson actually did not alter the text radically, but some of his excisions and additions in the essay on "Eight Ages of Man" are revealing. In the first edition, the eight-stage diagram had been placed at the end of the chapter with a one-paragraph description. The 1963 edition added a five-page commentary on the "epigenetic chart."[31] Erikson significantly rewrote passages discussing the early stages far more than he did those concerning the latter stages. He doubled the length of Stage Two (Autonomy vs. Shame and Doubt) and Stage Four (Industry vs. Inferiority) but made only minor changes in Stage Eight (Ego Integrity vs. Despair.)[32]

Besides *Childhood and Society*, Erikson is probably best known for two psychohistories. *Young Man Luther* (1958) proposed that "the life crisis of adolescence" was "in some form normal for all youth."[33] During his monastic moratorium "marking time" between childhood and adulthood, Luther "accepted for his life work the unconquered frontier of tragic conscience, defined as it was by his personal needs and superlative gifts." The monk's identity and talents, in turn, were "molded" and "channeled" by tradition and "the metabolism of generations." Luther reshaped history when "the stages of individual life and of basic human institutions" dovetailed.[34] Erikson won both a Pulitzer Prize and a National Book Award 11 years later for *Gandhi's Truth*, which explored Gandhi's transformation from organizer of the Ahmedabad strike (1918) to "father of his country." Faithful to his epigenetic model, Erikson analyzed the "developmental probability" manifest in Gandhi's existential being throughout his life. But the focus was on generativity in the middle years. "Identity," Erikson claimed in *Gandhi's Truth*, "becomes most evident in unhesitating commitment—when the time is ripe."[35]

The author's choice of subjects was influenced by many factors, but the auto-historical parallels are not coincidental. Erikson had suffered an identity crisis and had done extensive clinical studies of childhood and youth before writing about Luther. Erikson turned to Gandhi only after he had become renowned. The analyst saw how Gandhi was impelled by "a mighty drivenness, an intense yet flexible energy, a shocking originality, and a capacity to impose on his time what most concerns him."[36] Like Gandhi, Erikson exercised moral suasion; he raised professional concerns about the future of psychoanalysis and increasingly spoke out on controversial issues, such as the identity of Negro youth (1964), the potential of women (1965), and student unrest.[37]

As he aged, Erikson awakened more fully to the possibilities and contrarieties of the second half of life: "It is only too obvious that, so far in man's total development, adulthood and maturity have rarely been synonymous."[38] Moving back to California in 1975, he and his wife became involved in joint community ventures designed to combat racism, sexism, ageism, and prejudices against the "mentally disturbed." Twelve years later, the couple returned to Cambridge, where they were lionized as wise elders.[39] Both Eriksons thereafter focused on maturity and old age in their writings.

Like Abraham and Sarah, the Eriksons stayed the course and in the process, discovered that their awakening was even richer than first imagined. As with Adam and Eve, they subjected their hypotheses to critical analyses and relied on empirical insights. Shifts in the historical climate altered the context of late-life choices. There is, the Eriksons reported in their 70s, "something paradoxical . . . happening to those 'self-governing' middle years: today, when death seems to be more definitely postponed, there is almost a search for dangerous transitions and critical passages *within* life, threatening the survival of the individuality of the person now that physical survival seems so much certain."[40] The elderly had to prevent negativity from debilitating their search for wisdom, for wholeness. "Old people can and need to maintain a *grand*-generative function," the Eriksons declared. "Much of their despair is, in fact, a continuing sense of stagnation."[41] Late life thus provided the couple a new arena for studying human potential. Baldly put, the trust and hope experienced earlier in life paid off, but dystonic elements (such as mistrust, shame, inferiority) could trigger severe depression.[42]

Far from being a mere rehearsal of earlier traumas and triumphs, late life had its own distinctive agonistic features. In eulogizing Paul Tillich, for instance, Erik Erikson stressed the importance in the "existential design" of accepting and transcending boundaries. The German theologian at 50 "combined his opposites— and his occasional extremes—in . . . his blend of realism and faith, his utter sensual and spiritual Hereness." Grounded in the present, Tillich could look back "on the powers that formed him, and ahead to what he yet intended to make of himself.[43] Had he written a third biography in his old age, Erikson said that he would have selected an older figure (possibly that "great compatriot" Kierkegaard), who had wrestled at the borders of ethics, religion, and existentialism.[44] Instead, Erikson spent his latter years perfecting motifs at last coming into perspective.

From evolutionary biologists such as Konrad Lorenz and Julian Huxley, Erikson examined age-based rituals in school and adulthood that he felt gave life cycles and institutions their interdependent integrity in modern times. "By combining and renewing the ritualizations of childhood and affirming generative sanction, [rituals] help to consolidate adult life once its commitments and investments have led to the creation of new persons and to the production of new things and ideas."[45] Some critics felt that the emphasis on ritualization made the epigenetic model of human development too mechanistic. This fed a larger suspicion that the Eriksons unduly homogenized the varieties of human growth.

The charge was unfair; their work with Native Americans in the 1930s showed that early on they placed importance on human diversity. In the 1960s, both Eriksons wrote about gender differences. In a special issue of *Daedalus* on "The woman in America," Erik Erikson noted the "severe theoretical handicap" caused by insufficient attention to the problem of identity among young women. A "total configurational approach," claimed Erikson revealed that "anatomy, history, and personality are our *combined destiny*."[46] To the same volume, Joan Erikson offered "Nothing to Fear: Notes on the Life of Eleanor Roosevelt," which traced how F.D.R.'s virtues, shortcomings, and disability all provided a context to foster his wife's "increasing ability to think for myself." It is revealing that Joan Erikson ended her sketch by asserting that "transcendence of the human condition through activity on a large scale, then, could characterize Eleanor Roosevelt's career." This emphasis on transcendence in old age became a major theme in the couple's writings.[47]

The Eriksons' appreciation for gender complementarity ran deep. All along, Erik acknowledged Joan's role in his work. "Joan Erikson always edits what I write," he wrote in the preface to *Identity* (1968). "Nobody knows better what I want to say, and nobody could be more careful to let me say it in my own way and, if need be, in overlong sentences."[48] Those who watched how the pair interacted recognized Joan's critical role as "able editor, collaborator, and supporter of his efforts . . . Joan Erikson has confirmed and enhanced Erikson's clinical understanding and clarity of style."[49] In addition, they laughed together; theirs was a working partnership from the start. Still, Joan approached life-cycle issues differently from the way her husband did. She taught school while nursing her eldest child. In 1951, Joan Erikson was invited to develop an arts activities program for patients at Austen Riggs and later established similar programs elsewhere. She wrote poetry and pursued her interests in the arts.[50]

It is worth noting that initially Joan Erikson did not fully verbalize her sense of her own awakening or her distinctive contributions to refining the epigenetic model. "Weaving with words has not come easily for me," she acknowledged.

"Dancing, doing, making were my ways of saying something." During the last quarter century of their marriage, however, Joan Erikson wove words. "I have spent years living with and examining the relationship of the senses to the wisdom that is supposed to come to fruition in old age. The search has been an expansive one encompassing the life cycle."[51] Joan Erikson thought that she understood the model "completely in all of its ramifications," but she "never really thoroughly *grasped* all of its implications . . . until the threads themselves had duplicated the black-and-white chart."[52] Erikson's weaving enabled people to see and to feel how contrapuntal waves of colors set up a warp of rich shadings. "All knowledge begins with sensory experience," she asserted. First impressions are important, but "a central part of the imaginative process, the power to recall, is one of the sensory vitalizers of any age, but especially the later years of the life cycle."[53] Erik Erikson in his old age rightly claimed that Joan "has enlivened the whole imagery of the life cycle."[54]

The Eriksons' artistic side is manifested in the previously quoted passages; they appreciated the aesthetic element in ordinary life. Just as Walter Benjamin once summed up the aesthetic aura of an object as the "strange weave of space and time: the unique appearance or semblance of distance, no matter how close the object may be,"[55] Erik and Joan did the same for life. In their capacity to see the panorama of life from a distance, to demarcate its internal pattern or "weave," and to empathize with the object or life being experienced, the Eriksons transposed the artistic viewpoint to the imagery of real life. "This is the meaning of existence," the existential Jewish theologian Abraham Joshua Heschel observed, "to reconcile liberty with service, the passing with the lasting, to weave the threads of temporality into the fabrity of eternity."[56] The weave of which Joan and Erik spoke ultimately carries over to the spiritual dimension of life.

Honoring the logic of their shared model, Erik and Joan watched and listened attentively. "This century's discovery of relativity and of the unconscious gave new dimensions to our experience."[57] One of these "new dimensions" occurred in the spiritual realm. Science enabled people to go further in the modern era, Erikson believed, to look within themselves for the kingdom of God. He cited the example of Albert Einstein, a "childlike scientist" capable of getting in touch with primal suffering while realizing his potential. Commenting on the "amazement at the beauty and grandeur of this world" expressed in the Psalms, Einstein found "this joy [that] is the feeling from which true scientific research draws its spiritual sustenance."[58] The 1969 moon landing inspired Erikson to predict that

> what we are learning and teaching will help create truly relevant priorities only gathered into a new kind of religiosity. And here, I think, the conquest of the outer space may yet help in a paradoxical way: That men now invade the boundaries of the heavens as concrete goals of science could force man at last to center heaven down on earth, which has, in fact, so patiently and tormentedly waited for it.[59]

Late in life, both Eriksons pondered the relationship of religion and spirituality to well-being in old age. Erik's roots in Judaism were an integral part (but only one facet) of his identity. By his mid-70s, if not before, he was "not only willing but determined to live on the shadowy borderline of the denominational ambiguities (whether national or religious, political or professional) into which I seem to have been born."[60] In his 1973 Jefferson lectures, Erikson described how our third president searched for the "authentic" sayings of Jesus. Erik's own interpretation of "The Galilean Sayings and the Sense of 'I' " several years later traced the symbolic nexus "of the *I* with an inner eye full of light."[61] The tension between wisdom and despair in the last stage fused a transcendent "integrity of experience" admid declining bodily capacities and fleeting time. "Wisdom, then, is a detached and yet active concern with life in the face of death."[62]

To Joan, the daughter of an Anglican minister and author of a book on Saint Francis, reverence for God inspired poetry. Through her hymns of praise she could sing about what filled her whole being with optimism and vivacity:

> God is an awesome spirit—and we must worship the awesome in spirit and in truth.
> The spirit has and does offer us the gift of love—love of one another—the ability and means of reaching out with tact, with contact and understanding and the forming of bonds of inspiration.
> We have been blessed with the capacity to focus all our senses and thus to apprehend, reach out for and experience beauty. We are all artists and in love with art.[63]

Like her husband, Joan felt that experiential wisdom was one of the fruits of a full life: "As one ages, one becomes more interested in endurance and in those capacities so necessary in old age, those that make a life of integrity possible . . . One is inexorably bound to one's entire life."[64] Enlightenment came from seeing "eye" to "I."

For both Eriksons, reverence, wonder, and awe, words usually associated with the ultimate reality, were all related to human qualities impossible to attain vicariously. "A richness of experience *is* a potential generator of wisdom," asserted Joan Erikson, "a recognition through the senses of the richness and diversity of life which on the surface might seem to have been an uneventful one."[65] Current history added significance to the last stage of life. "Historical changes have recently mobilized a general, and somewhat alarmed, awareness of the rapidly changing conditions of old age and an intense interest in the special nature of this last stage," Erik Erikson opined. "Old age must eventually find a meaningful place in the economic and cultural order—meaningful to the old and to the occupants of all other age groups, beginning with childhood."[66]

In the last 2 decades of his life, Erik revised his impressions of the eighth stage. In 1978 and 1988 he published interpretations of Ingmar Bergman's motion picture *Wild Strawberries*, a film featured for years in his Harvard course on The Human Life Cycle. Comparing the articles attests to both his growing acuity about the last stage and his ability to integrate various truths about historical, generational, and individual developments into a fluid conceptual context.

Both essays reconstruct the protagonist, Dr. Borg's life history within generational terms. Both underscore "the specific affinity of childhood and old age which is marked by the interplay of what, psychosocially, I call Integrity (if not without Despair) at the end of life and Trust (if not without Mistrust) at the beginning."[67] Interestingly, Erikson mentions the love the biblical Isaac had for his mother Sarah, relating to the psychodrama in the motion picture between the main character Isak and his first love, Sara.[68] Both essays might apply equally well to the relationship between Isaac and Abraham, however. Erikson's model aptly describes the remarkable trust Isaac had in his father's judgment as Abraham placed him on the altar and the father's conflict between integrity and despair. Lifting the knife meant severing the generations but consummating a father's devotion to God's commandments.

Despite commonality of themes, there are critical differences between the 1978 and 1988 interpretations. In the earlier piece Erikson was didactic; he used his analysis of Dr. Borg's crises to "present a conception of the life cycle and the generational life cycle . . . in my own words."[69] Rewriting the article for *Vital Involvement in Old Age*, Erikson let Bergman's storyline dictate his interpretation: "We can best begin to demonstrate more pictorally some of the dynamics of the interwoven stages of human life, as they culminate in old age, by outlining the scenes and themes that reveal, in Bergman's drama, an old man's search for his life's transcendent meaning; and by claiming that all old people are involved in some such search, whether they—or we—know it or not."[70] Whereas Erikson's singular "I" and "eye" predominate throughout the 1978 essay, the perspectives of many characters from *Wild Strawberries* are juxtaposed in the later version. "Only in a communal context can we judge how the same individual's relationships have remained developmentally underinvolved or whether, in the course of a lifetime, they have become defensively disinvolved," Erikson concluded. "Old age brings with it an effort to get reinvolved in typical patterns of living, as it were, in the past."[71]

The Life Cycle Completed (1982) placed the epigenetic theory into a psychosocial, historical context. While reaffirming that adulthood "*is* the link between the individual life cycle and the cycle of generations," Erikson decided to "go further and begin my account of the stages with the last one, *old age*, to see how much sense a re-view of the *completed* life cycle can make of its whole course."[72] The tone was autobiographical: "It was in our 'middle years' that we formulated it—at a time in which we certainly had no intention of (or capacity for) imagining ourselves as really old. This was only a few decades ago; and yet, the predominant image of old age was then altogether different."[73] Even after publication, Erikson recognized that "the role of old age had to be reobserved, rethought." He returned before his death to his copy of *The Life Cycle Completed*, underlining in red, green, and blue ink those passages that pleased him and others that irked him. He told his wife that he intended to make additional revisions. Erik's own aging awakened in him a sense that he did not yet fully comprehend the limitations of the last stage.

Joan Erikson, meanwhile, became prolific in her eighth decade. She probed dimensions of old age in ways that went beyond Erik's thinking in at least two ways. First, Joan questioned whether the eighth stage, as formulated in 1950, fully embraced the experiences that came with added years of longevity. In *Wisdom and the Senses* (1988), Joan envisioned a confrontation in "final maturity" activated by withdrawal, not wisdom: "Perhaps there should be a ninth stage indicated, because there is, inevitably, one further challenge. The struggle may be a long or short one, but one would surely face it and live it through with integrity."[74] Second, in a study of Prometheus, Orpheus, and Socrates published 5 years later, she made gender differences a central motif. *Legacies* explored three legendary figures who continue to serve as "conduits of the wisdom of the ages." As if reflecting on her own life, Joan noted that the book's central characters were "guided in essential decisions by womanly figures who shine out persistently and powerfully."[75]

Joan Erikson in her 90s has become a modern Muse, undeterred by barriers that constrained women in biblical and classical times. In contrast to her husband's clinical tenor, she writes in a more personal tone. Living independently on Cape Cod, Joan has an intense need to "see" nature, human and otherwise, and to "touch" the "inner" recesses of the self, despite pains and feelings of emptiness. To wit, ruminating about Orpheus's fall "moves me to think that Orpheus's very humanness was expressed in this small but heartbreaking misstep." To accentuate this idea, Erikson places in the text her translation of one of Rilke's "Sonnets to Orpheus." To make the point accessible from yet another perspective, she offers this image (a memory of one of her sons decades ago?): "Or perhaps one should be reminded of a small boy venturing across an open space like an empty kitchen floor, who stops suddenly in his tracks to look back, to check for reassurance that the parent and safety are still there—that very human moment of self-doubt, of need for approval or another gulp of courage, yearned for by that child within us all."[76]

After Erik's death, Joan Erikson revisited *The Life Cycle Completed*, updating the epigenetic model with her own ideas and experiences. Joan fleshed out possible stage(s) of life beyond the one called "Old Age" in the original formulation. Whereas the positive (syntonic) element was mentioned first in describing earlier stages of life, she reversed the pattern for the ninth stage. Joan Erikson placed "the dystonic element first in order to underscore its prominence and potential strength. I am persuaded that if elders can come to terms with the dystonic elements in their life experiences in the ninth stage, they may successfully make headway on the pathway leading to Gero-transcendence . . . [which] demands of us an honest and steadfast humility."

Joan Erikson's sense that there is more beyond what had broadly been called "the last stage" brings to mind the final saga in Abraham's life recorded in Judaic folklore, in which he viewed from on high the sinners of the world. The legend highlights that element of detachment from both self and the world that emerges in advanced old age. Individuals in the final stage, like Abraham, finally let go of egocentric, judgmental viewpoints. They can see life's antimonies from both sides and a higher perspective. This sensibility has resonance in Eastern cultures. In response to a question from former prince Ananda, "What is the contemplation of distaste for the whole world, the Buddha answered, "It is simply, Ananda, the abandonment of any desire to cling to the world. It is the abandonment of mental prejudice, wrong beliefs, and latent tendencies concerning this world."[77] World religions apparently share similar views about the transcendent "I." They endorse Joan Erikson's assertion that a global shift in one's outlook, which moves toward withdrawal from life's dualities, becomes possible in the ninth stage.

Joan Erikson also coined the word "*transcendance*," which played deliberately on the language of the arts. The term goes beyond the category of dance Erik described in his analysis of Bergman's *Wild Strawberries*, involving a collective need of adults caught between the complex process of having been "brought up" and "terminal decline" to affirm ceremonially with whom they have grown up and whose standing in the world they now share.[78] Quite the opposite, the term characterizes what becomes, ultimately, "a surpassing of all human knowledge and experience." The old-old can "feel shabby" and are "forced to slow up and reconfirm [their] decision to proceed." Nonetheless, they still can be animated by the syntonic powers acquired over their lives, a psychic accumulation that Abraham was able to escape only at the end of his life. "The great dance of life can transport us into all the realms of making and doing with every item of body, mind, and spirit involved."[79]

CONCLUSIONS

Like Eve and Adam, Joan and Erik Erikson in middle age imagined a course of human development that they dared to test with the best scientific and practical means at their disposal. At first, like Sarah and Abraham, they did not comprehend the full dimensions of their awakening. Perhaps they were just too young; they needed to learn that it takes years of experience to ripen the receptive eye. Still, like the biblical figures, they sought wisdom in an interactive, epigenetic process; they tested their insights, came to terms with their doubts as well as their feelings of generativity, and acted upon on ever-richer array of experiences.

Unlike Adam and Eve or Abraham and Sarah, it is clear that Erik and Joan Erikson were true intellectual collaborators, soul friends committed to reforming the world in which they lived. Theirs was a shared awakening of equal partners. As a sounding board with a good ear, Joan improved her husband's prose so that his theories about the life cycle could become accessible to millions. Erik encouraged his wife to advance her own career as she brought her artistic sensibilities to their project. The Eriksons' awakening was not a private matter; they relied on their children and friends around the world. That said, their pathways to wisdom became individuated in manifestly complementary ways.

NOTES

1. Goldstein, J.J., & Kornfield, J. (1987). *Seeking the heart of wisdom* 1987, Boston: Shambhala.

2. Unless otherwise noted, all quotations from the Bible come from the New Revised Standard Version: We relied on the commentary in *Genesis 1–11*, by R. Davidson, 1973, Cambridge: Cambridge University Press.

3. The Bible differs in interpretation. Compare Gen. 15:6, which stresses righteousness, with Heb. 11:8, 10, which says that Abram acted out of faith. For more on the relationship between "faith" and "righteousness," see *The Interpreter's Dictionary of the Bible*. Freidman, D.N. (Ed.). (1992). New York: Doubleday.

4. For information on Abraham, see *Anchor Bible Dictionary*, I:39; For more on Sarah, see *Genesis 12–50*, p. 59, by R. Davidson, 1979, Cambridge: Cambridge University Press.

5. From *Aging and God* (p. 125), by H.G. Koenig, 1994, New York Haworth Pastoral Press. For parallels with Job, see "Becoming Wise," 1991, 21–39, by W.A. Achenbaum and L. Orwoll, 1991, *International Journal of Aging and Human Development, 32*, pp. 21–39.

6. From *The Binding of Isaac & Messiah*, (pp. 64–65), by A. Agus, 1988, Albany: State University of New York Press. It is also possible to draw parallels in the Gospels and Pauline texts to the sacrifice on Golgotha. See *The Last Trial* by S. Spiegel, 1967, New York: Pantheon Books.

7. For more along these lines, see "Cruelty Is Not Destiny," by M. Lerner, 1994, *Tikkun, 9*, pp. 33–40, 115–116.

8. Elsewhere in Hebrew scripture there is the same pattern: Trust in God contains within it a fear of God. "Many when they see will be filled with awe, and will learn to trust in the Lord." (Psalm 40:3). On the perfect Davidic king, Isaiah announced (11:2), "the spirit of the Lord shall rest . . . a spirit of wisdom and understanding, a spirit of counsel and power, a spirit of knowledge and the fear of the Lord."

9. From "A panegyric upon Abraham" (p. 35), by S. Kierkegaard, 1973, in *Fear and Trembling and the Sickness Unto Death*, Princeton, NJ: Princeton University Press. See also *Comprehensive Developmental Psychotherapy* (p. 4), by R.J. Wright et al., 1992, Chicago: Human Effectiveness.

10. From "A panegyric upon Abraham" (p. 64), by S. Kierkegaard, 1973, in *Fear and Trembling and the Sickness Unto Death*, Princeton, NJ: Princeton University Press. See also

Kierkegaard's Thought, by G. Malantschuk, 1971, Princeton, NJ: Princeton University Press.

11. From *Legends of the Bible* (pp. 144–146), by L. Ginzberg, 1956, Philadelphia: Jewish Publication of America.

12. From *Symposium on the Healthy Personality* (p. 93), by M.J.E. Senn, 1950, New York: Josiah Macy, Jr. Foundation.

13. Reprinted in *A way of looking a things* (p. 475), by E.H. Erikson, 1987, S. Schlein (Ed.), New York: W.W. Norton.

14. Reprinted in "Problems of infancy and early childhood," in *Ways of looking* (pp. 548–549), S. Schlein (Ed.), New York: W.W. Norton.

15. On the significance of this paper, See *Erik Erikson: The growth of his work*, by R. Coles, 1970, Boston: Little, Brown.

16. From "Children's Picture Books" (p. 38), by E.H. Erikson, 1931, in *A way of looking*.

17. From *Legacies* (p. 9), by J.M. Erikson, 1993, New York: W.W. Norton.

18. From "Identity crisis in autobiographic perspective" (pp. 19, 25–26), by E.H. Erikson, 1975, in *Life history and the historical moment*. New York: W.W. Norton.

19. Erikson stated that "ego identity accrues through childhood" in the special meeting of June 8–9, 1950, at the Conference on the Problems of Infancy and Childhood, reprinted in *Symposium on the Healthy Personality* (p.18), by M.J.E. Senn (Ed.), 1950, New York: Josiah Macy, Jr. Foundation.

20. For more on this, see Steven Weiland's essay on Erikson in *Intellectual craftsmen* (pp. 41–66), 1991, New Brunswick, NJ: Transaction Publishers. Coles suggests, p. 134, Erikson's connection with the "existentialist" psychological literature, in *Erik Erikson: The growth of his work*, by R. Coles, 1970, Boston: Little, Brown.

21. From Fact Finding Committee, Midcentury White House Conference on Children and Youth, Helen Witmer, Director (p. 13), reprinted in *Symposium on the Healthy Personality*, by M.J.E. Senn (Ed.), 1950, New York: Josiah Macy, Jr. Foundation.

22. From "Growth and crises of the 'Healthy personality'" (p. 98), in *Symposium on the Healthy Personality*, by M.J.E. Senn (Ed.), 1950, New York: Josiah Macy, Jr. Foundation.

23. From "Growth and crises of the 'Healthy personality'" (p. 99), in *Symposium on the Healthy Personality*, by M.J.E. Senn (Ed.), 1950, New York: Josiah Macy, Jr. Foundation. Erikson used a similar chart to analyze Freud's psychosexual stages. See also *Erik Erikson: The Growth of his work* (p. 77), by R. Coles, 1970, Boston: Little, Brown.

24. From "On the generational cycle," by E.H. Erikson, 1980, *International Journal of Psycho-Analysis, 61*, p. 219; and "Thoughts on the city for human development" (p. 522), by E.H. Erikson, in *A Way of looking at things*, S. Schlein (Ed.), 1987, New York: W.W. Norton.

25. From "The eighth stage reviewed and revised . . . ," by J.M. Erikson, 1995. Unpublished manuscript. I am grateful to Joan Erikson for sharing this text and for discussing this incident.

26. From B. Spock (p. 77) in *Symposium on the Healthy Personality*, by M.J.E. Senn (Ed.), 1950, New York: Josiah Macy, Jr. Foundation.

27. From B. Spock (p. 28) in *Symposium on the Healthy Personality*, by M.J.E. Senn (Ed.), 1950, New York: Josiah Macy, Jr. Foundation.

28. Among his U.S. colleagues were Henry Murray, who taught him personality theory; Lawrence Frank, who involved him at Yale in a study of incipient infantile neuroses; and distinguished anthropologists such as Gregory Bateson, Ruth Benedict, Alfred Kroeber, and especially Margaret Mead. For more on multidisciplinarity, see *Crossing frontiers*, by W.A. Achenbaum, 1995, New York: Cambridge University Press.

29. All quotations from the Foreword of *Childhood and society* (pp. 11–14), by E.H. Erikson, 1950, New York: W.W. Norton.

30. From "Foreword to the second edition" (pp. 11–13) in *Childhood and society*, E.H. Erikson, 1963, New York: W.W. Norton.

31. It is also worth noting that in 1950 the Eriksons placed the first stage (trust vs. mistrust) in the upper-lefthand corner of the table. Commentators at the Macy Foundation symposium asked whether Erik was trying to "symbolize American culture" or show the nation's preference for youth. "Oh no," Erikson replied. "That's merely because in reading a page we begin that way." From *Symposium on the 'Healthy personality'* (p. 27), by M.J.E. Senn (Ed.), 1950, New York: Josiah Macy, Jr. Foundation. In the 1963 edition the sequence is represented by an ascending diagonal.

32. Interestingly, in light of the "spiritual" nature of his later work, Erikson toned down some of the religious content in his 1950 publications for the second edition of *Childhood and society*. In his Macy paper, he had sounded disinterested: "As a psychologist it is not my job to decide whether religion (or, for that matter, tradition) should or should not exist . . . To me the important thing is whether or not religion and tradition are living psychological forces creating the kind of faith and conviction which permeates a parent's personality and thus reinforces the child's basic trust in the world's trustworthiness." (From *Symposium on the 'Healthy personality'* [p. 108–109], by M.J.E. Senn (Ed.), 1950, New York: Josiah Macy, Jr. Foundation.) Although the 1963 edition mentioned "religion" and "ritual" at various points in the text, such references were excised from the revised essay on the "Eight Stages of Man."

33. From *Young man Luther: A study in psychoanalysis and history* (p. 8), by E.H. Erikson, 1958, New York: W.W. Norton. Erikson's assumption that he had uncovered a universal human trait probably accounts for the allusions to young Hitler (p. 105) and his own views on the young at Guadalajara, Mexico (p. 266). See also "Erik Erikson on America" (pp. 43, 48), by S. Weiland, in *Intellectual craftsmen*, 1991, New Brunswick, NJ: Transaction.

34. For moratorium, *Young man Luther: A Study in Psychoanalysis and history* (p. 43), by E.H. Erikson, 1958, New York: W.W. Norton. For Luther's distinctive role, *Young man Luther* (p. 195). For the interdependence of individual, generational, and historical cycles, *Young Man Luther* (pp. 253–254).

35. From *Gandhi's truth: On the origins of militant nonviolence* (p. 169), by E.H. Erikson, 1969, New York: W.W. Norton. Note how consistent this is with Erikson's reformulation of the Golden Rule: "An adult should strive to do to another what will enhance the other's growth (at his age, in his condition, and under his circumstances) while at the same time enhancing his, the doer's, own growth (at his age, in his condition, and under his circumstances." See "Remarks on the 'Wider Identity'" (p. 502), in *Ways of looking*, 1966.

36. From *Gandhi's truth: On the origins of militant nonviolence* (p. 395), by E.H. Erikson, 1969, New York: W.W. Norton.

37. For more on this, see "Becoming a biographer: Erikson, Luther, and the problem of professional identity" (p. 193–215), by S. Weiland, in *Contesting the subject*, W. Epstein (Ed.), 1991, West Lafayette: Purdue Indiana Press.

38. From *Life history and the historical moment* (p. 109), by E.H. Erikson, 1975, New York: W.W. Norton.

39. From "Erik H. Erikson" (Vol. 18, p. 174), by M.W. Piers & G.M. Landau, in *International encyclopedia of the social sciences*, D.L. Sills (Ed.), 1979, New York: Free Press. See also Erikson's obituary (1994, May 13), *The New York Times*, p. C14.

40. From "Introduction: Reflections on aging" (p. 2), by E.H. Erikson & J.M. Erikson, in *Aging and the elderly*, S. Spicker, K.M. Woodward, & D.D. Van Tassel (Eds.), 1978, Atlantic Highlands, NJ: Humanities Press.

41. From *The life cycle completed: A review* (p. 63), by E.H. Erikson, 1982, New York: W.W. Norton. They attributed the idea itself to *Ego Psychology and the Problem of Adaptation*, by H. Hartmann, 1939, New York: International Universities Press.

42. From *Erikson: Identity and Religion* (p. 12), by J.E. Wright, Jr., 1982, New York: Seabury Press. According to Wright, Erikson.

43. From "Words for Paul Tillich" (pp. 726–728), in *A way of looking at things*, by E.H. Erikson, 1966, New York: Norton.

44. See *Life history and the historical moment* (p. 31), by E.H. Erikson, 1975, New York: W.W. Norton; and "On generativity and identity: From a conversation with Erik and Joan Erikson, 1981, *Harvard Educational Review, 51*, p. 260.

45. From *Toys and reasons: Stages in the ritualization of experience* (p. 113), by E.H. Erikson, 1977, New York: W.W. Norton. First phrase in "The Ontogeny of Ritualization in Man" (p. 590), in *Way of looking at things*, 1987, New York: Norton. See also "Jefferson and Erikson, politics, and the life cycle," by S. Weiland, 1986, *Biography, 9*, p. 303; and "The structure of Erikson's model of the eight ages: A generative approach," by P. van Geert, 1987, *Human Development, 30*, pp. 236–254.

46. From "Inner and outer space: Reflections on womanhood" (pp. 4, 20–21), by E.H. Erikson, in *Daedalus*, (1965) reprinted 1975, Westport, CT: Greenwood Press.

47. From "Notes on the life of Eleanor Roosevelt" (pp. 285, 287), by J.M. Erikson, in *Daedalus*, (1965) reprinted 1975, Westport, CT: Greenwood Press.

48. From *Identity: Youth and Crisis* (p. 11), by E.H. Erikson, 1968, New York: W.W. Norton.

49. From "Erik H. Erikson" (Vol. 18, p. 174), by M.W. Piers & G.M. Landau, in *International Encyclopedia of the Social Sciences*, D.L. Sills (Ed.), 1979, New York: Free Press. See also *Erik Erikson: The Growth of His Work* (pp. 256, 408), by R. Coles, 1970, Boston: Little, Brown; and "Erikson in His Old Age Expands His View of Life," by D. Goleman (1988), June 14), *The New York Times*, p. C1.

50. From *Activity, recovery, growth: The communal role of planned activities*, by J.M. Erikson, 1976, New York: W.W. Norton; and "The arts as healing," by H.Q. Kivnick & J.M. Erikson, 1983, *American Journal of Orthopsychiatry, 53*, pp. 602–618.

51. First quotation from *Legacies* (p. 8), by J.M. Erikson, 1993, New York: W.W. Norton; second quotation from *Wisdom and the senses* (p. 11), by J.M. Erikson, 1988, New York: W.W. Norton.

52. From *Wisdom and the senses* (pp. 78–79), by J.M. Erikson, 1988, New York: W.W. Norton.

53. From "Vital senses: Sources of lifelong learning," by J.M. Erikson, 1985, *Journal of Education, 167*, pp. 85, 95.

54. From *The life cycle completed: A review* (p. 11), by E.H. Erikson, 1982, New York: W.W. Norton.

55. From "Edward Bullough's Aesthetics and Aestheticism: Features of Reality to be Experienced," By N. Boulting, 1990, *Ultimate Reality and Meaning, 13* (September), p. 204.

56. From *Man is not alone: A philosophy of religion* (p. 296), by A.J. Heschel, 1977, New York: Farrar, Straus & Giroux.

57. From "On generativity and identity." From a conversation with Erik and Joan Erikson, 1981, *Harvard Educational Review, 51*, p. 250.

58. From "The Galilean sayings and the sense of 'I', " by E.H. Erikson, 1981, *Yale Review, 57*, p. 360.

59. From "Landing on the moon" (pp. 746–747), by E.H. Erikson, in *Way of looking*, 1987, New York: Norton. See also *Encounter with Erikson: Historical interpretation and religious biography*, by D. Capps, W.H. Capps, & M.G. Bradford (Eds.), 1977, Missoula, MT: Scholars Press.

60. Letter to Mrs. Curfman, dated December 30, 1976.

61. From "The Galilean sayings and the sense of 'I', " by E.H. Erikson, 1981, *Yale Review, 57*, p. 361.

62. From "The human life cycle" (pp. 608–609), by E.H. Erikson, in *Way of looking*, 1987, New York: Norton.

63. I thank Joan Erikson for sharing this hymn, written in 1995.

64. From *Legacies* (pp. 9–10), by J.M. Erikson, 1993, New York: W.W. Norton.

65. From *Wisdom and the senses: The way of creativity* (p. 177), by J.M. Erikson, 1993, New York: W.W. Norton.

66. From "Reflections on the last stage—and the first," by E.H. Erikson, 1984, *Psychoanalytic Study of the Child, 39*, p. 156.

67. From "On the generational cycle," by E.H. Erikson, 1980, *International Journal of Psycho-Analysis, 61*, p. 216.

68. From "Reflections on Dr. Borg's life cycle" (p. 39), by E.H. Erikson, in *Aging and the completion of being*, D.D. Van Tassel (Ed.), 1979, Philadelphia: University of Pennsylvania Press.

69. From "Reflections on Dr. Borg's life cycle" (p. 2), by E.H. Erikson, in *Adulthood*, E.H. Erikson (Ed.), 1978, New York: Norton. This essay originally appeared in a volume of *Daedalus*.

70. From *Vital improvement in old age* (p. 241), by E.H. Erikson, J.M. Erikson, & H. Q. Kivnick, 1988, New York: Norton.

71. From *Vital improvement in old age* (p. 291), by E.H. Erikson, J.M. Erikson, & H. Q. Kivnick, 1988, New York: Norton.

72. From *The life cycle completed* (p. 8–9), by E.H. Erikson, 1978, New York: Norton.

73. This and the clause quoted below are from *The life cycle completed* (p. 62), by E.H. Erikson, 1978, New York: Norton.

74. From *Wisdom and the senses: The way of creativity* (p. 109–110), by J.M. Erikson, 1993, New York: Norton.

75. From *Legacies* (pp. 6, 10–11), by J.M. Erikson, 1993, New York: Norton.

76. From *Legacies* (pp. 86–87), by J.M. Erikson, 1993, New York: Norton.

77. From *Buddha: The quest for serenity* (p. 164), by G.N. Marshall, 1978, Boston: Beacon Press.

78. From "Reflections on Dr. Borg's life cycle" (p. 54), by E.H. Erikson, in *Adulthood*, E.H. Erikson (Ed.), 1978, New York: Norton. This essay originally appeared in a volume of *Daedalus*.

79. Joan Erikson, "Gero-Transcendence," unpublished manuscript. I am grateful for permission to quote from this text but more especially for the privilege to talk with Joan Erikson about these matters.

PART TWO

Spirituality Writ Large and Small in Late Life

Religious and Ethical Strivings in the Later Years: Three Paths to Spiritual Maturity and Integrity

Melvin E. Miller

> *At fifteen I set my heart upon learning.*
> *At thirty I established myself [in accordance with ritual].*
> *At forty I no longer had perplexities.*
> *At fifty I knew the Mandate of Heaven.*
> *At sixty I was at ease with what ever I heard.*
> *At seventy I could follow my heart's desire without*
> *transgressing the boundaries of right.*
> —Confucius, *Analects*

> *Each individual, to become a mature adult, must to a sufficient degree develop all of the ego qualities . . . , so that a wise Indian, a true gentleman, and a mature peasant share and recognize in one another the final stage of integrity.*
> —E. Erikson

What is the full complement of attributes or ego qualities needed to become a mature adult enroute to something akin to integrity? What is it that "a wise Indian, a true gentleman, and a mature peasant" share and recognize in each other? Are both Erikson and Confucius, in the above passages, getting at something similar? What are the ubiquitous attributes that might be realized by women and men who have fought the good fight? What are the perennial qualities experienced by those who have struggled to reach maturity, a spiritual way of being, wisdom, and integrity?

In this chapter, I hope to cast some light on what I have found to be some of the attributes that lead to spiritual maturity. I also hope to reflect on the kinds of images of the ultimate, images of the good, and the good life that are developed and sought by those striving toward ego integrity, by those searching for ways of experiencing and expressing their spiritual aspirations or, if you will, their spiritual possession. I do not presume to be able to give any definitive responses to these complex matters, but I do intend to present a distillation of my ponderings, arrived at through research, clinical experience, and ongoing personal and theoretical tug-of-war with these concerns.

To begin with, there is something essential about the drive, the motivation, to experience a full, individuated, actualized life. In addition, the drive for a spiritual way of being, and for a moral and ethical way, are essential motivations for many.

If there are such drives, when in the life span might they "kick into gear"? Are we born with the spiritual instinct in a manner similar to Kant's categorical imperative? Does a spiritual inclination of sorts reside in people from the beginning in a manner similar to the drive to actualize or individuate as discussed by theorists such as Maslow (1968) and Adler (1927)? Perhaps there is a developmental stage, such as that espoused in Jung's midlife transition, where a spiritual instinct is awakened? Does one's search for a spiritual way of being, religious understanding, moral improvement, and genuine connectedness ever end? Is this propensity the same for all people? Does this need or desire increase or perhaps decrease in the later years? What are the forms that these strivings take?

The above represent the types of questions that interest me. From their inchoate formulation, I began to devise a strategy and a device to help me explore such questions. Out of this effort, and my long-standing interest in exploring philosophical narratives, evolved the World View Interview,[1] a structured interview procedure through which the vicissitudes of an individual's beliefs, values, motivations, and meaning-making efforts could be explored (Miller, 1982, 1988, 1994; Miller & West, 1993).

Through the use of this instrument, I found myself in a very privileged position. I was, through intermittent interviews in a longitudinal format, able to listen to the stories and narratives of people as they aged. I was able to listen to expressions of their interest in, and yearnings for, the spiritual dimension; I was able to listen to their questions of ultimate concern. Throughout this process, I became increasingly interested, both academically and personally, in exploring this often hidden dimension of human experience. In my research on world views and personality, and from my clinical experience, as I listened more and more carefully to my respondents, I heard stories and tales about the deep yearnings of the soul. It was usually when I listened more sensitively and patiently that this would happen. When I did listen carefully, I heard respondents talk about spiritual needs, ethical needs, and the need for authentic ways of being. It is this set of needs and drives—and the attendant outcomes of such drives—that I hope to explore in more detail in this chapter.

Before turning to the narratives of my research participants, I believe it would be helpful to have a collective understanding of key terms used in this chapter. First, we must come to an understanding of how the notion of spiritual maturity will be employed. In general, I plan to take my lead from Joann Conn (1989) as outlined in her book Spirituality and Personal Maturity:

> Maturity . . . [is] a matter of loving relationships and fidelity to one's personal call and gifts. Radically new possibilities and re-examination of religious authority reinforce the need for discernment which demands that one both trust and evaluate personal decisions. (p. 25)

In a similar vein, we shall draw on Erik Erikson for a working understanding of integrity. Most likely the reader is aware that integrity or ego integrity is the optimal outcome of Erikson's eighth stage of development. Erikson (1950) initially articulates his understanding of this term in his outline of the Eight Ages of Man (p. 268). Through this concept of integrity, Erikson is describing those attributes or qualities the actualized or fully developed individual may experience in the later years of life.

> Only in him who . . . has taken care of things and people and has adapted himself to the triumphs and disappointments adherent to being the originator of others or the generator of products and ideas—only in him may gradually ripen the fruit of these seven stages. I know no better word for it than ego integrity. Lacking a clear definition, I shall point to a few constituents of this state of mind. It is the ego's accrued assurance of its proclivity for order and meaning. It is a post-narcissistic love of the human ego—not of the self—as an experience which conveys some world order and spiritual sense, no matter how dearly paid for. (p. 268)

Erikson (1950) continues with this description of ego integrity.

> [Integrity] is the acceptance of one's one and only life cycle as something that had to be and that, by necessity, permitted of no substitutions . . . It is a comradeship with the ordering ways of distant times and different pursuits. Although aware of the relativity of all the various life styles which have given meaning to human striving, the possessor of integrity is ready to defend the dignity of his own life style . . . For he knows that an individual life is the accidental coincidence of but one life cycle with but one segment of history, and that for him all human integrity stands or falls with the style of integrity of which he partakes. (p. 268)

We shall be looking for the emergence or unfolding of these qualities, both maturity and integrity, in my participants as we follow the development of their spirituality in the interview excerpts to follow. Spiritual maturity and integrity will not necessarily be used interchangeably in this chapter. Nonetheless, it is assumed that there is a significant overlap present in these attributes. Those who have led thoughtful and reflective lives, guided by hard-won values, principles, and a spiritual orientation, may reflect both virtues in the later years of life.

Before we move on, we also must look further into the concepts of spirit and the spiritual, and the related notion of spirituality. What does it mean to be spirited? Might we contemplate what it means to be a spiritual person? As we do this, let us look at some early contributions to the narrative surrounding spirit and spirituality, and get a sense of how these notions might inform this study.

ON SPIRIT AND THE SPIRITED

What is this thing called spirit? Without going into the Greek, Hebrew, or early Latin etymological derivatives, we find that the notion of spirit has had a long, gradually unfolding history. Spirit has been called: "the animating or vital principle . . . that gives life to the physical organism; the breath of life. [It has been called] being or intelligence conceived as distinct from . . . anything physical or material" (*Oxford English Dictionary* [OED], p. 617).

Spirit, historically, also has been used to mean one's "mettle; vigor of mind; courage; disposition or readiness to assert oneself or hold one's own" (OED, p. 617). In addition, it has been defined as "a brisk or lively quality in things . . . liveliness, vivacity, or animation in persons, their actions, discourse, . . . " (OED, p. 617).

Spirit has also been used as a verb—meaning "to infuse spirit, life, ardor, or energy into (a person); to inspirit [inspiration]; to animate; to encourage; to lead or urge on as encouragement; to excite; instigate; or stir up; to invest with a spirit or animating principle, (and) to invest with a particular spirit, disposition or character" (OED, p. 617).

> Spirit moves one as does the wind. In . . . [the Bible], for example, spirit is said to "blow where it wills"; . . . In keeping with its wind nature, spirit is vivifying, firing, stimulating, inciting, and inspiring. Spirit is always an active, winged, swift-moving being. In addition to its characterization as wind, spirit is also said to be breathed into one. (Fuller, 1994, p. 102)

Let us think for a moment about how we use the term spirit in common, everyday language and expressions. We say things such as as the spirit moves you, he is a spirited chap, she is in low spirits today, she is in high spirits today, that was a spirited discussion, and so on.

Carl Jung is one modern thinker who boldly spoke of such unconventional and daring topics. Jung had some rather fitting notions about the importance of spirit in people's lives. Jung argued that the only life to be lived was the spirited life—

the inspired life. He wrote as if to say that it behooves a person to find what animates him or her and to live out a life in accordance with this sense of spirit. This seems to be the essence of the following passage. "[L]ife needs to be lived *in a certain spirit* [emphasis added], needs to be taken hold of and possessed by the wider consciousness that is spirit—for the fulfillment of its destined potentialities" (Jung, 1969, p. 333).

Thus, to be spirited is to have an animating energy, an energy that can be freed up for certain actions and commitments. Similarly, Andrew Fuller (1994) argues that "Life needs the superiority of independent, dominant spirit, the inspiration that spirit alone can bring. Spirit gives life meaning and allows its fullest unfolding" (p. 103).

It is important at this juncture to see how Jung and others tie together and unite the notions of spirituality and meaning. The union of these concepts is especially critical for our understanding of essential development in adulthood and the later years.

Jung proposes that the wish to find meaning—the struggle to find meaning—is an "instinct" that is initiated or sparked as one makes the turn into the second half of life. Spirit, according to Jung (1968), "is the archetype of meaning, and the spiritual is that [through which and] towards which life moves to its goal. Spirit inspires us with good and creative ideas, fills us with enthusiasm, and spurs us on" (p. 214).

Perhaps a few points on the distinction between spirit and the spiritual need to be made. Spirit, in its most basic sense, as we have seen above, can be called the animating force, the energy of life. Spirit is the breath of life and of inspiration. Yes, it may spur us on. In contrast, I shall argue that the spiritual has to do with the focusing of spirit. According to this way of thinking, the spiritual orientation comes from a focusing of spirit in a particular direction, toward salient objects or events. Spiritual refers to a particular kind of orientation to another object or being.

Sam Keen, a contemporary theologian, contends that spirituality should be understood as a soulful quest, path, or journey. To Keen (1994), this spiritual orientation or journey manifests a striving

> to discover our higher selves and to explore the depths, to allow ourselves to be moved, animated, inspired, by that sacred "no-thing" that keeps us human . . . [It is] the impulse to go beyond the ego and to explore the heights and depths, to connect our individual life with something beyond the self, something more everlasting than the self." (p. 58)

To be spiritual then, is to take the energy of spirit and direct it to commitments and connections, to personal development, or to that which is perceived as the ultimate.

Rollo May (1977) and other existential theorists speak of people with a blocked or inhibited propensity to individuate, in contrast to those possessed by spirit.

Similarly, Marion Woodman, a contemporary Jungian, writes about individuals who are reluctant to orient themselves spiritually; she speaks of those "not willing to find the river [of spirit] in their lives [nor] surrender to its current" (Anderson & Hopkins, 1991, p. 17). These reluctant souls seem alienated from themselves and cut off from the source of their inspiration and energy.

In my research, I was interested in discovering people who were willing to attempt to find the river or current[2] of spirituality in their lives, people who were willing to search for the source of their inspiration and surrender to it. Could I find individuals who were not only willing to surrender to the updraft, but also willing and able to talk about the process? As I set about my project, I wondered if I might discover research participants who invited this struggle with spirit, people who grappled with the presence of meaning in their lives. Might I find some special individuals who took an active, open orientation to such matters and who actually invited an ongoing relationship with the other, with the ultimate, regardless of the specific form in which the ultimate was envisaged? Might I find people who seemed to fit Jung's (1974) description of the spirited or spiritual life portrayed below?

> [The] . . . spiritual life—a life lived according to an ideal—in which one resolutely chooses one's own way, and demands a life beyond social, moral, religious, political, and philosophical conventionality. God's "true sons" [and daughters] are said to be those who break with convention and take the "steep and narrow path" that leads into the unknown. (Jung, 1974, p.175)

These were the individuals I hoped I might find.

MOVED BY SPIRIT: SPIRITUAL ENCOUNTERS ON THE WAY TO EGO INTEGRITY

At this point I would like to take excerpts from the interview protocols of three spirited research participants (a priest, a minister, and a professor). Here we will attempt to highlight their struggles with issues of ultimate concern and their ever-evolving relationships with matters of spirit. We shall focus on their consistent efforts to become more spiritually committed and enlivened as they strive toward ego integrity and a mature, spirited life. We will attempt to highlight their search for an ethical stance or ethical way. We will also attempt to understand their relationships with other people, with the mysterious, and with the source of their inspiration. We will briefly follow them on their spiritual paths as they move through interior, spiritual landscapes.

The excerpts from the stories of these individuals are like narrative snapshots taken from the lives of three fairly dissimilar men who are different in personal, interpersonal, and professional characteristics. These men, of course, share some commonalities as well. Thus, I ask the reader to be sensitive to both their similarities and their differences as we reflect on their lives and struggles. The reader is also invited to imagine himself or herself in some form of identification with these participants. (I imagine my own identification with them is conspicuously transparent.) Perhaps the readers will see themselves mirrored in the lives and struggles of these people and will not only observe but also experience how these noble souls confronted their demons and wrestled with the spirits of their interior worlds. Hopefully, the reader will see at least some aspect of herself or himself reflected in the lives of these three people.

There is no way that I can do justice to the breadth of the struggles encountered by these complex individuals in such a brief essay. I do hope, however, to present enough material to enable us to highlight their active, ongoing grappling with issues of ultimate concern and to focus on conflicts that emerged during their efforts to relate to the ultimate. I also would like to reflect on the personal, historical background relevant to their spiritual struggles and to explore some of the tentative resolutions at which they arrived. Finally, we shall examine some of the images of the ultimate created by them along the way.

CASE 1: THE PRIEST

The first individual is a 60-year-old research participant, a priest, who we will call Father Monti. This man has been, and continues to be, a very influential figure in his religious community, in his parish, and in his secular community. He inspires people with his ideas, his sermons, his music, and his charismatic personality. This man has been involved in seminaries and religious training for virtually his entire life. He has struggled diligently to have a special relationship with religion, spirituality, the key leaders of his order and church, and his God. This struggle has taken on many shapes and forms over the years.

In the early years, Father Monti had to struggle desperately, often against forces within himself, often against conscious will, to obey the rules and duties of his religion and his religious order. He wanted to learn how to be a "good priest." He had a lot of energy and high ideals, and he wanted to use it all for good. Thus, he resisted the inclination to disobey or challenge the rules of the church. Over time, however, he became almost sickened by the rules and by those who rigidly adhered to them, often in hypocritical ways. The customs and rules of the Church seemed to conspicuously and painfully conflict with his personal inclinations and inspirations. Even as he aspired to be a good Catholic and faithful priest, he felt tormented, exploited, and rather mishandled by the system in which he was struggling so hard to belong. He was angry with the system, with its leaders, with himself, and with God. He felt that the system—and people in the system—contributed to a reduction in his self-confidence and a fragmentation of his sense of self, and he believed that it unwittingly fostered an acute sense of inferiority, something that he struggled with most of his life. "Why is it that I have this feeling of insecurity? I mean I can take it far back into my life . . . the things that my parents have said, the things that my fellow students have said . . . (that I am irresponsible, selfish, etc.) . . . I feel a great amount of guilt [over these things]."

He continues:

I have this kind of inferiority feeling . . . I had a superior . . . who was very critical of things that I did and I don't know why and still don't to this day . . . why he hated my guts . . . and I never understood why. And I was very sensitive to this kind of feedback . . . He just simply treated me like I was a piece of dirt . . . I [also] developed this sensitivity to criticism from my peers.

He felt blamed and criticized and could not figure out why. Was he actually worthy of blame? What had he done wrong? Were the criticisms offered by his Church superiors and those issued by his parents and peers stemming from the same ugly and unsuitable traits? Were they all pointing out some indelible flaw within him? Were their responses evoked by some incredibly obvious defect? Why did he feel such an overarching inconsistency between the feelings and the yearnings of his heart and the mandates of the Church leaders? Why this overweening conscience? These are just a few of the struggles over which Father Monti agonized.

When I first arrived on the scene with the World View Interview in hand, Father Monti was almost 50 years old. He was actively working in a parish and carrying out his clerical duties while trying to come to terms with critical conflicts that had reached crises of conscience proportion. He was wrestling with the depths of his religious commitment and the challenges presented to it that took the form of questions relating to rules, dogma, morality, sexuality, interpersonal relations, and his relationship with God. He had vowed to himself that he would not give up on trying to resolve these matters, that he would not let his spirit be dampened. He pledged to work continually on his relationship with his Church, his God, and himself. He took these vows seriously—as seriously as he took his formal religious vows—and he struggled intensely. His confidence in the Church and in himself had been shaken.

The crisis of conscience seemed to focus around his reluctance to do what and act the way the superiors in his Church dictated. They wanted him to follow the Church's rules to the letter of the law. He felt distant, removed, and kept at arm's length by the church's behavioral mandates. This crisis also involved a midlife sexual awakening. The confusion and conflict surfacing around sexual urges befuddled him and led him to ask such questions of himself as how can I be a Christian and a priest and have such feelings? Am I bad or dirty? Must I actually be the evil sex monster they will say I am for having such feelings? In his own words, "The girls at the school—this sexual arousal—I found myself getting interested in girls and women, and I thought I was bad—an evil sex fiend. They always taught us the evils of sex, but never the nature of love. My order didn't teach me anything about spirituality. It taught me only to go through the motions."

Throughout this crisis period, he had been actively trying to develop a more personal relationship with his God. He had been frustrated by the effort required to live according to such a strict set of rules. He had been fighting for more depth in his relationship with God and the good. His was a striving for a more meaningful, natural relationship with God; he wanted a relationship with a more natural God, not a controlling and critical God. He did not waver or pull back from the struggle. He did not let his spirit be dampened. It was as if this ongoing quest was his job. It was more than his job; it was his duty, his vocation; it was his life's path. He was beginning to understand quite profoundly that he needed more than rules, that something more was needed in the form of relationship, to God, to the ultimate, to others, and to himself. His constant prayer at this point in his life was: "Dear God, I am your servant. Do with me whatever you will from this point on . . . I will be able to tolerate anything as long as I am in your good graces."

He continued with this prayer for some time, even as he continued to work on a new relationship with his superiors, his order, and God. At this same time, he grappled with new images of God, images that suggested a God who might be less punitive, more loving, and more relational. At some point, around midlife, Father Monti experienced something that he called a "mystical experience," an experience of God's presence. It was a transformative experience; he said it was a "turning point in my life." He went on to say that "It was about God's presence, my relationship to God, and it was a sanction of my OKness." It was as if God said, "Stop struggling so hard. You are OK the way that you are. Don't be so influenced by those Church leaders. Focus on your relationship with me, focus on your relationship with your parishioners, and let yourself be." According Father Monti,

I did have a mystical experience in my life . . . of God's presence, and I think that it was a turning point in my life. On the day that this mystical experience occurred to me, . . . I am almost sure I heard the voice [of God] say: "Monti, you are going to be my servant." I am telling you there was a feeling that came over me [as I heard something like] I'm going to use you and I am going to use your personality and your experiences. I am going to use all of that . . .

He goes on to describe this experience as a feeling of overwhelming love, a love that changed him and transformed him, and contributed to a kind of self-acceptance.

I am not afraid anymore . . . because I have been loved enough by God; he has really given me a lot of gifts. There is hope for us all, if we can just quit worrying about ourselves and just let the Lord love us and try to give love back as well . . . [T]he day that I found out I was lovable was the day that my life was changed.

He believed that this awakening or transformative moment happened to him because he continued to struggle with the issues that were tormenting him, because he continued to pray, to meditate, and to work on his relationship with God and his image of God and because he never gave up. Here are some of his reflections that followed the transformative experience.

I now have a kind of spirituality all my own . . . My prayer is the prayer of nature. My prayer is the prayer of being with people, and it is not the prayer that my order wants me to do out of a book.

He finally began to be comfortable with this prayer and with himself. He went on:

I think being a preacher is very important to me. But . . . I'm only as good as the relationship that I have with God because it's duplicity for me to get up there and talk about platitudes that I've been taught over the years . . . which is the way I was when I first became a preacher . . . [Early on] I wrote things that people should hear because I was trained to tell these kinds of things.

He could now describe himself as one who was formerly rule driven and as one who had been attempting to shift from such archaic ways to a more authentic and spontaneous style. He began to understand that the problem with rules and regulations—and the crisis of conscience—was tied in with his own psychology and, to some degree, with his personal conflicts relating to rules and direction imposed from outside. He was so pleased that some internal change had actually begun. In terms of being a religious speaker and studying scripture, he noted that, after the mystical experience, he finally began to take pleasure in ecclesiastical activities that used to be so tedious. Now he could do what he heretofore had resented, since he wasn't just following the rules.

I enjoy it. [Now, I can sit] down for a whole afternoon and simply read scriptures and the interpretations that great minds have given to us, and I'm not even aware that time had passed. It went [in time] from "you should" to "it would be nice if you did" to

"I want to." And, I think I've finally integrated all that . . . to the stage now that . . . nobody has to tell me that "you should do this." I'm speaking more about integration now . . . I would like to be a preacher who believes what he is saying because he has integrated it into his own life.

From this point on, he approached his calling with renewed vigor and energy. He began to feel more integrated emotionally; the personal and professional arenas of his life felt more integrated as well.

In the second interview a decade or so later, at almost 60, Father Monti was still working on developing his relationships with people and his relationship with God. He was trying to care even more for his parishioners. He also continued to make gains in self-confidence and self-esteem. He affirmed that he had made a lot of progress in his relationship with God, and he was still working on it. At this point in his life, he could imagine a God that was not a mean-spirited tyrant or a pusher of rules and regulations, but a loving God, a relationship God, a God of nature. He had now found a God with whom he could dialogue, as found in both nature and people.

It all seemed easier and more natural now. He believed that he was continuing to assimilate and integrate the meaning of this transformative experience into his everyday life, primarily leading to more self-acceptance and more care for his fellow human beings. Here are some examples of the dominant awareness articulated by Father Monti that were distilled from the second interview:

[T]he philosophy that was still underlying it all was my personal relationship with God as I viewed him and that view has changed dramatically over the years. That personal relationship with God now in my life at the age of 58 . . . is based on those who are ill, because He said, "When I was sick, you visited me." And this is my spirituality now; this is my prayer. I am in the position or I have the honor of serving . . . directly through dealing with His sick, because when I am dealing with them I am dealing with Him. So this is my prayer life, right here. The reason I love it so much is that my work is my prayer, and I am totally fulfilled in this work.

Concerning his response to guilt experienced over not abiding by the rules of the Church in a rigid, dogmatic manner, he comments: "There is no more guilt." He continued along this vein:

Now I could not, based on my philosophy, ever do an evil action deliberately. It is . . . far removed from my personality. I can literally and truthfully say to you, I have never done an action that I regarded as being an affront to God . . . even though it was contrary to what those guys [Church superiors] said . . . [I]f I were to do that, it would be like taking . . . [someone] you love deeply, and killing the relationship somehow. Now, that would be hell for me.

How consistent he feels his actions and behaviors to be with his conscience and his sense of the ultimate. His spiritual strivings, according to his
own report, have led him in the direction in which he was aiming. He claims
to be at peace. He goes on to say, "[Now] I have the very thing I've been trying all my life to get and that is a personal relationship with God and I find
it here in my people. I don't know what else could be given me that would
be greater than this. I am fulfilled."

In brief, we have come to see how a devout man of the cloth had to struggle diligently to come into his own—to move toward ego integrity and spiritual maturity. We see how he worked to direct his spirit and energy and how
he strove to do so through meditation, dialogue, and prayer. He developed
the ability to set limits and to say "no." He had learned to say "no" to the
more questionable rules of the order. He learned to say "no" or "hands off"
to the people who made him feel so inferior. In the process, he deeply struggled with impulses and yearnings that were contrary to the order and its
teachings; he learned that he could put them in a manageable perspective. He
actively worked to create, construct, and keep an image of God in mind, an
image that had more to do with relationship, nature, and peace than any he
had known previously.

CASE 2: THE MINISTER

The second research participant is a 50-year-old Protestant minister. We
shall call him Reverend Ernest. Reverend Ernest was born into a family of
ministers. His father, grandfather, uncles, and brothers were all ministers. He
inherited this tradition and believed that he had to follow it, as if he had no
choice in the matter. So, he did follow in the family tradition, albeit not without great ambivalence and conflict.

Since I came from a long line of ministers, I wonder if I am doing it for the wrong
reasons. I was inoculated with just enough Christianity for a long time to keep me
from catching the real thing. I learned Christianity as a culture, as family heritage,
as duty, and as ritual—all of which seem very, very close to the center of Christianity, but . . . missing the kernel.

In the first interview, Reverend Ernest described how being the youngest
in his prep school class negatively affected him and shaped his personality
and interpersonal style. He was always picked on; he was always beaten up.
Below, he mentions the impact that this dynamic played in his life.

When I was a child of 11, 12, 13 and was going off to prep school, I found that I was
2 years younger than the rest of the school. I was beat on [by the older students] and

thus I developed coping strategies which involved pleasing people and being self-evasive. Out of adapting to this situation, I came to feel that assertiveness was dangerous and probably wrong. And, therefore, since assertiveness was taboo, long-range goals were hard to set.

In many ways, Reverend Ernest believed that this early experience set the tone for and established the paradigm for much of his later professional life and interpersonal relationships. "If you think that you need to please people so that they will quit beating on you or affirm you, that tempts you to even more workaholism."

Reverend Ernest talked further about his early, formative years. He noted that throughout his college and graduate years he struggled to find his way. He felt lukewarm in his religious commitment. He even took a naturalistic, positivistic world view during his university years because it was popular to do so in his circle. He also believed he did so because it was difficult for him to understand and develop his own position, let alone take an unpopular stance. It was as if his center or core was offbase, misdirected. He was pleasing everyone else but not himself; personally, he was floundering. This was all so disconcerting. He had high energy and a wish to do good things but no real direction, except to please others, except to avoid harm.

Early in the first interview session, Reverend Ernest frequently articulated a struggle he had been experiencing related to an important professional decision. He had been offered an administrative position in the church just prior to the first World View Interview. He was torn between his own interest in academic teaching and writing and the call or the pressure to become more involved in administration and church leadership. He accepted the administrative position. In his own words: "Something needed to be done; nobody else seemed to be up to doing it. I am always eager to please, so I said I would do it. I am not comfortable with the decision."

He spoke often about the frequent struggle between what he thought he wanted from within versus the demands from without. He needed to please and to get the reinforcement; he longed for the positive feedback obtained from a job well done. In addition, he needed to keep people from beating on him. So, he more or less capitulated to the pressures from the church authorities to be the best administrator that he could be. It was as if he didn't want to give into such pressures, but he felt that he "needed to" or "had to." Interestingly, as he began to fulfill this new role, he began to discover an urge for power emerge within himself. It was as if these newly found feelings of power could make up for the years of being picked on. Nonetheless, at times during the interview, he berated himself for selling himself to the highest bidder. In some respects, he felt like he had sold his soul to the devil.

On the other hand, at a very deep level, Reverend Ernest wanted to grow, to develop, to feel the freedom to individuate but instead felt seduced by the reinforcements found in administration. He needed to please people; he wanted to please people; he liked the adulation and positive feedback. He enjoyed the approbation but found that, meanwhile, he had overlooked family, friends, and, perhaps most importantly, himself. His relationship with God seemed to disappear in the process as well.

When asked about his most important life goals or objectives, he responded,

I am re-evaluating whom I want to please and acknowledging very painfully that I can't please everybody. I really want to live; I really want to live in God—the trying God . . . In terms of long range goals? I define the primary long range goal as knowing God and enjoying him forever. The specific . . . form this takes at the present is— working through this *mid-life crisis* [emphasis added] or whatever, and trying to come to a resolution between an emphasis on teaching and an emphasis on administration.

It was in midlife, in the midst of a midlife crisis of sorts, that he began to look at himself more closely. He began to look more systematically at his personality style, his people-pleasing, self-effacing tendencies, and the untoward consequences of these qualities. He also had begun to realize about this time that he had been fighting against the updraft; he had been resisting the current of the river of self-transformation. Reverend Ernest had great intellect, great skills, and great energy, and he eventually came to understand that these strengths were not unified or focused in the most self-enhancing manner. He berated himself for following the plans of others—for responding so readily to the "call to please." He desired to be truer to himself and his unique spiritual journey. This was his prayer. He continues with this line of thought:

Whom do you play to? Firstly, in the spiritual quest, learning how to relate to God, not as a cosmic taskmaster, not as a policeman in the sky, not in those categories that one tends to use compulsively as a child, but in some way as He really is. I have come to discover that this is the spiritual quest at the deepest level. Secondly, as a priority, would be the family. The family and I do not want to let work come above the family in order of priority. What does a man profit if he gains the whole world and loses his family?

Despite this awareness, and his attempt to fight against his workaholism and the tendency to please, he did take the job in administration. He continued to be ruled by the people-pleasing demon for a while longer. He went on to attempt to develop the perfect Christian community. As he did so, he lost his relationship with himself, with God, and, to a degree, with his wife and family.

Finally, he decided to put an end to these counterproductive ways. In the second interview, at age 50, he talked more about an increased awareness of his self-declared foibles. "I pushed my needs on the community, and not God's needs or wishes." Reverend Ernest is now able to admit to himself that he remained a workaholic during the administrative years. Yes, he was getting good feedback and praise for the job he was doing, but he remained discontented and unhappy. Yes, he had been getting the job done; he had helped create a very exciting learning and religious environment. He had been infusing others with energy and spirit, and with a sense of mission and passion. Something was missing for him, however.

So . . . if there was a career to which I was committed, it was this dream of being part of a "perfect Christian community." And, what I've discovered, of course, is that dreams can be savagely devouring . . . that the price of participation in that type of project is often higher than you want to go on paying indefinitely . . . And, also, I guess you discover that the dream is not susceptible of realization . . . that in some ways the harder you work at it, the worse you do.

He continues,

All of this has become clear to me, I think, in the last year or so. I'll be fifty this year. Realizing how much my need to recapture . . . a family I missed out on at some point earlier on, and also my need to be part of something "important" drove my partici-pation in this dream . . . or this career . . . and how I was embedded in it . . . I could-n't get any distance on it . . . and just got really burned out trying to make a perfect Christian community happen on the basis of my own application of energy.

At this point, it seems that Reverend Ernest really wanted to do things dif-ferently. He sincerely wanted to let relationship be the centerpiece or key-stone of his existence, e.g., his relationship with his wife, with family, with a Christian community, and with God. Relationships became central to him, as opposed to hard, driving work. As this began to happen, he no longer felt burned out; his spirit and energy became more focused, and he believed him-self to be heading in a healthier, more integrated direction.

What I think I got a little distance on over the last year has been the needs that were driving my participation in this dream, and a little distance on the ideology of the community that I belong to . . . realizing that it has a lot of strengths . . . but doesn't incorporate other significant themes quite as well. For example, it has strong com-mitments to truth, . . . and it is a strongly thinking type orientation . . . but maybe not so strong commitments to relationships. While the truth commitment is necessary, an overweening preoccupation with truth is really unhelpful to a lot of people.

It seems that something rather transformative had been occurring within Reverend Ernest. He was now more critical of the community that he was trying so hard to please. In addition, it appears that he was noticing within his church community the very same kinds of psychological issues and dynamics with which he had been struggling over the years. He spoke from first-hand experience. As all this was developing, he began to get an even sharper image of what he wanted for his own continued psychological and spiritual development. In his own words again, "Now, I would like to develop a network of acquaintances and colleagues who are interested in the same kinds of questions I am . . . namely . . . adult development . . . spirituality, and the reconciliation of men and women."

When asked about his level of satisfaction with his present personality and what he envisaged for future growth, Reverend Ernest replied,

I feel like I'm just out of the egg . . . just beginning to grow. I read the literature of Christian spirituality over twenty centuries, and I look at these people and I think . . . oh man, they were light years beyond where I am. I'm just getting to the point where I might get to the starting line . . . I want to be more receptive and open—listening and paying attention, . . . and yet I'm grateful to God for who I am. I don't feel that the solution to the remaining deficiencies in my personality—of which I'm so painfully aware—is repression or willful imposed discipline, but rather a deeper relationship with God.

He continued, "So in terms of goals and objectives . . . I am waiting and seeing, in part. I certainly would like to emphasize relationships in the next phase of my life . . . much more than ideology and the defense of the institution . . . which is where I've been the last 15 years or so.

Thus, we find Reverend Ernest continuing to individuate while promoting relationships that included committed and connected involvement. At this juncture in his life there seems to be much less of a need to please. We find more of a sense of personal integrity, more a sense of self, and self-possession. We should note that he worked hard at arriving at this place in his growth. He never gave up on himself. He kept re-envisioning what he wanted in his life. Through an ongoing exploratory process, he eventually arrived at an expanded understanding of God, a newly constructed image of God, and a more personal relationship with God. In turn, the roles of relationship and dialogue became privileged in every facet of his life. Through the process of these changes, his gifts of care and spirit to the community became even greater.

CASE 3 : THE PROFESSOR

The third participant, a 73-year-old retired college professor, is a self-proclaimed humanist and atheist. We call him Professor Ansel. He is included for purposes of contrast with the clergymen and because his journey is fascinating in its own right. He is a secular figure who is not interested in God talk or God imaging per se but he spoke passionately of kindness, decency, good deeds, and the good. Despite not being a clergyman or theist, we found that he too attempted to orient himself to spirit and the spirited life. Perhaps, in part, because his spirit and energy were not as obvious or as out-there-in-the-world as those of the other two participants, he became an interesting figure for us to examine. As we will see, his energies and interests in the earlier years appeared to be somewhat unfocused. He seemed to struggle even more than the others to channel them and have them flow with his creative force.

Professor Ansel described being brought up in a very comfortable, conflict-free environment where people were nice, kind, and respectful with each other. Professor Ansel reports: "My mother was a terrific woman and my stepfather was a very gentle guy." Professor Ansel noted that excessive demands were not placed on people by his family but that they did promote a kind of curiosity, a curiosity about nature, ideas, religion and the world. Kindness, decency, and a moral way were advocated, but not much was offered in the way of focused direction or goal achievement. When asked about life goals and life directions in the first interview (conducted at age 57), Professor Ansel replied, "I'm not sure how I escaped forming goals as most people think of them. I don't really think I have developed any . . . any goals . . . any life goals . . . I am one who lives very much in the present . . . and I have a good bit of trouble planning something a year . . . or five years from now. I've never really done that."

He continued along these lines:

Almost everything I've done has been kind of almost . . . well, it hasn't been planned like you like to think of people saying "well in ten years I want to do so and so. I need to do this and this and this to get there." I've never done that, and since I don't have it in my habit pattern, I find it impossible to do now . . . I'm just so caught up in the moment.

This inability to set goals seemed to be a perennial concern for Professor Ansel. He has many talents and gifts, and interests, (science, art, teacher, craftsman) but typically was not able to focus them in any particular direction. So, Professor Ansel went out into the world of education, academia, the sciences, and the arts. He tried to make his way. He'd move in one direction and then in another. He had talent in the sciences, arts, and the liberal arts. He was interested in philosophy, religion, and literature. He just couldn't focus on any one thing. In his own words,

I've been interested in too many things to be really good in one area, and I've never had the discipline to put everything else aside and pursue only one thing. If I had done nothing else and just pursued . . . [painting], you know, it might have worked out better. I spent a lot of time and effort getting "tooled up." This has kind of followed me along. I guess it is a kind of characteristic. I'm still in the process of getting "tooled up."

In looking for an explanation or reason for this phenomenon, Professor Ansel noted,

I never felt that I had a very strong ego . . . This has probably done me some harm, because it never gave me the confidence in my abilities, although I know I have some [abilities]. But, ones that I know I have are never really developed very well . . . in any purposeful way.

It is interesting to note Professor Ansel's awareness of his own lack of ego strength. We get the impression that he felt this way from early on. Despite this awareness, he kept moving forward; he kept trying to find a way to orient himself in the world. He drifted for a while, from college to college, from one graduate program to another. He seemed aimless. He eventually married a woman who was an attorney. She was very ambitious and very focused. According to Professor Ansel, she was also very angry and an alcoholic. He tried to take care of her and support her, even though she put him down and degraded his work and his interest in the arts. Meanwhile, he put his own needs on hold.

When asked about early guiding principles or philosophical influences, Professor Ansel replied,

I had rather a sheltered upbringing, and I never had to worry about security. I was always with people who dealt reasonably with each other and with their associates, and I guess I just kind of absorbed that. And, so, the way I operate is really fairly simple. I just try to generally be as helpful as I can . . . to those I'm working with, etc., . . . and treat people reasonably. It really isn't very grandiose.

Being reasonable, kind, helpful, and decent became operative values for Professor Ansel. Upon further thought about the formation of his values and philosophy, he remarked,

I think my guiding principles are really fairly simple. I suppose this is because I was raised by a mother who . . . might have been termed a free thinker, and as a result didn't have any firm theological ideas. She was much affected by people around her, and she knew enormous numbers of people and would periodically be influenced by one group or another . . . There was no evidence that organized religion ever really did much for my stepfather either. As a result, I had a rather eclectic background.

He continued,

When I was a teenager . . . and I started to ask questions about the world and life's meaning and so on, I was unlike other teenagers who would go to their pastor or priest and ask questions. I couldn't. I went to the library and dug things out. And, because I was exposed to Christian Science and a Catholic private school and Christian Sunday School and a synagogue, I got exposed to a variety, and this led me to be aware that there were many points of view. It led me to read extensively and be rather amazed at how many viewpoints on the world there were.

Further, along these lines,

Rather than help me solidify things [this background] helped me kind of be "on the fence" longer . . . Maybe it caused me to take a more detached look at the world and the human condition and say that people are [the way they are] for historical reasons. As a [scientist] . . . my world view does not include a supreme being, . . . and I resent people from some special group going in and saying this is the way things ought to be . . . [They do this] in the face of a plethora of world views saying this is the right one, and therefore you change the way you live.

Despite his diverse background in religious and philosophical matters, Professor Ansel persisted in the struggle to develop a workable philosophy. He continued to work on himself—to get into the flow of his long-standing interests, preoccupations, and creative outlets. Although his strivings were exclusively in the secular world, at times they had a sense of urgency and ultimacy not unlike those of Father Monti and Reverend Ernest.

After 10 difficult years of marriage, and after much self-questioning and vocational drifting, he divorced his wife. At this point, he was finally able to settle down with himself and his talents, and he began to focus a little more. He continued to ask questions, such as where have I been in life, where am I going, and what do I believe in? What is the best way for me to actualize my potentials? He stayed with the search and he tried to become more focused.

He eventually settled into college teaching. He did not give up on the arts nor his philosophic questioning; he did not give up on himself. He found a mate who appreciated his many talents, someone who did not demand that he be in a prestigious profession. Somehow he began to feel that there was room for him to develop and explore. In his 40s and 50s, he began to thrive. He began to find himself. Perhaps it was the security of this new relationship and his determination to make it work that enabled him to begin to find himself. Although he taught sciences at the college level as a vocation, he permitted himself to indulge in the arts as much as he wanted. He continued to pursue his studies in philosophy and religion. Things began to come together for him.

His second marriage was to a woman he could support and nurture, and she was someone who could reciprocate these gifts. He described his second marriage as a turning point in his life. He was now with someone who shared his interest in art, science, and religion. His wife could also fully engage him in relationship, something he had yearned for. Relationship was so very important to Ansel. He loved the reciprocity of a warm, caring relationship. He also loved the fact that he could debate philosophy, art, and religion with his new mate. She was equally involved in connecting to spirit and creative expression. He talked about these changes in the second interview as well.

In the second interview, at age 69, Professor Ansel talked even more about the development of his philosophical outlook and the minor changes and fine tuning that took place over the years. He also said more about the connections his philosophy had with his creative and professional strivings and the way he lived his life.

I developed my own philosophy [a kind of scientific, humanistic atheism] and I don't need support for it from somebody else . . . you know, to keep it going. I can't imagine anything that would upset my worldview. I think it is really serviceable. Maybe we all like to think ours is the correct one, but it is as close as being correct as I can imagine. So, I'm going with it; it is a workable philosophy.

He continued, "You know there are good, religious people who believe . . . in God, and they treat people with respect too. And, probably if you put us side by side in the way we dealt with people, there might not be any difference."

In addition to the philosophical changes evident in the above, we also see a gain in self-confidence evidenced by Professor Ansel. He seemed to exhibit a greater confidence in his philosophy of life and in the focusing of his energies. In fact, the more he consolidated his view of the world, the more he found his sense of self, his way of being in the world, and his way of relating to the world all improving.

At other places in the second interview, Professor Ansel talked about being happy and content with life. He exhibited a greater focus on his avocations—woodworking and painting. He presented more one-man art shows. He felt the freedom to concentrate more fully on his creations. He has remained very active intellectually, reading prolifically, and attending humanistic and philosophical meetings. He articulated an awareness that things were coming together for him in very constructive ways. He summed up his perspective quite nicely in the following: "Yes, I am still kind of a jack of all trades . . . and I have plenty of room to improve. I keep trying to do things better than I have. I keep taking classes in [art] and seminars. If I just improve what I'm into now, I'll be quite happy. Actually, . . . my cup runneth over."

DISCUSSION

In the preceding we witnessed three men struggling with their infection of spirit in very different ways. We noted how they attempted to get into relationship with it and how they attempted to direct it. They seemed almost possessed by spirit early on. Their lives seemed to be engrossed in an attempt to get with the updraft, even as part of them seemed to struggle against it. Sometimes defenses, conflicts, or interpersonal issues got in the way of their involvement with the spiritual. We saw them wrestle with many impediments to their spiritual focus, but they continued to "fight the good fight." They continued to struggle with relationship, ethical and leadership issues, as well as with personal conflicts and their respective modes of being in the world.

Almost all research participants, in addition to these three, seemed committed to and passionate about giving themselves over to spirit. (This phenomenon was not always described in a religious sense; often it wasn't.) Nonetheless, these people resolutely struggled to find their ways during the midlife period and beyond. As they did so, they often evidenced an uncanny ability to infuse others—to stir up and animate others—with life, spirit, and courage. They influenced most who met them; they inspired those with whom they came in contact. Yet, as we have witnessed, they did not have an easy time of it themselves. They were often plagued by self-doubt, confusion, and uncertainty. They never gave up, however.

Little did I realize, as I began my world view research, that it would develop into a project of such magnitude and dimension. I never quite imagined that this project would evolve into a vehicle through which I could begin to get some insight into these essential spiritual strivings and the forces behind them. In essence, I had been asking people about what possessed them, and I didn't quite realize this at the time. I did have a strong hunch that those things (those ideas, those passions) that possessed people would have a motivating, driving influence in their lives. I didn't realize the power or energy behind these possessions and forces, however. I didn't realize how they could streamline a life in a particular direction, nor move one along with such force.

I have presented only three people, but they seem to be representative of the entire sample. What I heard from Father Monti, Reverend Ernest, Professor Ansel, and the other men in my study was a kind of longing for integration, actualization, and maturity. I also witnessed a tension in many of them. Sometimes it was a twofold tension. There was the tension experienced through being estranged from the updraft, from being out of the current. There was also a tension between the demands of and the longing for individual growth (the need to individuate) and the need to be involved in and grow through relationship. The call toward experiencing both seemed to get louder and louder for some as they aged. The passage of time seemed to create a sense of urgency for most. All three participants evidenced an integration of both individuation needs and the need for intimate relationships, with partners, friends, and the ultimate. As they approach the twilight years and their eventual deaths, the level of activity in their searches appears to have intensified; they do not divert their eyes from the path.

In short, I found each man iterating a call for meaning, a cry towards integration. They were attempting to situate their lives within the context of something greater than themselves. For some, this meaning was found in the re-creation or revamping of images of God. For others, deeper meaning was found in a new relationship with nature. For many, meaning was discovered in a revitalized relationship with friends and lovers or perhaps in a new relationship with the ultimate as they continued to rethink and revision their images of the ultimate.

Finally, this project, in addition to all the above, is a study of individual motivations to change, the capacity to change, and the dynamics of change. It is a study of how people construe and act upon the wish and need to transform their lives. This chapter is also an examination of the role that the formation of images can have in one's spiritual life. Likewise, it is an examination of the role of self-reflection, meditation, and prayer. It is a study of how spirit and energy (the vitalizing force) become channeled in individual lives. In this light, one could also say that we have been looking at how spirited people become spiritual beings. This chapter, in that respect, is a tribute to both the determination and the indomitable spirit of humankind.

Here is a question to ponder in closing: Can we imagine, can we conjure up, a fantasy of a meeting among these three men (Father Monti, Reverend Ernest, and Professor Ansel) at some point down the road, perhaps at a mutually shared chronological crossroads at age 75 or possibly 80? Perhaps we can imagine these men saying to themselves (and to each other) the words of Confucius noted at the beginning of the chapter: Yes, I am at ease with whatever I hear; I can follow my heart's desire without transgressing the boundaries of right. Might we dare to think that each could see in the other (that they could share with and recognize in one another) a kind of spiritual maturity—a kind of integral fullness—despite the differences in background and orientation? Might these men also realize in themselves and in each other the attributes of Erikson's final stage of ego integrity? Such a fantasy is a rich one. Yes, I can imagine it.

NOTES

1. For a transcript of the complete World View Interview, contact Melvin E. Miller, Department of Psychology, Norwich University, Northfield, Vermont 05663. For a further discussion of the overall worldview project and details on the development of the World View Interview, see Miller (1982, 1994, 1996).

2. For a further discussion of this concept, see Pierre Teilhard de Chardin's *The Phenomenon of Man* (1965) and *The Divine Milieu* (1957). Mihaly Csikszentmihalyi's (1990) explication of the concept of flow is fairly consistent with the idea of giving oneself over to the current of one's spiritual inspiration as well.

REFERENCES

Adler, A. (1927). *The practice and theory of individual psychology.* New York: Harcourt, Brace & World.

Anderson, S.R., & Hopkins, P. (1991). *The feminine face of god: The unfolding of the sacred in women.* New York: Bantam Books.

Conn, J.W. (1989). *Spirituality and personal maturity.* Lanham, MD: University Press of America.

Csikszentmihalyi, M. (1990). *Flow: The psychology of optimal experience.* New York: Harper Collins Publishers.

Erikson, E.H. (1950). *Childhood and society.* New York: Norton.

Fuller, A.F. (1994). *Psychology and religion: Eight points of view.* Lanham, MD: Littlefield Adams.

Jung, C.G. (1968). *The archetypes and the collective unconscious.* Princeton, NJ: Princeton University Press.

Jung, C.G. (1969). *The structure and dynamics of the psyche.* Princeton, NJ: Princeton University Press.

Jung, C.G. (1974). *The development of personality.* Princeton, NJ: Princeton University Press.

Keen, S. (1994). *Hymns to an unknown god: Awakening the spirit in everyday life.* New York: Bantam.

Maslow, A.H. (1968). *Toward a psychology of being.* New York: Van Nostrand.

May, R. (1977). *The meaning of anxiety.* New York: Norton.

Miller, M.E. (1982). World views and ego development in adulthood. *Dissertation Abstracts International, 42,* 3459–3460.

Miller, M.E. (1988). Developing a world view: The universal and the particular. *New England Psychological Association Newsletter, 5,* 3–4.

Miller, M.E. (1994). World views, ego development, and epistemological changes from the conventional to the postformal: A longitudinal perspective. In M. E. Miller & S. Cook-Greuter (Eds.), *Transcendence and mature thought in adulthood* (pp. 147–179). Lanham, MD: Rowman & Littlefield.

Miller, M.E. (1996). Ethics and understanding through interrelationship: I and thou in dialogue. In R. Josselson (Ed.), *Ethics and process in the narrative study of lives* (pp. 129–147). Thousand Oaks, CA: Sage.

Miller, M.E., & West, A.N. (1993). Influences of world view on personality, epis-
    temology, and choice of profession. In J. Demick & P. Miller (Eds.) *Develop-
    ment in the workplace* (pp. 3–19). Hillsdale, NJ: Lawrence Erlbaum.
Oxford English Dictionary (compact ed.). (1971). New York: Oxford University
    Press.
Teilhard de Chardin, P. (1957). *The divine milieu: An essay on the interior life.*
    New York: Harper & Row.
Teilhard de Chardin, P. (1965). *The phenomenon of man.* New York: Harper &
    Row.
Wei-Ming, T. (1978). The Confucian perception of adulthood. In E. Erikson (Ed.),
    Adulthood (pp. 113-127). New York: Norton.

Reading Between the Lines: Aspects of Transcendence and Spirituality in One Group

Susan A. Eisenhandler

T he renowned ethologist, Konrad Lorenz, suggested late in his life that the time for reflection "and the freedom that one needs for this is a human right." (Lorenz, 1987, p. 147) The value Lorenz placed on freedom and thought as basic human rights underscores what might seem self-evident to many about humans and their contemporary existence: The process of reasoning and the occasions that stimulate reflective thinking are wedged more and more tightly into smaller and smaller portions of an adult's life. Whether daily, weekly, monthly, or yearly, the pauses and places for reading and reflection have been diminished in the helter-skelter of postmodern life. The old have not escaped this diminution of times and occasions available for reflection.

Indeed, the inflation in the social value placed on "leisure consumption" by the old as a group has placed them in a precarious position with respect to spirit and soul. They are in the mainstream of movement away from occasions and times of sustained reflection and contemplation, times and occasions formerly thought to be associated with retirement, or in the contemplation of death, that in developed countries is most closely associated with late life. To put it bluntly, the old are increasingly sought as consumers, a market segment, not merely for health care or allocations therein but as purchasers of products and of a wide range of experiences. Old age as a steady stream of time spent in front of slot machines, bingo cards, television shows, or sporting events somehow seems an affront to the great gift of thinking and reasoning that is the distinctive mark of the humanity of our species in contrast to other nonhuman species. When consuming experiences becomes a modus vivendi, it matters little what the content of an activity may be. For example, age-specific programs whose products or experiences may be beneficial in many respects are themselves in the midst of being transformed into beguiling substitutes for substantive activity and thought by market forces. One need not fully subscribe to Ivan Illich's extreme statement that death is the ultimate act of consumer resistance in order to understand the implications of buying into a paradigm of late life as merely another stage of consumption.

Younger cohorts among the old may soon find themselves even less likely than the oldest of the old to find or follow a regimen that presents opportunities for thought, be it spiritual or secular. Contrary to some powerful evidence about a renaissance of concern with religious and spiritual matters, it is the young-old cohorts who were most dramatically affected in their adulthood by post–World War II trends of secularization and apostasy. The aging babyboom cohort will, in a decade, bring its own imprint of secular and spiritual matters to the stage of late life. The effect on this cohort of instantaneous communication and access to information has yet to be carefully examined, but dedication to traditional forms of intellectual and spiritual activity has not been a hallmark of this generation. Thus, the limited expression and range of intellectual opportunity available to older adults may already be evaporating; the future may present more in the way of "psychic friends" than philosophical pondering or opportunity for reflection.

THE EXPERIENCES OF ONE READING GROUP

In order to develop some perspective on the kinds of social settings and occasions conducive to reflection and thought before such settings disappear or are altered to fit the dimensions of Internet chat rooms, I would like to discuss some experiences that emerged over the course of a 12-week reading group. The particular group experiences I describe are those associated with the most recent reading group I directed. Drawing on my participant observation in this group and my experiences over the years with other reading groups, I suggest that this primary group represents one of the strongest possible ways to arrange social actors and social settings conducive to and necessary for intellectual and spiritual growth in late life. This particular chapter describes a time, occasion, and group—a set of social actors—where reading, thinking, and talking shaped social interaction for 12 weeks in the late spring and early summer of 1995. The group, which met weekly, was not devoted to autobiography, oral or written, or life review. It was not a group with any particular religious or theological orientation or dogma, nor was it a psychotherapeutic group or a group that actually produced or purchased any tangible product. The group was a purposive reading and discussion group: a small group of women, occasionally hovering around the tipping point of a large group, a handful of whom knew one another very well from church and community work, some of whom had only met previously in other reading and discussion groups, and some who were unacquainted with one another until the group formed.[1] Most of the women were familiar with the process and purpose of this kind of group, but most were not intimately acquainted.

CONTEMPLATIVE ROOTS OF READING

I detail some of our experiences with reading and share some of the reflections engendered from time spent reading and responding to others. I call this group spiritual and moral by virtue of the themes, ideas, and debates educed in the turns of our conversations. Specifically, I propose that this kind of group experience approximates something akin to *ruminatio*. This richly laden word captures the meditative and active component of contemplation found at its peak development among western European monastic communities during medieval times (LeClercq, 1962; Needleman, 1993). From the contemporary perspective advanced here, *ruminatio* is understood as an active form of reading and contemplation that encourages attentiveness and stimulates receptivity to and curiosity about spiritual matters. My use of the term is consistent with both its monastic roots and the complementary liturgical practices that educed *ruminatio*, though quite obviously the social setting and group ties of a small group of elderly women reflects a very different sociohistorical period worlds away from the cloister.

The nature of focused contemplation or *ruminatio* that typified this elderly reading group stands in stark contrast to the portent of megachurches managing religion or, alternatively, charismatic religious groups and media ministries capturing lost, isolated souls. Moreover, this image is the opposite of contemporary institutionalized religions and their attendant practices, although the activity of small groups reading, thinking, and discussing what they've read has traditionally been at the heart of religious epistemology. Group interaction in response to sacred text is the heart of liturgy, prayer, and some forms of scriptural study. Manguel's (1996) recent work on the history and development of reading documents turning points in the process and method of reading (e.g., reading out loud in a group; reading as a solitary act) and amply illustrates the great variety of size and setting in experiences with text. It is through the medium of group interaction that worship and reading are joined as ways of knowing and of seeking connections with others and with that which is holy. As Bellah, Madsen, Sullivan, Swidler, and Tipton (1991, p. 285) have commented, "The impulse toward larger meaning, thankfulness, and celebration has to have an institutional form, like all the other central organizing tendencies in our lives, so that we do not dissipate it in purely private sentiment." The reading group had the lightest institutional form one can imagine. Lest I wander ahead of my narrative and sociological perspective, however, I will now turn to outlining a conceptual framework for understanding this reading group, a description of our experiences, and the thesis that these experiences are filaments of transcendent meaning, tangible albeit evanescent occasions that enlarged the spirits of older women.

READING AND INTERACTION: A SPIRITUAL EVOLUTION

Sociologists and social psychologists have long held that it is our group membership and participation, our association with others, as well as the size and dynamic nuances of intragroup and intergroup relations that shape our individual perspective of self-identity and our social lives. Another significant feature of shared experience in small groups, including religious and spiritual ones, is the character of interaction and the nature of attentiveness to the purpose or task of the group. With respect to religious attachment, sociologists and social psychologists interested in religion (e.g., Festinger, 1956; Lofland, 1966; Berger, 1967; Greeley, 1989; Demerath,1974; Roof, 1978; Bellah & his associates, 1991), although differing in perspective and in emphasis, would concur with Durkheim's (1915/1965) functionalist formulation that "the idea of society is the soul of religion." Durkheim's observation that it is the cohesive and integrative elements of group belonging, social bonds themselves, that encourage people to come together religiously is a sociological insight that endures. People gather together and search for or reaffirm religious and spiritual meaning and belief because congregating makes real the social connections among them and gives life to a future they are in the process of creating. It is precisely this connection that has been vitiated by modern and postmodern forms of social organization that do not depend on the close ties once established by neighborhood and community.

Indeed, some gerontologists, Gutmann (1987) is one example, have suggested that the process of deculturation has placed the elderly and others in a devalued status. Although it is not news to say that the way we live our lives has changed dramatically, the consequences of the loss of communal ties and the accompanying stripping away of social status remain noteworthy. Consequences of weakened group affiliation and solidarity during the late 20th century include the following: (1) the increasing privatization of religious experience; (2) secularization and apostasy; (3) the growth of what Weber (1922/1991) would term charismatic religious groups; and, (4) the diminution of religious, spiritual, or moral socialization for a great proportion of the post-World War II generations. This has created the irony, observed elsewhere (Eisenhandler, 1994), that secular texts supplant traditionally defined sacred texts and may constitute the most viable source of material for a new generation of thought and discussion centering on religious and spiritual themes and ideas. In other words, other-worldly concerns and a sense of transcendence may emerge as people work closely to understand a particular secular text.

The contemplative and spiritual elements of reading emanate from the basic sociological processes of group activity and the individual act of reading. The nature of the experience also stems from the content of the reading material itself and from the expectations and life experiences of group members. Perhaps the continued existence of Western religions depends on the repository of secular literature and the activity of reading as much as on participation in formally organized religions and an understanding of sacred texts.

EVOKING SPIRITUALITY FROM TEXT

This turn of events, a secular body of literature spawning an interest in the sacred, presents a wrinkle to our historical and social scientific understanding that the formation and organization of religion gave rise to written language, literacy, and "the love of learning." Centuries of social and technological change and earnest efforts to promote widespread literacy have been built on the notion that the purpose of learning and the meaning of life were intrinsically associated not merely with an improvement in material well-being, but with a qualitative improvement of the human spirit, a drawing closer to the divine within us and around us. It is not accidental that the mass production and dissemination of texts is closely associated with the formation of many religious movements. Altick's (1957) analysis of John Wesley's role in endorsing secular and religious reading as a valued activity is one important example of the centrality of literacy or at least of a certain level of literacy to the life of mainstream denominations. Although reading for pleasure has been disapproved across time, especially with respect to common folk, the notion of derogating reading as "escapist" is a rap reserved for the mid-20th century (Nell, 1988).

Efforts to sustain the processes of literacy, the underpinning of learning in all its forms, and the processes of religion, the wellspring of the perfectibility of the spirit, were often left to the clerical castes and classes and to the intelligentsia instead of to a mass readership of the laity. In terms of Western civilization, literacy, that is, fluency in reading, writing, speaking, and thinking, has had a life course filled with peaks and valleys. Writing about medieval times and the sustenance of literacy, Jean LeClercq notes that there were many monastic forms of "active reading" ranging from *lectio meditatio* and *oratio* to *lectio divina* (1962, p. 78). In addition, LeClercq writes that the activities of "reading and meditation are sometimes described by the very expressive word *ruminatio*." It is this word *ruminatio* that most closely captures the quality of parts of the reading group experience. Indeed, Keating states that the "spontaneity" of lectio was lost as part of the congregate and individual activity of worship (1994, p. 54).

One was expected to do spiritual reading and discursive meditation for x number of years; if one lived to be very old—or maybe on one's deathbed—one might hope for an experience of contemplation. But in actual fact one rarely or never expected it and hence did not take steps to prepare for it. As a consequence, it got to be more and more identified as a form of prayer that belonged exclusively in a cloister—and not even commonly there. (Keating, 1994, p. 54)

At the most general theoretical level, spirituality is often associated with the idea of transcendence; a spiritual experience or set of experiences is understood to transform the individual's relationship to God or to a divine force and to intensify the person's engagement with life by deepening an appreciation for life's struggles and joys. Although other categorical arrangements are plausible, it follows logically that religion, morality, and ethics are subsumed by this general category of spirituality. Moreover, I contend that spirituality is evinced in the intellectual awareness of enlightenment or insight that moves a person forward in life. For the sociologists among us, it is Paul Lazarsfeld's "aha" experience coming from a higher plateau than social science.

As its etymology suggests, spirituality has greater evanescence than either religion or morality. Implicit in this definition is the notion that heightened spirituality does not merely sit in the person nor can a person be plugged into a continuous stream of spirituality. Instead, spirituality is a quality whose concrete or tangible component is manifested ultimately in some form of behavior, whether that is the most sublime contemplation to the most active interaction associated with helping others or acting to further social justice. Spirituality simply dissipates or becomes encrusted in sterile ritual if it does not become the basis for some, however infinitesimal, act of transformation.[2]

In order to illustrate some of the foregoing points, I wish to highlight four spiritual themes that arose in response to reading short stories and novels in a 12-week reading group series entitled "Family Scrapbooks." This series was purposefully designed to engage older adults in reading and discussion. It did this and more.

THE NEEDS OF OTHERS COME BEFORE THOSE OF THE INDIVIDUAL

In reading groups I have directed and observed previously, several themes were paramount in the ensuing discussions by older readers. Questions regarding the proper balance between an older person's need for intellectual and spiritual growth and the opposite pull, the pragmatic need to respond to family responsibilities and obligations, particularly those coming from adult children and from grandchildren, figured prominently in discussions (Eisenhandler, 1994). In the "Family Scrapbooks" series this question was elevated to a more abstract or spiritual level, particularly with respect to several of the excerpts from the short story anthology we used. Specifically, writings from Henry David Thoreau (1979) and Theodore Roosevelt (1979) were discussed not merely as emblematic of self-centeredness (living apart from others [Thoreau]; using time and money in pursuit of adventure [Roosevelt]) on the part of transcendentalists or Bull Moose Party members, but also as illustrative of adventurism and selfishness rampant today in the United States. The group of older readers was adamant about its uniform perception that narcissism was not simply tied to younger generations but was also linked to older adults who spent their retirement almost exclusively in pursuit of leisure. The group was unanimous in its disdain for solitude or adventure as a legitimate or good purpose for life and living. Strong appeals made by the discussion leader on behalf of the "special" experiences that solitude (i.e., the contemplation of Thoreau) or novelty (i.e., the travel and unique encounters of Roosevelt) conferred on the meaning of life fell on deaf ears. According to group members, the purpose and meaning of life was to be found in other kinds of lives with very different purposes. There were no men in this group, so it is difficult to say if that made the group more tenacious about holding to an other-connected (perhaps gender-influenced conception of moral interests) moral imperative.

UNJUST SITUATIONS NEED TO BE SET RIGHT

Several excerpts from the anthology used by the group, as well as two of the three books (*Papa Martel* [Robichaud, 1961] and *The Living Is Easy* [West, 1969]), generated considerable discussion of personal and social injustice. These two books and the majority of the readings featured autobiographical or fictional accounts of individual lives. Growing up, coming into adulthood, and other phases of adult life were principal features of many of the narratives we read. Group members often responded initially to the readings by sharing anecdotes and longer stories of events in their own lives. Yet inasmuch as we engaged in exchanging tales of youth or of the present, there were commentaries, both indirect and direct, that focused on fairness and injustice as spiritual and moral matters, not civil or legal ones. For example, in 2 successive weeks we considered two different readings that described experiences involving native North Americans. One biographical essay detailed a White woman's captivity; another modern fictional essay portrayed a father's attempt to retrieve his daughter from her maternal grandparents. Although the writers' perspectives were dissimilar, group members (who were often ahead of the scheduled reading) referred to both stories when they vehemently voiced their opposing views about the treatment of Native Americans. The meaning and nature of being dispossessed from the land were hotly debated. Injustices of the past that crowded into the present and demanded some settling of accounts now or in the near future were brought forward for discussion. Responses to the kind of treatment Native Americans received historically were offset by references to the equalizing force that gambling receipts brought to a particular Connecticut tribe. The fact that animals figured prominently in "Chee's Daughter" (Platero & Miller, 1979), one of the two readings, and were valued unanimously by group members as unifying links among themselves, the environment, and Native Americans, soothed some ruffled human feathers. Group members agreed that on the whole, Native Americans had been treated shabbily, but there was considerable disagreement on how such injustice rooted in the past could be equitably resolved in the present.

The theme that unjust situations need fair resolution but that humans frequently lack the power to resolve serious injustice was taken up in readings about the Depression and in an essay on a temporary experience of homelessness. What people in the group truly struggled with spiritually was how to correct social inequity without undermining or undoing the hard-won, not ill-gotten, gains of others. In some sense the group was asking just when will we get to evaluating the content of character rather than the color of skin or the vicissitudes of history? Can we do this now? What are we, as individuals or in groups, called to give up in order to attain this? What does God have to do with overseeing this vast sea of injustice?

WHAT IS GOOD IN LIFE NEEDS ACKNOWLEDGMENT AND APPRECIATION

Another spiritual concern educed from the reading series was the idea of how profoundly good some aspects of life are and how shameful it is that many people cannot recognize and appreciate the gifts, "blessings," that are presented to them. This spiritual theme was not advanced as a theorem of Pollyanna or as an attempt to deny real difficulties. It was a constructive appeal for honesty in spirituality; that is to say, group members suggested, almost as a prerequisite to uncovering transcendent meaning, that people had to acknowledge and appreciate what was good in their lives. This idea helps me understand the appeal of what I'd otherwise consider a stale and contrived novel, *Papa Martel* (Robichaud, 1961). According to the regional program director for the "Family Scrapbooks" series, this novel was almost universally applauded by older readers and consistently disliked by the reading group discussion leaders. One of the major themes identified in the text was Papa's gratefulness to God for all things in his life. This level of spiritual awareness is not, I think, a trivial one. It may be the hallmark of a mature, or perhaps wise, spirituality. In another qualitative study, in the context of a nursing home an elderly resident phrased this theme in terms of prayer, but the sentiment was as strong as the one in our group. ". . . a lot of people don't say 'thank God' for nothing. That's the thing that's destroying the world" (Gubrium, 1993, p. 131).

CONNECTIONS TO OTHERS NEED RENEWAL

For nearly all of the readers who stayed for most or all of the sessions, there was a concrete sense that the activity of getting together regularly, with serious work (reading and discussion) to complete, was in and of itself a practical kind of exercise of spirituality. Despite the aches and pains and the assortment of serious family problems, this was a special time for quiet yet extraordinary talk. This renewal of connections gave special meaning to individual reading and provided a fractional but significant boost to the sense of symbolic immortality that often proves elusive to the elderly as an ongoing feature of behavior (Lifton & Olson, 1974). Without intense drama, there were rather small but observable shifts that occurred in the perspectives of older adults. One small shift was observable in the renewal of interest in the process of reading and thinking about the nature of a good life. Without possessing a connection to text of one sort or another (i.e., pictographic or alphabetic) and without group engagement with a text, spirituality is magical rather than mystical, self-centered rather than expansive, and illusory rather than transcendent.

CONCLUSIONS

Conspicuously absent from the discussions, except with respect to *Papa Martel* (Robichaud, 1961), were overt references to institutionalized religions or theological or canonical interpretations of the written texts. The French-Canadian fictional narrative surrounding Papa was the only text closely connected to a specific theology and set of rituals (Roman Catholic). The spiritual dimensions of our discussions focused overwhelmingly on concerns related to social justice and within this realm on the ideal of fairness—the way to allocate materials and experiences so that individuals and groups could prosper and thrive without stamping out or being stomped on by others.

There is an apt phrase used among perspicacious readers: Understanding calls for reading between the lines. We read between the lines of texts to find a meaning beyond that of self; to recollect our connection to others across time and place; to formulate, however inchoate, reasons to move forward from moments we then comprehended as the present. It is precisely in this way that secular texts evoke the spiritual as often as spiritual texts evoke the secular: The direction taken lies in the nature of interaction surrounding the text itself, what we read between the lines in our emergent analysis as well as within the words themselves. Reading as active apprehension and responsive interaction shapes the meaning, sacred or profane, and influence of words and books. In order to fully grasp this idea, prevailing views of religion as a dualistic or compartmentalized activity must be revised. The words of a Chasidic thinker make the point this way: ". . . life provides many aesthetic and philosophical situations affording opportunities to enjoy the Divine through music, literature, scriptural commentary, and so forth. God can even become a respectable hobby" (Steinsaltz, 1988, p. 65). Such hobbies are precisely the ones that cannot be purchased with hard currency or within the resounding sanctuaries of sacred sites. They are, on the contrary, the hobbies of wisdom that flow from some regular engagement with active contemplation. The question remains as to which domain will recognize the value of this kind of engagement, the secular world of programming for older adults or the religious programs of ever-shrinking congregations? If one outcome of engagement with ideas and others is the enhancement or creation of "spiritual well-being" (Blazer, 1991), the culture has much to do in order to prepare and reserve a place, and not necessarily a solitary or remote one, in late life for reading both with and between the lines of text.

NOTES

1. This reading group received support and cooperation from local senior organizations, including Mt. Olive A.M.E. Zion senior center, the Connecticut Humanities Council, Reading Connections, and the Waterbury campus of the University of Connecticut. Primary sponsorship for the group described in this paper came from the National Endowment for the Humanities and the New England Foundation for the Humanities. The program, "Family Scrapbooks," ran from March 6 to May 22, 1995. As is both customary and sincere, the author gratefully acknowledges this support and adds that these research observations are the sole responsibility of the researcher and author.

2. Within the Jewish tradition, this sentiment finds expression in the Hasidic vision of spirituality. For example, as Kegan (1980, p. 438) notes in an acknowledgment of Buber's work, "The Hasidic vision testifies to a sacredness in the everyday, a spirituality to be found in the concrete world." Some insight into the sacredness of the everyday emerges in group discussions of literature when questions are raised about justice, love, and the meaning and purpose of living.

Such sacredness in the everyday world and in each human being was also recognized by this group of readers even when we changed our physical setting. We began in the Mt. Zion A.M.E. senior center and moved, midway through our sessions, to the university library. Although the two buildings are less than one quarter of a mile from each other, they are in very different social worlds. This fact, perhaps indicative of many kinds of social injustice as well as a shortsighted appreciation for who is sacred, was recognized by everyone. It was with the highest degree of humanity and spirituality that these women rejected the real obstacles they confronted in the contrast of their personal backgrounds and in the stark reality of their social experiences in late life. In this group, at least for a time, we were all in a place where those considerations could be set aside, however short-lived, and no matter how easily we all crossed back into our own worlds at the end of each meeting.

REFERENCES

Altick, R.D. (1957). *The English common reader: A social history of the mass reading public 1800–1900*. Chicago: University of Chicago Press.

Bellah, R.N., Madsen, R., Sullivan, W.M., Swidler, A., & Tipton, S. (1991). *The good society*. New York: Knopf.

Berger, P. (1967). *The sacred canopy: Elements of a sociological theory of religion*. Garden City, NY: Doubleday.

Blazer, D. (1991). Spirituality and aging well. Generations, 15, 61–65.

Demerath, N.J. (1974). *A tottering transcendence: Civil vs. cultic aspects of the sacred*. Indianapolis, IN: Bobbs-Merrill.

Durkheim, E. (1965). *The elementary forms of religious life* (J.W. Swain, Trans.) New York: Free Press. (Original work published 1915)

Eisenhandler, S.A. (1994). A social milieu for spirituality in the lives of older adults. In L. E. Thomas & S.A. Eisenhandler (Eds.), *Aging and the religious dimension* (pp. 133–145). Westport, CT: Auburn.

Festinger, L. (1956). *When prophecy fails: A social and psychological study of a modern group that predicted the destruction of the world*. New York: Harper & Row.

Greeley, A.M. (1989). *Religious change in America*. Cambridge, MA: Harvard University Press.

Gubrium, J.F. (1993). *Speaking of life: Horizons of meaning for nursing home residents*. New York: Aldine de Gruyter.

Gutmann, D. (1987). *Reclaimed powers: Toward a new psychology of men and women in later life*. New York: Basic.

Keating, T. (1994). *Intimacy with God*. New York: Crossroad.

Kegan, R. (1980). There the dance is: Religious dimensions of a developmental framework. In C. Brusselmans & J.A. O'Donohue (Eds.), *Toward moral and religious maturity* (pp. 404–440). Morristown, NJ: Silver Burdett.

LeClercq, J. (1962). *The love of learning and the desire for God* (C. Misrahi, Trans.). New York: Mentor.

Lifton, R.J., & Olson, E. (1974). *Living and dying.* New York: Bantam.

Lofland, J. (1966). *Doomsday cult: A study of conversion proselytization and maintenance of faith.* Englewood Cliffs, NJ: Prentice-Hall.

Lorenz, K. (1987). *The waning of humaneness* (R.W. Kickert,Trans.). Boston: Little, Brown. (Original work published in 1983)

Manguel, A. (1996). *A history of reading.* New York: Viking.

Needleman, J. (1993). *Lost Christianity: a journey of rediscovery to the centre of Christian experience.* Rockport, MA: Element. (Original work published in 1980)

Nell, V. (1988). *Lost in a book: The psychology of reading for pleasure.* New Haven, CT: Yale University Press.

Platero, J., & Miller, S. (1979). Chee's daughter. In R.A. Alvarez & S.C. Kline (Eds.), *A family album: The American family in literature and history* (pp. 67–87). Washington, DC: National Council on Aging.

Robichaud, G. (1961). *Papa Martel.* Garden City, NY: Doubleday.

Roof, W.C. (1978). *Community and commitment: Religious plausibility in a liberal Protestant church.* New York: Elsevier.

Roosevelt, T. (1979). Autobiography. In R.A. Alvarez & S.C. Kline (Eds.), *A family album: The American family in literature and history* (pp. 8–11). Washington, DC: National Council on Aging.

Steinsaltz, A. (1988).*The long shorter way* (Y. Hanegbi, Trans.). Northvale, NJ: Jason Aronson.

Thoreau, H.D. (1979). Walden. In R.A. Alvarez & S.C. Kline (Eds.), *A family album: The American family in literature and history* (pp. 33–38). Washington, DC: National Council on Aging.

Weber, M. (1991) *The sociology of religion.* Boston: Beacon Press. (Original work published 1922)

West, D. (1969). *The living is easy.* New York: Arno Press.

PART THREE

The Nature of Beliefs:
Cross-Cultural Perspectives

Quarreling with God: Belief and Disbelief Among Elderly Jewish Immigrants from the Former USSR

L. Eugene Thomas

I would like to begin this chapter with a personal note. I have been engaged in cross-cultural study of successful aging, or "optimal personality development" (to use the more academic term), during the past 15 years. From research with the elderly in India and England, as well as the United States, I have been impressed with the importance of beliefs, particularly those regarding religion and the transcendent, in determining how a person handles the inevitable losses of old age. In India, England, and the United States, I have noted the importance of a sense of transcendence in helping many individuals make meaning of their lives, which enables them to come to grips with the prospect of continuing loss and eventual death.

More recently, my colleagues and I have undertaken research with a group of elderly Jews who recently emigrated from the former Soviet Union. In these interviews I have been impressed with the incredible suffering most of them have undergone and the integrity with which they have faced and overcome adversity. From the beginning, however, I have been puzzled that, unlike my Hindu and Christian respondents, few of these Jewish elderly reported having an interest in religion and the transcendent. In other sample groups I have interviewed (Thomas, 1994; Thomas & Cooper, 1978), about one third have reported experiencing transcendence to some degree (a percentage that has been found consistently in surveys conducted in this country and in England [Gallup, 1976; Greeley, 1974]). In contrast, not a single one of our Russian informants answered yes to the question I have asked other respondents over the years: "Have you ever found yourself in the presence of a power greater than yourself, which lifted you out of yourself?" Even those few who had become active in organized synagogue life after coming to the United States gave a quick no when asked this question.

Only in rereading Barbara Myerhoff's (1978) classic study of elderly Jews at the Aliyah Senior Center in southern California have I come to better understand this

difference. Interestingly, the elderly that Myerhoff studied came from backgrounds similar to those we have studied in Connecticut. Both groups were born in small villages in Eastern Europe, where they were immersed in the "Yiddishkeit" of *shtetl* life. The main difference between the groups was that Myerhoff's sample emigrated to this country as children, whereas our respondents emigrated to this country in their later years and their families remained in Russia. The other major difference between the groups was that they represented different cohorts: the members of the Aliyah Center, who were on the average in their mid-80s when Myerhoff conducted her study in the 1970s, would have been born before the beginning of this century, whereas members of our sample were born in the present century, a generation later. In addition, of course, the latter group had remained in Russia and lived through the tumultuous period of Russian history that included the Bolshevik Revolution, Stalinism and the Cold War. Most of our respondents had immigrated from the former Soviet Union within the past 3 to 5 years.

The present study is based on interviews and participant observation, somewhat similar to that on which Myerhoff based her book. Life-narrative interviews were conducted with nine individuals over a period of 2 years, with the number of interviews with each individual ranging from two to seven. Because the respondents (six women and three men ranging in age from 72 to 92 years, with an average age of 80) spoke very little English, interviews were conducted in Russian through an interpreter (unlike Myerhoff's respondents, who spoke English). Interviews were conducted in the homes of respondents, most of whom lived alone in their own apartments.

Although our respondents attended the day care program of the local Hebrew center, we did not conduct systematic participant observation there, as Myerhoff had done at the Aliyah Center. Data somewhat comparable to the observations made by Myerhoff of her Living History class were provided by focus group sessions conducted at the Hebrew center with six of our respondents, where they were asked to share their personal experiences. A Russian-speaking research assistant provided simultaneous translation of the interviews and focus-group sessions. Each of the interviews and focus-group sessions were audiotaped, and the tapes were subsequently transcribed verbatim.

THE ALIYAH CENTER AND CONNECTICUT SAMPLES

When I reread Myerhoff's book (1978) after having conducted interviews with the elderly immigrants in our sample, I experienced a strong feeling of déjà vu. From their expressions, their concerns, their outlook, and much of their behavior, our respondents could have stepped out of the Aliyah Center and off the pages of Myerhoff's book. It occurred to me that, in some ways, our study serves as a replica-

tion of Myerhoff's work. The fact that striking similarities emerged, despite
marked differences in time and locale, provides strong suggestive support that Myerhoff's results are not idiosyncratic to her isolated group and that her highly personal style did not "create" the data that she gathered. The real difference in our
studies lies in the interpretation that is made of the "findings," which will be considered later.

First, the differences in the setting and background of the respondents should
be noted. As indicated earlier, the individuals in Myerhoff's sample had left Russia as children, before the revolution and the formation of the Soviet Union. As
children and young adults they had learned English, made their way in this country, educated their children and seen them enter the professions, and later found
themselves more or less abandoned by their families. Our respondents, on the
other hand, experienced the revolution as children, lived through the Stalin purges
as adolescents, participated in World War II as young adults, and lived through the
Cold War and experienced growing state anti-Semitism in their mature years.

There were vast differences between the groups then, in historical and cultural
experience, having literally grown up in two different worlds. There were significant differences in their present situations also. In regard to family, most of our
respondents emigrated to the United States to be near their children, who kept in
almost daily contact with them. The groups differed in economic status, as well.
Our respondents did not live in poverty like most of the members of the Aliyah
Center; on the contrary, they had been well cared for by Jewish and other social
service agencies since their arrival in this country. Finally, whereas Myerhoff's informants were bilingual, our respondents spoke little or no English. Their inability to speak English isolated them from the larger culture; through an interesting
twist of fate, they now live in an ethnic ghetto not unlike that of the elderly of the
Aliyah Center.

Striking similarities to the Aliyah Center sample became more obvious in the
focus group sessions we conducted and emerged in our interviews. Like their
Aliyah counterparts, our respondents told about their early *shtetl* experience and
their hopes that their children would have a better life. Particularly interesting was
the similarity between the groups in their members' desire to tell their life stories
at every opportunity. Our respondents, like Myerhoff's, wanted to have their stories recorded to pass on to their grandchildren, and they wanted their names used
in our subsequent research reports (like Myerhoff, we adopted the strategy of
maintaining anonymity, however). This desire to have their personal narratives
recorded facilitated the individual interviews, where they could tell their stories
without interruption and we could give our undivided attention to each individual.
But the drive to have their own stories heard presented initial problems in the focus
group sessions. Like the members of the Aliyah Center, our respondents found it
difficult to listen to others in the group setting, where they tended to talk at the
same time, sometimes trying to shout each other down.

We also noticed in our respondents, particularly in the women, the tendency to be assertive, not only in the group sessions but also in other situations. In an early interview, Tasha, who had left the Soviet Union several years earlier when it was difficult and dangerous to get immigration papers, told about her battle to get a visa for her adopted daughter, who had stayed behind.

TASHA: My daughter was left there with two grandsons. Even before we passed the border my daughter was fired from her job. And she had two children. Here my fight began. We began to struggle to get her permission to leave. And there was always a negative answer.

INTERVIEWER: For how many years?

TASHA: Until my daughter came. For 7 years and a half, I wrote to every person around. To the governor (sic) of San Francisco. She promised us to help bring children here. I met with Barbara Kennelly (Congresswoman) in a Catholic church, and she promised that she would try to help. I received a letter from Barbara also (trying to find the letters). I cannot find. Reagan helped us. I even have a letter from him (still rummaging in her purse).

This assertiveness was not limited to political areas, we soon learned, but was characteristic of much of their behavior. They were particularly concerned that they have all the privileges that others enjoyed and were outspoken in seeking to have wrongs, whether real or imagined, righted. One social worker, for example, described to us with exasperation her experience with Anna, a healthy 78-year-old immigrant, who became incensed that she was not provided with nitroglycerine tablets like her friend who had a heart problem. Another social worker told of the quarrel between two women, who won't speak to each other now, over who would get authorship of a small news story that was to appear in the center newsletter. Moreover, we were told that this group of elderly is well-known among the local social service providers for insisting on being heard and on having their rights respected.

At first we assumed these behaviors were the residue of survival skills they had learned from years of scarcity and struggle with Soviet bureaucracy. Later, in rereading *Number Our Days* (Myerhoff, 1978), I was struck by the fact that Myerhoff observed similar behavior in her Aliyah sample. These individuals had left Russia before the revolution and had had no experience with Soviet bureaucracy, yet they, too, were assertive and, to use Myerhoff's descriptive phrase, "argued to keep themselves warm."

Finally, we were impressed with the fact that both groups, although identifying with Judaism, were mostly secular in their religious outlook. We didn't find this surprising for our sample, as they had spent their formative years in the Soviet Union, where all religious observance was suppressed. Brym (1994) notes that members of the cohort were "relatively assimilated Jews whose families had lived under Communism since 1917, who had passed through the Soviet education system, and who thought of Russian culture as their own" (p. 15).

Curiously, most of the elderly that Myerhoff reports on in her study, although they had lived their adult years in the United States, had arrived at a similar position regarding religion. Most of the individuals in both groups no longer considered themselves religious, although they felt a strong allegiance to cultural and ethical Judaism. This reflected, no doubt, their early shtetl experience, where both groups had been exposed to "Yiddishkeit" Judaism. This domestic religion of childhood, to use Myerhoff's term, remained a powerful, although subterranean force, in their lives.

The combination of the emotional pull of domestic religion and the adult rejection of Jewish religious practices seems to have produced not a little cognitive dissonance for many of her respondents. Indeed, the tension between the religious and the social-cultural aspects of Judaism seemed to be one of the defining characteristics of the elderly that Myerhoff describes in her study and was clearly present in our sample as well. Examining how they handled this ideological, or cultural, tension proved to be a key to understanding various aspects of their lives.

GREAT AND LITTLE TRADITIONS

In analyzing her respondents' religious beliefs and world view, Myerhoff drew on Redfield's (1960) concept of great and little cultural traditions. This distinction enabled her to disentangle the strands of Judaism that were relevant to her respondents and to understand the ideological tensions with which they struggled. The great tradition of a society, she notes, refers to the abstract, literate, and formal beliefs and usages of a culture, which would correspond to formal Jewish law and ritual, conducted in Hebrew. Little traditions relate to local, oral, and more informal ideas and practice, which correspond to the "Yiddishkeit" of *shtetl* life. Concerning this tradition, Myerhoff observes: "The first experiences of domestic life, transmuted into Domestic Religion, are permanent and powerful, for their roots have been set down in the deepest layers of the heart" (p. 258).

This distinction proved useful in her study, in that it clarified how the elderly of the Aliyah Center could express strong allegiance toward both the domestic religion of their childhood and Zionism (the *Eretz Yisroel* tradition), while feeling little affinity for either *Klal Yisroel* (which requires knowledge of Hebrew) or American-temple Judaism. She found unpacking these layers of the Judaic tradition, and noting the tensions that existed within individuals and the group toward these various dimensions, to be very useful in understanding the role that religion played in the lives of the elderly members of the Aliyah Center.

As useful as this distinction was in understanding Myerhoff's sample, analysis of our sample highlighted the importance of considering an additional great tradition that had an impact on both groups, in other words, that of modern secular society. Actually, for those in our sample who lived their adult lives in the Soviet Union prior to coming to the United States, there was the further tension between the great tradition of Soviet communism and the great tradition of the Western society to which they had recently immigrated.

In order to analyze how these tensions played out in the lives of individuals, we found it useful to draw on dialogic theory, pioneered by Russian literary scholar Mikhail Bakhtin (1978), whose work has recently begun to receive attention in the West. Based on his view of the objective nature of belief systems, Bakhtin insists that ideologies do not reside "in the soul, not in the inner world, and not in the detached world of ideas and pure thought" (1978, p. 8). Following the Marxist position of the objective reality of ideology, he insists that "every ideological product (ideologeme) is a part of the material social reality surrounding man, an aspect of the materialized ideological horizon" (p. 8).

The classic statement of Bakhtin's dialogic theory was developed in his book *Problems of Dostoevsky's Poetics* (Bakhtin, 1984), in which he argues that the notion of internal dialogue is not just a metaphor for Dostoevsky's literary style but that it is the essence of personality (Florenskaya, 1989). Mary Watkins (1986), who came to a similar conclusion working from a Jungian framework, argues that imaginal dialogues are not limited to preoperational children but constitute an essential part of the adult psychological world. She maintains that these imaginal voices engage in dialogues that are played out in our heads and that these imaginal dialogues, as well as the actual dialogues we engage in with real others, are an essential component of our narrative construction of the world.

In a curious convergence of intellectual currents, historian Benedict Anderson's (1983) concept of "imagined communities," which he developed in quite another context, helps provide conceptual understanding of how cultural ideologies impinge on an individual's cognitive world. Anderson argues that nationalism, a historically recent invention, is based on the concept of "imagined communities." These communities are imagined, he suggests, "because the members of even the smallest nation will never know most of their fellow-members, meet them, or even hear of them, yet in the minds of each lives the image of their community" (p. 15).

It does not stretch this concept unduly to suggest that imagined communities can be based on ideologies other than nationalism, reflecting identification with different great and small traditions. This is the distinct image one gets from the description Basha gave Myerhoff of her dinner preparations, when she ate alone in her tiny room:

> No matter how poor, we would eat off clean white linen, and say the prayers before touching anything to the mouth. And so I do it still. Whenever I sit down, I eat with

God, my mother, and all the Jews who are doing the same things even if I can't see them. (p. 22)

In this narrative we see the blending of ideological commitment and imagined communities into a continuity-affirming personal narrative. In another instance of theoretical convergence, feminist scholar K.M. Langellier (1989) argues that all personal narratives are ideological. The ideological function of narrative, she suggests, is to legitimate meanings, to "privilege certain interests over others" (p. 266) and to delegitimate or contest the meanings of others. Although Langellier doesn't make the point, it would follow that it is possible for the individual to engage in dialogue with what might be called the "larger cultural narrative," or ideology. When there is congruence between personal narrative and the larger cultural narrative, such a dialogue would be muted or latent. In times of social change, when cultural ideologies are in transition or when individuals no longer resonate to received ideologies, such tension would lead to dialogue between ideologies within the individual.[1]

QUARRELING WITH GOD

David, an 80-year-old immigrant who came to this country 5 years ago, was one of the first persons we interviewed in our study. In both the individual interviews and in the group sessions, he strongly voiced his anger at the treatment he, and other Jews, had suffered at the hands of Soviet bureaucrats. Trained as an engineer, he had risen through the ranks of his profession through ability and hard work and was in line to become head engineer for a large plant. Because of growing anti-Semitism in the Soviet Union at that time, however, he was denied the position. In protest, he left engineering and eked out a living in various menial jobs.

Although he grew up in the Yiddishkeit of the *shtetl*, where he had belonged to a very religious family, and although his commitment to ethnic Judaism had hindered his professional career, David expressed little interest in religion. In fact, religion for him had a negative valence. When asked how long he wanted to live, he replied:

DAVID: I'm not afraid of death. I could die tomorrow, a day after tomorrow.

INTERVIEWER: What will happen to David when he dies?

DAVID: I would be thrown to a ditch, and that's it.

INTERVIEWER: What happens after death?

DAVID: They say that you go to paradise. That it would be good there. I don't take it seriously.

INTERVIEWER: You don't believe that?

DAVID: I studied religion a lot. And prayed. Believed in God. But after my father . . . He was religious. Very religious. And God killed them alive. Buried them alive. They were covered with ground. Alive.

INTERVIEWER: Do you still believe in God?

DAVID: No. He (David's father) prayed every morning. He was very religious. And my father-in-law and mother-in-law were also. They were 45 years old. For what? Buried alive for what?

INTERVIEWER: Does that make you bitter? Angry?

DAVID: It is painful. Painful is not even the word. It is much worse.

Later, when David was asked what epitaph he would like to have, he replied, still referring back to his father's death:

DAVID: We even wanted to buy a place in a cemetery. A tomb...

INTERVIEWER: What do you want written for your tomb?

DAVID: Only my name. Date of birth, date of death. That's all. My name and two dates. He was alive; he has died. That's all.

INTERVIEWER: What would people say about you?

DAVID: If my father is not alive... He was a very good person. If he had committed some sin. But this was for nothing.

At first we were puzzled by David's insistence that he didn't believe in God although it was clear that he could not forgive God for what He had done. For over half a century, like Job, David has quarreled with God about the injustice he has endured. Unlike Job, David refuses to accept the fate to which he has been subjected. In his hurt and anger he rejects the existence of a God who could let such senseless suffering take place. In revenge he refuses to leave an account of his life in God's unfair world. He will, like a soldier held captive by enemy agents, give only his name, rank, and serial number, actually, less than that, since he will have on his tomb only his name and the dates of entry and exit from this plane.

There is a certain irony in David's quarrel with a God in which he purports to no longer believe. At first, we perceived this incongruence as a humorous non sequitur. But we came to realize that a better way of conceptualizing the issue, one in which the integrity of David's anguish could be honored, was to see his quarrel as a dialogue with the small tradition of Yiddishkeit that he had known in his childhood. He, in effect, is demanding to know of this religious community why a righteous man like his father could be allowed to suffer so needlessly. David's ostensible answer was to reject this small tradition for which belief in God was central.

Despite his repudiation of the religious culture of his childhood, David maintained his moral integrity by refusing to assimilate into the Soviet culture and give up his Jewish ethnic identity, even though anti-Semitism cost him his career. Of course, the fact that he was unwilling to give up his identity as a Jew suggests that his repudiation of Jewish culture was far from complete. He was still in dialogue with it; one might say, still arguing with its religious content. In any case, he had clearly rejected the great tradition of the Soviet state. When asked if he would like to go back to Russia to visit, he replied,

DAVID: No, never!

INTERVIEWER: You don't want to see it again?

DAVID: If I was given a free ticket, even a private plane . . . I still don't want it.

Later, in the group session, he was even more emphatic:

DAVID: There is no Jew who is not trying to escape from there (said with strong emotion).

HIS WIFE: Calm down. Calm down.

DAVID: I would tear them in pieces with my own hands.

HIS WIFE: Stop, stop. It's enough.

From these extracts, and throughout our interviews with David, it became clear that he was in dialogue with both the little tradition of his childhood Judaism, and with the great tradition of Russian state socialism. In David's case, he was in conflict with both traditions; his only allegiance was to the great tradition of the country to which he had immigrated. This had to be at a more theoretical level, however, since his inability to speak the language of this tradition greatly limited his access to, and full participation in, it.

The elderly of the Aliyah Center exhibited similar tension in their identification with the strands of the great and little traditions of Judaism. As Myerhoff observed, most of the elderly who frequented the center did not identify with the religious, observant part of that tradition. In fact, one of the dramatic and decisive events she witnessed in her participant observation at the center occurred when a visiting Hasidic rabbi attempted to impose observances that were inconsistent with their more secular orientation. In the commotion that followed the rabbi's attempt to impose a kosher kitchen on the center, Basha, speaking for the group, stated emphatically,

"I can't go along. With God, without God, with kosher, without kosher, a Jew is a Jew" (Myerhoff, 1978, p. 138).

Shmuel, one of Myerhoff's key informants, reflected this secular, or ethnic, form of identification with Judaism. Perhaps the reason he proved to be such a good informant was due to the fact that his connection with the center was marginal because of his rejection of Zionism (the *Eretz Yisroel* tradition), to which most of the other center members were dedicated. Like most of the other members, however, he claimed not to believe in God. Despite his avowed agnosticism, Shmuel, like David, was far from indifferent to the religious elements of the tradition. In quoting from a *midrash* (a philosophical commentary), Shmuel makes a humorous, but telling, observation:

> After the Day of Judgment, all the Jews will be found in Heaven. There they spend eternity studying Torah together, at last arguing with the Lord Himself about the right interpretation of His Law. This is the Jew's idea of Paradise. Do we have angels peacefully riding on clouds with their harps playing, like the Gentiles? No, we have a big debate with God, a pilpul (Talmudic debate) in the sky. (Myerhoff, 1978, p. 126)

Interestingly, Myerhoff's other "main character" in *Number Our Days* (1978), Jacob, also struggled with the tensions between the different strands of the Judaic tradition of his youth. Although an agnostic, he fervently identified with cultural-ethical Judaism. Concerning these tensions in Jacob's beliefs, Myerhoff observed,

> He struggles with the contradictions between his internationalist beliefs and his nationalism, in the form of Zionism and American patriotism. And he managed to embrace contradictions generated by his agnostic, even antireligious attitudes, on one hand, and fervent identification with cultural-ethical Judaism, on the other. (p. 218)

Myerhoff (1978) notes that these conflicts were not unique to Jacob's individual psychology but were characteristic of the center membership. With the eye of the anthropologist, she observed how these tensions were played out and often resolved in the ritual handling of events at the Aliyah Center. Her portrayal of the ritual surrounding Jacob's 95th birthday party is one of the most moving, and insightful, accounts in the ethnographic literature. In the presence of center members, relatives, and visiting dignitaries, Jacob presided over an elaborate birthday ceremony in what proved to be the final minutes of his life, postponing his fatal collapse until after he had completed his valedictory address. Tension at this secular-sacred event had been heightened by rumors that the Angel of Death was waiting for Jacob in the wings of the room. Despite the fact that Jacob made no secret of his religious skepticism, members of the center, most of whom were also agnostic, talked for days about the possible transcendent meaning of the event, comparing Jacob's death to the deaths of Elijah and Moses. It seemed natural that the Kaddish prayer be invoked by the visiting rabbi at the end of the ceremony. The communal ritual, in this case, had managed to encompass the conflicting ideologies that informed Jacob's life and the lives of many other members.

Myerhoff suggested that for Jacob, and for members of the center, "It may be that an active engagement with ideological conflict played a part in the ability of the Center elders to age well" (p. 219). Whether Jacob's life strategy, particularly of creating his own "sacred myth," can be taken as a prescription for successful old age in general is a question I will address presently. For the moment it is interesting to note that the pseudonym (Jacob) that Myerhoff chose for this 95-year-old informant, carries rich symbolic associations. In the Bible it was Jacob who wrestled with a divine emissary all night and exacted a promise of a blessing from him before releasing his grip. The blessing Jacob received was a new name, Israel, "He who strives with God" (Gen. 32:28, Revised Standard Version). It would seem that members of the Aliyah Center and respondents in our study (as well as Myerhoff, as we shall note later) carry on this honorable tradition of quarreling with God.

QUARRELING WITH MYERHOFF

In seeking to understand the qualities that contributed to Jacob's "successful aging," Myerhoff noted the importance of his autobiographical writing in maintaining a sense of continuity and identity. Jacob also used his writings to teach, hoping to pass on to his children and grandchildren his life story and the meaning that he had wrestled from life. Indeed, the importance of protecting and passing on one's life story was a dominant theme among Myerhoff's informants, and one that we found in our respondents as well. Ensuring that one's story did not go to the grave with the physical body constituted an important form of "symbolic immortality" for them, to use Lifton and Olson's (1974) term. Concerning Jacob's autobiographical efforts, Myerhoff observed,

> In these writings, Jacob constructed a sacred story, a personal myth, which took up the ultimate eschatological questions, "What has it all meant?" "Why was I here?" In traditional, religious settings, answers to these questions are provided collectively. In our secular world, the individual must provide one's own, and this Jacob undertook. (p. 221)

Concerning the way her informants created meaning for their lives, Myerhoff observed. "The discovery of personal unity beneath the flow and flux of ordinary life is the personal counterpart of myth-making" (p. 222). Although she identifies other qualities that accounted for the high level of life satisfaction among the elderly she studied—"good health, resilience, endurance, imagination, courage, and a childhood passed in a society that cherished its children" (p. 219)—the focus of much of her book is on the importance of the individual having a chance to narrate his or her own story in order to create a meaningful personal, even sacred, myth.

Marc Kaminsky (1992), in a sympathetic and moving analysis of Myerhoff's work, observes that in her hands the stories told by her informants became "impassioned lay sermons" (p. 318). Kaminsky notes that the story, the lay sermon, "tells us how to live . . . In speaking to us in 'our common humanity,' the story tells us how to die" (p. 319). Although Kaminsky doesn't mention the fact, such lay sermons are, of course, based on "lay theology." It is this implicit theology, or prescription for the good life, that I would like to examine in evaluating the implications of the findings from Myerhoff's and my own research.

Sociologist Peter Berger (1969) has defined religion as the establishment of "an all-embracing sacred order, that is, of a sacred cosmos that will be capable of maintaining itself in the ever-present face of chaos" (p. 51). This "socially established comos," although seemingly durable and unchanging, especially when enshrined in institutions, is in fact a gossamer web that is easily disrupted. Berger observes, "The precariousness of every such world is revealed each time men forget or doubt the reality-defining affirmations . . . and most importantly each time they consciously encounter death" (p. 51). In addition, of course, religion is the primary institutional vehicle through which the sacred cosmos is established and maintained.

Myerhoff would not have quarreled with this formulation; in fact, she was keenly aware of how communal ritual is used in the enterprise of nomos maintenance. But her formulation diverges from that of Berger in her Promethean prescription that each individual create his or her own sacred myth. Berger notes that this has been precisely the agenda of "neo-liberalism" theology since World War II.

> The new liberalism "subjectivizes" religion in a radical fashion . . . the *realissimum* to which religion refers is transposed from the cosmos or from history to individual consciousness. Cosmology becomes psychology. History becomes biography. (Berger, 1969, pp. 166–167)

Transposing history into biography is the genius of the folklorist; it enables storytellers like Myerhoff to give concreteness and immediacy to their subjects. As lay theology, however, with its implicit prescriptions for life satisfaction and fulfillment, it runs the danger to which Berger alludes H.R. Moody (1986), in a seminal essay, has commented insightfully on this tendency, particularly as it relates to gerontology. He observes that Western society, in its penchant for privatism, has made an increasing separation between public and private worlds. Claiming Voltaire's dictum "cultivate your garden," contemporary society has shrunk these privatized "gardens" to the size of window boxes. In the process, Moody argues, "We have shrunk the question of meaning down to the lowest denominator, the psychological meaning of *my* life." "The bankruptcy of privatism," he observes, "becomes all too evident in old age" (p. 13).

Moody associates this trend toward privatism with our national drift toward narcissism, as exemplified in the "me generation." It was not narcissism, however, that motivated Jacob, or the elderly we interviewed, in their passion to construct a meaningful life narrative, or "sacred myth." Rather, it was their fierce search for purpose in seeking to construct a personally meaningful world rather than narcissistic self-indulgence that motivated them. The "lay sermon" that Moody himself expounds concerning the dangers of narcissism serves as a reminder of the danger inherent in Myerhoff's "lay theology," however. Left to their own devices to create personal meaning, without the support of a collective enterprise and without a mooring in a wider cosmic setting, there is no guarantee that the elderly will attain the high level of life satisfaction that Myerhoff pictures for the members of the Aliyah Senior Center. Instead, there might well be the darker undertone of narcissism about which Moody cautions us. The danger implicit in conflating history with biography and cosmology with psychology is spelled out vividly by Ronald Blythe (1979) in his *The View in Winter: Reflections on Old Age* (which, incidentally, was published in the same year that Myerhoff completed the final "Afterword" of her ethnography):

> It may soon be necessary and legitimate to criticize the long years of vapidity in which a healthy elderly person does little more than eat and play bingo, or consume excessive amounts of drugs, or expects a self-indulgent stupidity to go unchecked . . . One of the most dreadful sights in the country of the old is that of the long rows of women playing the Las Vegas slot machines. Had Dante heard of it he would have cleared a space for it in Hell. It is symbolic of the specially self-indulgent mindlessness of old age which is its most intolerable aspect. (pp. 22, 23)

This is, of course, hardly the picture of the socially and politically involved members of the Aliyah Center. The fact that the individuals had such a need to have their stories told, however, made it hard for them to listen to each other, Myerhoff admits. She sees this tendency as necessary in order for them to forge their own sacred myths. Their competitive jousting she dismisses with the light-hearted explanation given by one of the center members: "We fight to keep ourselves warm" (p. 153). But Kaminsky, despite his admiration of Myerhoff's work, raises questions about her valorization of the individuality and competitiveness of her informants. Kaminsky (1992) observes that Myerhoff ignores the effect of "storms of privatization that do violence to *communitas* and the competitive individualism that in practice tears apart 'moral social relations'" (p. 308).

THE DIALOGUE OF BELIEF AND DISBELIEF

Although most of the elderly immigrants in our sample considered themselves nonreligious Jews, not all did. Of the nine informants we studied in depth, four had established synagogue connections. Of these four, two attended only occasionally and expressed reservations about their belief in God, and one was both a nominal believer and attendee. One respondent, however, was a devout believer and had maintained religious convictions at considerable personal risk throughout her life in the former Soviet Union. As an act of faith, and in defiance of state-ordered suppression of religion, she had secretly kept the mezuzah (a small case containing parts of the Torah) that her grandmother had given her as a young woman. As a final act of faith, after she arrived in this country, she sent it to Israel with her grandson to be donated to a synagogue depository there.

Although Zina did not lose family members to the Nazis, the *shtetl* where she grew up was annihilated during the war, and the thought of all her friends who died there still haunted her. Unlike David, she did not blame God for this loss, nor did it cause her to lose her faith. In an early interview with Zina (we conducted seven interviews with her in all), when asked if she considered herself religious, she replied,

> ZINA: Yes. I strongly, strongly believe in God. I'm not an orthodox. I don't keep all the laws. I can miss a prayer. But I always follow the Ten Commandments.

In our last interview with Zina, we tested to see how she was able to reconcile her religious beliefs with the senseless pain and suffering she had encountered. Her response was in marked contrast to what David had told us:

> INTERVIEWER: How do you make sense of all this inhumanity? How do you make sense that God allows such suffering and injustice?

> ZINA: I will not answer this question. I don't argue with God. And I don't interfere with God's deeds. Only my own.

> INTERVIEWER: Right, I understand. But do you have any speculations?

> ZINA: I cannot answer such questions. Hitler lived. There was an Inquisition of the Jews in Spain in 1492. But those who do bad things die. What was Hitler's end? He destroyed half of Germany. And poisoned himself. God punishes them. I don't know why. I can answer about myself but not about God. I am myself God's creature. I cannot judge him.

But hers was not a distant, stoic assent to the workings of some remote deity. In an earlier interview, when the subject of God came up, she made a particularly interesting observation:

INTERVIEWER: When you said God was caring about you, it sounded very personal. I wonder if you could comment on that.

ZINA: It is my God. He treats me personally. I treat him personally.

INTERVIEWER: Are there things you do on a daily basis to be closer to God?

ZINA: I go to synagogue every Saturday. I participate in everything.

INTERVIEWER: (laughs) Is it your second home?

ZINA: (laughing) When I pray, it is my first home. When I go to synagogue I pray. I always kiss mezuzah, the Torah. But it is not the most important thing. I would have God in my heart, in any case. It is not important to do something special. I don't perform. It is not a theater. You have to do good things for people without exhibiting it.

Zina's faith stood in sharp contrast to most of the members of our sample and to Myerhoff's respondents. Symbolically, a year after the original (1978) publication of *Number Our Days*, Myerhoff appended an "Afterword," in which she described a final visit to one of the members who had been forced to give up her apartment and move into a nursing home. When Myerhoff entered Hannah's room she found her alone, crying quietly into her pillow. Hannah was unaware of the appearance of the barren room, because a stroke some months earlier has rendered her blind. Hannah complained that her children neglected her and that center members seldom visited. Her main complaint, however, was that she continued to live in a body that was disintegrating while her mind remained sharp. She was furious at God and observed, "Look at me. I'm completely awake. My body is strong. I'm 91. Why has God cursed me to keep on living this way?" (p. 278)

Myerhoff tried to relieve Hannah's distress by reminding her that it was the time of the ancient Jewish festival of Yom Kippur. She urged Hannah to forgive her children, who seldom visited her now, and to take a more positive attitude toward life. Myerhoff reminded Hannah that in the Yom Kippur tradition the Book is open until Kol Nidre at the conclusion of the festival the next night and that it is not too late for a new beginning. It was all to no avail, however; Hannah reminded Myerhoff that she was an atheist. Then she went on to tell Myerhoff of the visit of a friend who brought a shofar, the goat's horn used in the Yom Kippur ceremony: "Right here in the hospital he blew the horn! These sounds could break your heart" (p. 278). To Myerhoff's astonishment, in a strong voice Hannah began to chant the ancient New Year service. "Despite the plaintive melody," Myerhoff noted, "she smiled as she sang."

On the surface, Hannah and David, who was described earlier, would appear to be at the opposite pole from Zina in their religious beliefs. Closer analysis suggests a similarity, however; despite the different feelings they had for the great tradition of Judaism, all three were in dialogue with God. In Hannah's case, the strength of this tradition was apparent in her response to the ancient symbols of the *Klal Yisroel* tradition, the ram's horn and the ancient chant of the Yom Kippur service. For all three, however, despite differences in their stated beliefs, the great tradition of Judaism is not a matter of indifference. Despite their stated belief or disbelief in the Divine, they were in dialogue with the strands of the great and little traditions, and to a greater or lesser extent they felt themselves part of the sacred community to which these traditions belonged.

It is also clear that Myerhoff herself was engaged in a "quarrel" with the great tradition of Judaism. Toward the end of her book she tells of attending an Orthodox Sabbath service held in the lounge of the Ocean Beach Kosher Guest Home where some of her informants lived. Myerhoff's description of the scene, from the drab walls and seedy furnishings of the room to the male-dominated service itself, indicates something of her negative reaction to the Orthodox tradition. She notes that since adolescence she has avoided the "beautiful temple services" of the Reform tradition as well, because she had never found in them "the kind of religious experience I wanted" (p. 261). It was therefore surprising to learn that she returned to the Ocean Beach Kosher Guest Home Friday afternoons as often as she could, "even though as a woman I would have to stand outside," because of the male-dominated service (p. 261).

The extent of Myerhoff's religious conviction, despite her quarrel with the great tradition, is poignantly portrayed in the last paragraph of the "Afterword" that she appended to the book in 1979. Concluding her story of Hannah's positive response to the shofar, symbol of the ancient Yom Kippur service, Myerhoff noted that Hannah still refused to forgive her family for neglecting her. When Myerhoff asked Hannah if she at least would accept her wishes for another year, Hannah replied, "No. I don't accept. It's all over. It's too late to forgive" and turned her head away and seemed to sleep. In a final instinctive act, Myerhoff drew on the resources of the great tradition of Judaism, paraphrasing the words of blessing the Lord gave Moses in the wilderness of Sinai (Num. 6:24–26). Myerhoff recounts,

> I placed my hand in hers and haltingly, in English, said the blessing that I had often heard but had never before pronounced aloud. 'May the Lord bless and keep thee. May the Lord cause His countenance to shine upon thee and grant thee peace.' (p. 281)

CONCLUSIONS

Myerhoff's ethnography of the elderly Jewish immigrants at the Aliyah Center in California was based on research conducted some two decades prior to the time we conducted our study in Connecticut. Despite the differences in time and circumstance that separate the two studies, her research helped clarify some of the paradoxes that puzzled us about the recent immigrants from the former Soviet Union in our study. In particular, it helped us make sense of the seeming contradiction between the avowed atheism of most of our respondents and their clear identification with their Jewish heritage and the intensity with which some of them "quarreled" with the God they claimed not to believe in.

By unpacking their religious beliefs, as Myerhoff had done with her sample, it was possible to understand how our respondents could remain loyal to aspects of the great tradition of Judaism, such as the Zionism of *Eretz Yisroel*, as well maintain their dedication to other aspects of cultural and ethical Judaism while rejecting the religious beliefs and practices of the great tradition, *Klal Yisroel*. Her conceptualization of the way they handled these contradictory strands was useful, in so far as she framed it in terms of the communal ritual that often encompassed conflicting aspects of Judaism.

The rediscovery of Bakhtin's work (1978, 1984) and the development of dialogic theory for which it proved seminal allow us to better understand how the ideological strains Myerhoff identified in her informants could be incorporated into their sense of identity. Rather than representing just intellectual strain, the dialogic model holds that they are part of the inner dialogue by means of which individuals know who they are. Further, the inner ideological dialogue allows the individual to feel part of a larger "imagined community," such as that implied by Basha when she explained that even when she ate alone in her tiny room, "I eat with God, my mother, and all the Jews who are doing the same things, even if I can't see them" (Myerhoff, 1978, p. 22).

I am sure that Myerhoff would have no trouble with this different way of conceptualizing the stories that she recorded. Where we have more substantive differences relates to the way she valorizes competitive individualism and the creation of individual master narratives. The notion that life satisfaction is related to individuals being able to create their own "sacred myths" raises serious theoretical, even theological, questions.

Moody (1986), Berger (1969), and others have reminded us of the dangers of privatism in the matter of ultimate beliefs. Meaningful sacred myth must be more than individual stories, however carefully crafted. At times of crisis, particularly in the face of death, individuals tend to forget the answers that they have accepted intellectually. What is needed in those times are the corporate symbols and rituals that speak to the core of one's being. Individual effort and belief systems are never adequate in producing such healing symbols and rituals. Not only that, but the very attempt to place oneself in the center of sacred myth and symbol puts one in danger of self-centeredness and narcissism, which is a besetting temptation of old age.

But this does not mean that the only alternative is to fall back on the received beliefs of one's tradition, to return to the "old-time religion." The challenge of the modern secular world means that for most individuals, whether young or old, it is impossible to go back to the simple faith of childhood. It is not possible to single-handedly forge our own sacred narrative, de novo, either. Here Bakhtin's dialogic theory proves useful, in that it helps to clarify how an individual can be in internal dialogue with different ideologies that confront him or her. For our informants, these tensions reflect not only strain between various strands within the Jewish tradition that Myerhoff identified, but also tensions between a belief in a transcendent dimension of the world and the secular vision of the postmodern West.

Viewed within this dialogic framework, it is possible to understand that a person who claims to be an agnostic or atheist can continue to quarrel with God. In a real sense, they can be seen to be carrying on a dialogue with the ideologies of the communities of which they are part. What I failed to realize at the beginning of our study was that through these dialogues they were able to identify themselves as part of a larger "imagined community." It is from this sense of being part of a larger, transhistorical community that many of them derive a sense of transcendence. When their life stories can be seen to intersect with the larger narrative of this faith community, they are able to feel themselves part of a meaningful, orderly world, despite the chaos of individual change and vicissitude. This imagined transcendent community provides them with the "sacred canopy" of a shared cosmos that helps shield them from the specter of physical decline and the threat of isolation in old age and, above all, the terror of eventual death.

ACKNOWLEDGMENTS

Support for this research was provided by the University of Connecticut Research Foundation and a grant from the Vera Townsend Foundation. I would like to express my appreciation to Matvey Sokolovsky, who served as very able research assistant, translating for the interviews and group sessions, to Richard Feinberg, who conducted the focus group session, and to Barbara Rosen and Susan Eisenhandler for reinterviewing some of the informants.

NOTE

1. Dialogic theory holds considerable promise in extending our present personality theories. In particular, it enables us to understand how beliefs and ideological commitments are maintained and how they have an impact on self-identity. For a fuller discussion of this issue see Thomas, Sokolovsky & Feinberg (1996).

REFERENCES

Anderson, B. (1983). *Imagined communities: Reflections on the origin and spread of nationalism*. London: Verso.

Bakhtin, M.M. (1978). *The method in literary scholarship: A critical introduction to sociological poetics* (A.J. Wehrle, Trans.). Baltimore: Johns Hopkins University Press. (Original published 1928)

Bakhtin, M.M. (1984). *Problems of Dostoevsky's poetics* (C. Emerson, Trans.). Minneapolis: University of Minnesota press. (Original published 1963)

Berger, P. (1969). *The sacred canopy: Elements of a sociological theory of religion*. New York: Doubleday.

Blythe, R. (1979). *The view in winter: Reflections on old age*. New York: Penguin.

Brym, R.J. (1994). *The Jews of Moscow, Kiev and Minsk: Identity, antisemitism, emigration*. New York: New York University Press.

Florenskaya, T.A. (1989). Psychological problems of dialogue in light of the ideas of M.M. Bakhtin and A.A. Ukhtomskii. *Soviet Psychology*, 27, 29–40.

Gallup, G. (1976, December 11). 31% experience religious union. *Hartford Courant*, p. 6.

Greeley, A.M. (1974). *Ecstasy: A way of knowing*. Englewood Cliffs, NJ: Prentice-Hall.

Kaminsky, M. (1992). Story of the shoe box: On the meaning and practice of transmitting stories. In T.R. Cole, D.D. VanTassel & R. Kastenbaum (Eds.), *Handbook of the humanities and aging* (pp. 307-327). New York: Springer Publishing Co.

Langellier, K.M. (1989). Personal narratives: Perspectives on theory and research. *Text and Performance Quarterly*, 9, 243-276.

Lifton, R.J., & Olson, E. (1974). *Living and dying*. New York: Bantam.

Moody, H.R. (1986). The meaning of life and the meaning of old age. In T.R. Cole & S.A. Gadow (Eds.), What does it mean to grow old? (pp. 11–40). Durham, NC: Duke University Press.

Myerhoff, B. (1978). *Number our days*. New York: Simon & Schuster.

Redfield, R. (1960). *The little community and peasant society and culture*. Chicago: University of Chicago Press.

Thomas, L.E. (1994). Reflections on death by spiritually mature elderly. *Omega,*
   29, 1–9.
Thomas, L.E., & Cooper, P.E. (1978). Measurement and incidence of mystical experiences: An exploratory study. *Journal for the Scientific Study of Religion,*
   17, 433–437.
Thomas, L.E., Sokolovsky, M., & Feinberg, R.I. (1996). Ideology, narrative and
   identity: The case of elderly Jewish immigrants from the former USSR. *Jour-*
   nal of Aging and Identity, 1, 151–172.
Watkins, M. (1986). *Invisible guests: The development of imaginal dialogues.*
   Hillsdale, NJ: Analytic Press.

Some Correlates of Religiosity Among Turkish Adults and Elderly Within a Cross-Cultural Perspective

E. Olcay Imamoğlu

One's existence in life may be considered a quest for meaning. The social institutions one participates in and the developmental tasks one undertakes may be just vehicles to prepare or enable one to achieve satisfying answers for this ultimate quest. Viewed as such, old age may represent a period when one might be best equipped to do so. In fact, several theorists (e.g., Jung as reiterated by Goldbrunner, 1962) have suggested that during the second half of life the person becomes more inner oriented in order to find a meaning and wholeness in life that would enable him or her to accept death. An important associate of such an inner orientation may be the need for continuity of life, of being united to the world through children and through contributions to society so that the significance of one's temporary existence in this world might be extended beyond his or her time. Being unable to do so may lead to feelings of stagnation and despair (Erikson, 1968).

Thus, as one matures one may try to develop a personal meaning system or possibly seek help from some already-existing meaning systems such as religion. Religion has been regarded as a means of coping with and transcending death (Hood & Morris, 1983) and as having a strong effect on having a sense of meaning and purpose in life (Chamberlain & Zika, 1988). In congruence with the present formulation, Thomas (1994) reported that spiritually mature English elderly placed a positive value on death and viewed it as a continuation and source of meaning for their present life. Other studies have also reported attempts to find meaning in old age even with the prospect of declining powers (Dittmann-Kohli, 1989; Thomas & Chambers, 1989). For example, Thomas and Chambers (1989) found three interrelated themes in interviews with a group of Indian elderly: importance of family, salience of religious beliefs, and satisfaction with present life situation; which was related to family closeness and having done one's duty to one's children.

In a similar vein, E.O. Imamoğlu and V. Imamoğlu (1992b) reported that for the Turkish elderly frequency of interactions with social networks seems to have far-reaching effects for individuals' satisfaction with their sense of self and life situation. In this comparative study, involving Swedish and Turkish elderly, social contacts were found to help release feelings of loneliness and worries about aging; in Turkey, where values of interdependence seem more predominant (Imamoğlu, 1987), however, frequency of social contacts also seemed directly related to feeling satisfied with one's self and life, whereas they were unrelated in Sweden. Other studies mainly from Western societies have reported positive associations between religiosity and general well-being (Beit-Hallahmi & Argyle, 1997).

In view of the above-mentioned studies, the question may be raised whether the more religious Turkish elderly maintain closer social contacts and have a more positive outlook on their living conditions. The present report aims to explore the relationship between some religious beliefs and behaviors and social contacts, health and general well-being, preferences, and evaluations of general living conditions among Turkish adults and elderly. Because this study is part of a cross-cultural project, a comparison with the Swedish case is possible, thereby assessing the generalizability of the findings within a cross-cultural perspective (Küller, 1988; E.O. Imamoğlu & V. Imamoğlu, 1992b; E.O. Imamoğlu, Küller, Imamoğlu, & Küller, 1993).

METHOD

RESPONDENTS

The Turkish sample consisted of 574 respondents (229 females, 345 males) between the ages of 40 and 81, with a mean age of 61. The sample was selected by partly stratified random sampling according to area, age, gender and retirement-scheme considerations. The idea in sampling was not representation of the whole population but rather representation of different lifestyles in different geographical areas with varying levels of urbanization (see E.O. Imamoğlu & V. Imamoğlu, 1992a, b for detailed information about the areas). Of the respondents, only 17 had not yet retired; the great majority had retired under early retirement schemes available in the past. Although the majority of the respondents were not working, 12% of the women and 25% of the men were working full time after retirement and about 5% were working part time. All respondents were under some kind of Social Security.

As described more fully in Küller (1988), the Swedish sample consisted of 502 respondents (245 females, 257 males) between the ages of 60 and 71, with a mean age of 65. Thus, the Swedish sample was older, with a smaller age range. Still, 21% had not yet retired; 54% of the women and 62% of the men were not working; the rest were working either full or part time. In view of the differences between the two countries in terms of retirement schemes and life expectancy, the difference between the two samples in terms of psychological age might not be so great. Because the basic aim of the present report is to explore the trends in Turkey relative to those in Sweden, rather than to do direct comparison of the two samples, the whole Turkish sample was considered instead of a sample consisting mainly of the elderly more comparable to the Swedish sample, as was done in some earlier reports (e.g., E.O. Imamoğlu & V. Imamoğlu, 1992b; E.O. Imamoğlu et al., 1993).

INTERVIEW FORMS AND PROCEDURE

The interview forms consisted of booklets of 376 questions to be checked and 84 open-ended questions. The questions were adapted to the Turkish situation from the English version of the original used by Küller (1988), making some appropriate changes and additions. The questions were arranged to progress from the objective ones about housing, neighborhood, and mobility patterns to the more personal ones about the social living environments, retirement experiences, and recreation, health, and psychological status of the respondents. Then there were some questions to be filled in by the interviewers about the physical environment and the interview situation. On the average, interviews took 76 minutes in Turkey and 96 minutes in Sweden. The respondents generally were very favorable to the interviews, and most of them were willing to help again in the future.

In this chapter, only those questions concerning religiosity, social contacts, health and general well-being, dwelling conditions, and preferences are considered, in addition to some background variables involving age, gender, education, number of children, and employment. All responses were made on 3-point scales unless stated otherwise.

Religiosity

Religiosity was measured in terms of two religious beliefs concerning the degree to which the mosque or church was considered to have an important place in today's society and beliefs concerning life after death. Religious behaviors reflected whether the respondents had attended mosque or church or a religious meeting during the last 6 months.

Social Contacts

The index of the size of social networks consisted of the number of people in the household; children, grandchildren, siblings, and parents residing elsewhere; and neighbors, coworkers, and other close friends. Frequency of interaction with external social networks was measured using an index of the frequencies of interaction with children and their families, parents, siblings, neighbors, coworkers, and other close friends (each referring to people not included in the household). Five-point scales of almost never (1), about once a year (2), about once a month (3), about once a week (4), and almost every day (5) were used to measure each frequency.

The index of the need for social affiliation consisted of responses to questions concerning wanting to live next door to one's children and feeling a need to see one's friends often. The variable of interdependence with neighbors consisted of the following question: "Do you and your neighbors look after each others' homes when you go away? (e.g., look after plants, mail, etc.)." Respondents were also asked about the number of organized activities in their area that they participate in or are responsible for organizing.

Health and General Well-Being

The index of health functions consisted of being able to see, hear, and read ordinary print in a daily newspaper; not having problems with hearing on the phone or in noisy places; and walking, moving, or walking up and down stairs without difficulty.

The index of health problems consisted of whether the respondent often suffered from headaches, aches in joints or body, dizziness, high blood pressure, poor memory, anxiety, indigestion, pains in the stomach, eczema or allergies, colds or flu, general weakness, teeth or chewing problems, feeling sick and vomiting, and shortness of breath or pain in the chest. The index of sleeping problems concerned whether the respondent usually had trouble getting to sleep at night and whether he or she usually slept poorly.

The index of time spent outdoors concerned daily hours spent outdoors in winter and summer. The index of mobility addressed three questions concerning the frequency of going out of the neighborhood and doing one's own shopping to be responded to using 5-point scales of almost never (1), about once a year (2), about once a month (3), about once a week (4), and almost everyday (5).

The index of fear of accidents and robbery concerned whether the respondent feared that any sort of accident might happen to him or her and was afraid of mugging, purse snatching, and so on when out in the evenings.

The item of doctor visits concerned the number of times the respondent visited the doctor in the last year; that of days spent in bed asked the number of days the respondent had to stay in bed because of illness in the last year.

Questions related to loneliness asked whether the respondent often felt lonely and that no one needed him or her. The question concerning feeling rested enquired whether the respondent felt mostly rested or tired recently. Two other questions related to health habits asked whether the respondent smoked or abstained from alcoholic drinks.

The index of comparative self-image enquired whether the respondent felt younger or older, as having better or worse health and standard of living relative to most people of comparative age. The index of attitudes toward aging concerned worries of being sick and not being able to care for oneself, feeling insecure about getting older and whether getting older was better or worse than he or she thought it would be. Finally, the index of life satisfaction concerned satisfaction with one's life, considering one's current situation as better than 10 years ago, and satisfaction with one's current living conditions.

Dwelling Conditions and Preferences

Two indices were used to measure dwelling conditions; of these, dwelling standards was composed of the number of rooms minus the size of household; whether there was a separate kitchen, balcony, bathroom, toilet, and the type of toilet. Dwelling facilities involved cooking facilities, cold and hot water, drain, refrigerator, deep freeze, washing machine, dishwasher, and type of heating. To explore the respondents' subjective assessment of dwelling conditions, the index of evaluation of dwellings was used, involving evaluations of outside noise, privacy, pleasantness, and functionality of dwellings; problems with maintenance and maintenance costs; and considerations of changing dwellings (E.O. Imamoğlu & V. Imamoğlu, 1992a).

Dwelling preferences were measured in terms of attitudes toward institutional living, preferences for elderly or young companions, living in an area with mostly elderly people, and importance of having other-sex companions. Attitudes toward institutional living concerned considerations of living in a sheltered house, a communal living situation, or an "old folks or nursing home."

RESULTS

For each area considered, results of the Turkish study are reported first, and then some comparisons with the Swedish study are provided.

RELIGIOSITY

Most of the Turkish sample believed in both importance of the mosque (80%) and life after death (74%), with respective means of 2.66 and 2.60. The correlation between these two beliefs was found to be 0.29, $p < 0.0001$. The correlations between these beliefs and religious behavior were 0.26 and 0.22, respectively ($p < 0.0001$ for both).

In general, the Turkish sample appeared to be more religious than the Swedish sample; correlations with country being 0.12 for importance attributed to mosque or church, 0.31 for belief in life after death, and 0.20 for religious behavior ($p < 0.0001$ for all). For the Swedish sample, however, a somewhat stronger correlation was observed between the two beliefs ($r = 0.39$) and between belief in life after death and religious behavior ($r = 0.29$) as compared with the Turkish sample, whereas the correlation between belief in importance of church and religious behavior was 0.28 ($p < 0.0001$ for all).

RELATIONSHIP BETWEEN RELIGIOSITY AND SOME BACKGROUND VARIABLES

In contrast to Sweden, where age was not related to religiosity, in Turkey a weak trend was observed for the respondents to hold more religious beliefs with age ($r = 0.12$, $p < 0.005$ for belief in importance of mosque; and $r = 0.09$, $p < 0.04$ for belief in life after death). Age was not related to religious behavior in either country.

For the Turkish sample, gender was not correlated with religious beliefs; a correlation of 0.33 ($p < 0.0001$) was obtained for behaviors, however, implying that the Turkish men were more likely to engage in religious behavior. In fact, in contrast to 43% of the Turkish women, 74% of the Turkish men reported having attended mosque or a religious activity within the last 6 months, with respective means of 1.86 and 2.50. In contrast to Turkey, in Sweden women appeared to be more religious than men were, correlations being -0.14 ($p < 0.002$), -0.24 ($p < 0.0001$), and -0.19 ($p < 0.0001$) for beliefs in importance of the church, life after death, and religious behavior, respectively. Thus, in terms of the general religiosity index, consisting of both beliefs and behaviors, in Turkey men appeared to be more religious ($r = 0.23$, $p < 0.0001$), whereas in Sweden women seemed to be more religious ($r = -0.26$, $p < 0.0001$). Therefore, correlations between religious attitudes and behavior were relatively stronger for Turkish men and Swedish women ($r = 0.37$ and 0.35, respectively, $p < 0.0001$), less so for Swedish men ($r = 0.27$, $p < 0.001$), and least so for Turkish women ($r = 0.19$, $p < 0.003$).

For the Turkish sample, overall religiosity was negatively correlated with education ($r = -0.22$, $p < 0.0001$), with correlations of -0.23 for belief in importance of mosque ($p < 0.0001$), -0.14 for belief in life after death ($p < 0.001$), and -0.12 for religious behavior ($p < 0.003$). Furthermore, the Turkish respondents who believed in the importance of mosque and who engaged in religious behavior were slightly more likely to have more children, with respective correlations of 0.12 ($p < 0.002$) and 0.17 ($p < 0.0001$). For the Swedish sample none of the related correlations was significant.

Weak trends were obtained for the Turks who engaged in religious behavior to be currently employed ($r = 0.09$, $p < 0.02$) or for their past or current work to involve hard physical labor ($r = 0.11$, $p < 0.01$). The Turkish respondents' beliefs about the importance of the mosque were also weakly correlated with being involved in hard physical labor ($r = 0.15$, $p < 0.0001$). In Sweden, religiosity also appeared to be weakly correlated with being currently employed ($r = 0.23$, $p < 0.0001$), related correlations being 0.10 ($p < 0.03$), 0.17 ($p < 0.0001$) and 0.23 ($p < 0.0001$) for beliefs in importance of church, life after death, and religious behavior.

RELATIONSHIP BETWEEN RELIGIOSITY AND SOCIAL CONTACTS

The Turkish respondents who engaged in religious behavior appeared to have somewhat larger social networks ($r = 0.16$, $p < 0.0001$); to have relatively more frequent interactions with them ($r = 0.17$, $p < 0.0001$); to show more interdependence with their neighbors ($r = 0.16$, $p < 0.0001$); and to have higher needs for affiliation ($r = 0.13$, $p < 0.002$). Separate analyses indicated, however, that it was mainly the Turkish women for whom religious behaviors were associated with larger social networks and more social contacts ($r = 0.14$, $p < 0.04$, for both). In fact, Turkish women who engaged in religious behavior also showed a tendency to participate more in organized activities ($r = 0.16$, $p < 0.02$). Religious beliefs were not related to social contacts except for the relationship between belief in importance of mosque and interdependence with neighbors ($r = 0.13$, $p < 0.002$).

The Swedish respondents who believed in the importance of church and who engaged in religious behavior were also more likely to have somewhat larger social networks, respective correlations being 0.15 ($p < 0.001$) and 0.16 ($p < 0.0001$). Thus, a correlation of 0.18 was obtained between the religiosity index and size of social networks ($p < 0.0001$). The Swedish respondents who engaged in religious behavior were also more likely to have somewhat more frequent social contacts ($r = 0.19$, $p < 0.0001$). In fact, beliefs concerning importance of the church and engaging in religious behavior were weakly correlated with the number of organized activities in which the respondents participated ($r = 0.11$, $p < 0.02$ and $r = 0.14$, $p < 0.002$, respectively) and were actually responsible for organizing ($r = 0.15$, $p < 0.001$ and $r = 0.19$, $p < 0.001$, respectively). Separate analyses conducted for gender indicated that it was mainly the Swedish women for whom religious behavior was associated with being responsible for organizing meetings ($r = 0.28$,

$p < 0.0001$) and that for the Swedish men, engaging in religious behavior was weakly associated with having higher needs for affiliation ($r = 0.13, p < 0.04$). The other related correlations were not found to be significant in Sweden.

RELATIONSHIP BETWEEN RELIGIOSITY, HEALTH, AND GENERAL WELL-BEING

For the Turkish sample, religious behavior was not related to self-image, attitude toward aging, health functions or problems, frequency of doctor visits, smoking, or drinking. Weak correlations were obtained with the following variables, however: Those respondents who engaged in religious behavior tended to be less likely to have sleeping problems ($r = -0.16, p < 0.001$); to spend days in bed due to illness ($r = -0.13, p < 0.001$); or to feel lonely ($r = -0.11, p < 0.01$); they tended to be more mobile ($r = 0.17, p < 0.0001$), to spend more time outdoors ($r = 0.17, p < 0.0001$), to feel more rested ($r = 0.12, p < 0.005$), but to have more fears of robbery or accidents ($r = 0.15, p < 0.0001$). On the other hand, beliefs concerning importance of the mosque were weakly associated with poorer health functions ($r = -0.11, p < 0.01$), being less mobile ($r = -0.13, p < 0.003$), having fears of robbery or accidents ($r = 0.14, p < 0.001$) and never consuming alcohol ($r = 0.21, p < 0.0001$). Believing in life after death was weakly associated with being less likely to see the doctor within the last year ($r = -0.11, p < 0.008$) and less likely to consume any alcohol ($r = -0.15, p < 0.001$).

Separate analyses indicated that it was mainly the Turkish men for whom religious behavior was associated with fewer sleeping problems ($r = -0.12, p < 0.03$) and fears of robbery and accidents ($r = 0.28, p < 0.0001$). On the other hand, for the Turkish women, beliefs concerning importance of the mosque appeared to be weakly associated with a negative self-image ($r = -0.21, p < 0.001$), a negative attitude toward aging ($r = -0.12, p < 0.004$), poorer health functions ($r = -0.17, p < 0.01$), more health problems ($r = 0.14, p < 0.03$), and being less mobile ($r = -0.22, p < 0.001$); beliefs concerning afterlife were also associated with being less mobile ($r = -0.16, p < 0.005$).

On the other hand, the Swedish respondents who engaged in religious behavior showed weak tendencies to have more positive attitudes toward aging ($r = 0.10, p < 0.03$); to have better health functions ($r = 0.12, p < 0.006$); to have fewer health problems ($r = -0.15, p < 0.001$); to feel more rested ($r = 0.12, p < 0.007$); to feel more satisfied with life ($r = 0.12, p < 0.01$). They appeared less likely to feel that no one needed them ($r = 0.17, p < 0.0001$) and tended to be less likely to smoke ($r = -0.19, p < 0.0001$). Religious beliefs were only related to smoking and drinking behavior and life satisfaction. The Swedish respondents who believed in the importance of the church were more likely to abstain from alcoholic drinks ($r = 0.16, p < 0.0001$) and were less likely to smoke ($r = -0.15, p < 0.001$). Respective correlations for believing in life after death were 0.22 ($p < 0.0001$) and −0.11 ($p < 0.01$); belief in the importance of the church tended to be weakly but positively correlated with life satisfaction ($r = 0.10, p < 0.03$).

Separate analyses conducted for gender indicated that it was mainly the Swedish women for whom religious behavior was associated with more positive attitudes toward aging ($r = 0.16, p < 0.01$), higher life satisfaction ($r = 0.21, p < 0.001$), and fewer health problems ($r = -0.22, p < 0.0001$). Similarly, Swedish women who believed in the importance of the church appeared more satisfied with their lives ($r = 0.21, p < 0.001$); those who believed in life after death showed a slight tendency not only to feel more satisfied ($r = 0.13, p < 0.04$) but also to feel more positively about aging ($r = 0.15, p < 0.02$). On the other hand, for Swedish men religious behavior seemed to be associated with spending more time outdoors ($r = 0.24, p < 0.0001$), whereas belief concerning life after death seemed slightly correlated with being less mobile ($r = -0.15, p < 0.02$).

RELATIONSHIP BETWEEN RELIGIOSITY, DWELLING CONDITIONS, AND PREFERENCES

For the Turkish sample, weak negative correlations were obtained between religiosity index and both dwelling standards ($r = -0.12, p < 0.006$) and facilities ($r = -0.24, p < 0.0001$), respective correlations being −0.12 ($p < 0.003$) and −0.22 ($p < 0.0001$) for beliefs concerning importance of mosque and −0.10 ($p < 0.02$) and −0.18 ($p < 0.0001$) for beliefs in life after death. Separate analyses for gender, however, indicated that the correlations associated with dwelling standards were significant only for women ($r = -0.17, p < 0.009$ and −0.21, $p < 0.002$, respectively, for the two beliefs). Although correlations associated with dwelling facilities reached significance for both gender groups and beliefs, they were stronger for women compared with men, respective values being −0.30 ($p < 0.0001$) and −0.14 ($p < 0.01$) for beliefs concerning importance of the mosque and −0.24 ($p < 0.0001$) and −0.12 ($p < 0.03$) for beliefs in life after death. On the other hand, religious behaviors were only correlated with dwelling facilities ($r = -0.13, p < 0.001$) and mainly for men ($r = -0.26, p < 0.0001$). In spite of these trends for relatively poor dwelling standards and facilities, the Turkish respondents who believed in life after death and who engaged in religious behavior tended to evaluate their dwelling conditions somewhat positively, respective correlations being 0.13 ($p < 0.002$) and 0.15 ($p < 0.0001$).

In contrast, the Swedes who engaged in religious behavior tended to have somewhat better dwelling standards ($r = 0.10, p < 0.02$) and facilities ($r = 0.21, p < 0.0001$); still, however, they evaluated their dwelling conditions somewhat negatively ($r = -0.14, p < 0.003$). Similarly, the Swedes who believed in the importance of the church and in life after death also showed weak tendencies to evaluate their dwelling conditions negatively, respective correlations being –0.11 ($p <$ 0.01) and –0.14 ($p < 0.002$).

For the Turkish sample a weak negative correlation was obtained between religiosity index scores and attitudes toward institutional living ($r = -0.17$, $p < 0.0001$), related correlations being –0.13 ($p < 0.002$) for belief in importance of the mosque, –0.10 ($p < 0.02$) for life after death; and –0.13 ($p < 0.002$) for religious behavior.

In contrast to Turkey, in Sweden religiosity appeared to be positively correlated with attitudes toward institutional living ($r = 0.26$, $p < 0.0001$); respective correlations for religious beliefs and behavior being 0.16 ($p < 0.0001$), 0.13 ($p < 0.0003$) and 0.27 ($p < 0.0001$). Gender-related analyses indicated that correlations between religious beliefs and attitude toward institutional living were significant only for the Swedish men ($r = 0.19$, $p < 0.003$ and 0.14, $p < 0.02$ for beliefs concerning church and afterlife). Although the related correlations associated with religious behavior were significant for both men and women, they appeared to be stronger for the former ($r = 0.30$, $p < 0.0001$ and 0.21, $p < 0.001$, respectively). These results suggest that the religious Swedish men tend to be more favorable toward institutional living compared with Swedish women who hold religious beliefs and who already seem to have slightly better dwelling standards ($r = 0.12$ and 0.16, $p < 0.05$ and 0.01, respectively for beliefs concerning the church and the afterlife).

In terms of preferences, the Turkish respondents who engaged in religious behavior showed a weak tendency to prefer elderly companions ($r = 0.11$, $p < 0.007$) and living in an area mostly with older people ($r = 0.12$, $p < 0.004$). Beliefs were not associated with these variables; believing in life after death ,however, seemed to be weakly associated with a dislike for young companions ($r = -0.15$, $p < 0.0001$) and perceiving other-sex companions as less important ($r = 0.14$, $p < 0.001$). Beliefs about the importance of the mosque were also weakly correlated with regarding other-sex companions as less important ($r = -0.13$, $p < 0.002$). For the Swedish sample measures of religiosity were not related to the above-reported preferences, except for a weak correlation between religious behavior and preference to reside in an area mostly with older people ($r = 0.12$, $p < 0.01$).

DISCUSSION

In both Turkey and Sweden, religious beliefs were found to be associated with religious behaviors, in that beliefs about the importance of mosque or church and life after death were somewhat positively related to having attended mosque or church or a religious meeting within the last 6 months. In Turkey, most of the sample appeared to be religious; in fact, they tended to be more religious than the Swedish were.

Previous reports from the project indicated that the Turkish elderly have large social networks with which they interact frequently (E.O, Imamoğlu & V. Imamoğlu, 1992b; E.O, Imamoğlu et al., 1993). In fact, Turkey is more a culture of relatedness, where interpersonal bonds seem to be very important for the general psychological well-being of individuals, and Turks were found to have closer social contacts than the Swedes had even in metropolitan areas. At this point we may ask whether the more religious Turks maintain even closer social contacts. There appears to be such a trend, in that the Turkish respondents and mainly the women, who engaged in religious behavior showed a weak but positively significant tendency to have more social contacts with somewhat larger social networks and to exhibit more interdependence and feelings of affiliation. These findings are in accordance with the Islamic principles that demand close-knit interpersonal relationships among family members and encourage love and support among relatives (Serageldin, 1989). Accordingly, although the majority of Turkish families are nuclear (E.O. Imamoğlu & V. Imamoğlu, 1992a), the functions of an extended family are served, whereby close family ties extending into kinship relations serve an important function of providing material and psychological support when needed. Thus, in line with the Islamic and Turkish cultural conventions, support and sacrifice of parents for their children and obedience and responsibility of children in caring for their parents in old age are strong, widely accepted values (E.O. Imamoğlu & V. Imamoğlu, 1992a). In a similar vein, Sunar (1988) found that respect, gratitude, affection, and a sense of responsibility characterized Turkish students' feelings about elderly relatives, together with an ambivalence and impatience with their ideas and attitudes. Similarly, Bacanlı, Ahokas, and Best (1994) found that the Turkish university students' stereotypes about the elderly fell into two groups: one the "wise old man or woman," involving adjectives such as dignified, discreet, forgiving, mature, patient, reasonable, reflective, tolerant, and understanding; the other an "authoritarian old man or woman," with adjectives such as conservative, conventional, autocratic, hard headed, and thorough. Somewhat similar attitudes were found in Finland (Bacanlı et al., 1994).

In view of the negative correlation found between religiosity and education in Turkey, one may raise the possibility that the somewhat closer social contacts of the more religious Turks may be considered as merely representing traditional behavior in accordance with normative expectations. In Sweden, however, where religiosity was not associated with education, a similar trend was observed for the more religious respondents to maintain somewhat closer social contacts. Thus, in both societies, engaging in religious behavior appears to be associated with maintenance of closer social contacts. This finding is consistent with the related literature; for example, Beit-Hallahmi and Argyle (1997) have recently concluded that actively religious people appear to be more socially integrated and that religious involvement can provide a powerful means of social support, especially for the elderly who generally are more likely to be isolated and worried about death.

Moreover, in both countries religious behavior in general seems to be weakly associated with a more positive well-being. In Turkey, the religious respondents seemed more likely to have fewer sleeping problems, to spend fewer days in bed due to illness, and to feel less lonely, more rested, to spend more time outdoors, and to be more mobile. In Sweden, the religious respondents appeared more likely to have a more positive attitude toward aging, better health functions and fewer health problems; to feel more rested; to feel more needed and satisfied with life, and were less likely to smoke. Fewer and weak, but generally consistent, associations were also found for religious beliefs, except for the weak negative associations between belief in the importance of mosque and mobility and health functions; these associations, however, may be due to the weak but positive associations found between religious beliefs and aging in Turkey. In Sweden, where religiosity was not associated with aging, no negative relationships were found with well-being. Furthermore, in both countries, weak trends were obtained for religiosity to be associated with still being employed. In line with the present findings, several investigators have reported a relationship between religiosity and lower rates of morbidity (e.g., Beit-Hallahmi & Argyle, 1997; Levin, 1994). A meta-analysis of 56 studies indicated religion and happiness to be positively related, particularly for older samples (Witter, Stock, Okun, & Haring, 1985). Similarly, Willits and Crider (1988) found religious activity to be positively associated with happiness, life satisfaction, morale, quality of life, and general well-being. On the other hand, strictly following religious commandments might be a source of distress for some people (Lowenthal, 1993); and religiosity might have harmful effects when medical help is withheld for reasons of faith, and when physical punishment is advocated and practiced (Beit-Hallahmi & Argyle, 1997).

In Turkey the more religious respondents tended to live in dwellings with somewhat poorer standards and facilities; still, they tended to evaluate their dwelling conditions somewhat positively. In contrast, the more religious Swedes seemed to have somewhat better dwelling conditions but showed a tendency to evaluate them more negatively. These findings may indicate that religiosity is not directly associated with a more positive outlook about one's living conditions and instead may interact with other religious and cultural values. In line with the guiding ideas of Islam, the traditional values of the Turkish culture maintain that "This world is a temporary home where individuals must prepare themselves for the other world (heaven): hence they must live a humble, simple life avoiding the unnecessary frivolities and luxuries of this world" (V. Imamoğlu, 1992, p. 207). Such religious teachings are maintained in cultural values that encourage a positive acceptance of one's current situation and being thankful for whatever one has or whatever happens to oneself (E.O. Imamoğlu, 1995). Accordingly, Turkish cultural values advise that one should compare oneself not with those above but with the less fortunate below and that one should be thankful for whatever misfortune is bestowed on oneself because there could still be something worse than the seemingly worst things that have happened. In fact, one not only should show positive and thankful acceptance of unfortunate experiences but also should strive to find an enriched meaning in those seemingly unfortunate events or conditions because "there is a hidden fortune in every misfortune (even the worst), if only one could see it" (E.O. Imamoğlu, 1995). In a similar vein, Thomas (1992) noted that the elderly Hindu religious renunciates viewed pain as the will of God and as an opportunity to grow in spiritual awareness.

In Turkey, although gender was not associated with religious beliefs, men were more likely to engage in religious behavior. This seems to be due to Islamic conventions that do not hold women responsible for attending the mosque, whereas men are required to attend at least the Friday prayers ("namaz"). On the other hand, in congruence with the related literature, Beit-Ballahmi & Argyle (1997), the Swedish women appeared to be more religious in terms of both beliefs and behaviors. Thus, correlations between religious beliefs and behavior were found to be stronger for the Turkish men and Swedish women, less so for the Swedish men, and least so for the Turkish women. Of these four groups, religiosity seems to be associated with better outcomes for the Swedish women, particularly in terms of health and well-being, involving having fewer health problems, being more active in organizing meetings, having a more positive attitude toward aging, having better dwelling standards, and having higher life satisfaction. On the other hand, for the Turkish women, religious beliefs, particularly concerning importance of the mosque, seem to be associated with somewhat poorer health, negative self-image and attitudes toward aging, less mobility, and poorer dwelling conditions. Those women who engage in religious behavior, however, seem to experience the benefits of somewhat closer contacts with their social networks and tend to participate more in organized meetings. Thus, whether religiosity might be associated with positive or negative outcomes for an individual seems to be related to other interactive effects of the person's social status and cultural values. Other findings from the project indicated that gender differences seem to be more pronounced for Turkey compared with Sweden, which may reflect a sharper differentiation of lifestyles in Turkey as a function of gender (E.O.Imamoğlu & V. Imamoğlu, 1992b; E.O.Imamoğlu et al., 1993). Accordingly, the older Turkish women were found to have less frequent interactions with smaller social networks and to have more negative self-images than their male counterparts had, whereas in Sweden no such differences existed. In both countries, however, women reported more feelings of loneliness and worries about aging than did men. Thus, unlike this general picture, religiosity seems to have some positive correlates for the Swedish women, whereas the more negative state of the older Turkish women seems to prevail, except for the possibility of having increased social contacts associated with religious behavior.

Previous reports of the project noted that the Turkish respondents generally were more unfavorable concerning institutional living than the Swedish were (E.O. Imamoğlu & V. Imamoğlu, 1992b). Accordingly, in Turkey, an institution becomes an acceptable last resort for those who have fewer social contacts and feel lonelier and more negatively about aging and their lives. In contrast, for the Swedish elderly, only frequency of social contacts was found to be positively associated with attitudes toward institutional living. Present findings add to those previous reports by indicating that religiosity seems to be negatively associated with the attitude toward institutional living in Turkey, whereas in Sweden it seems to be positively associated. Thus, in Turkey, the more religious respondents who probably have stronger ties to the strong cultural values of interpersonal relatedness and embeddedness (E.O. Imamoğlu & V. Imamoğlu, 1992b), appear more likely to feel negatively about institutional living, although they seem to show a preference for elderly companions. On the other hand, in Sweden, where institutional living seems to represent an alternative living style for those with closer social contacts, the more religious respondents tend to have a more favorable attitude toward institutional living.

Unlike Sweden, where religiosity was not related to education, in Turkey, religiosity was found to be somewhat negatively correlated with educational level. In Turkey, acceptance of secularism in 1924, a year after the ending of the theocratic monarchy of 600 years, ruptured the formal ties of the state with religion and gave way to a more liberal type of living. Under the new state, secular education became widespread, leading the way "to regarding religious faith as a personal and private issue that concerns Allah and the individual. Such an understanding de-emphasized public attendance and the practice of the religious rituals" (V. Imamoğlu, 1995, p. 228), leading to a personalization of religious faith. This change toward personalization of religion led the way "to a weakening of the significance of mosques as central, indispensable places for prayer, as well as, social, political and cultural activities" (V. Imamoğlu, 1995, p. 233) among the more educated. "Mosques, however, continued to serve as indispensable places for the more traditional segments of the society whose understanding of religious issues . . . did not allow any changes. In the near future, as the internal consonance between religion and secularization is assimilated by larger portions of society, perhaps neither will be seen as a threat to the other by the respective representatives of each group" (V. Imamoğlu, 1995, p. 233–234), thereby preparing the way for more progressive attitudes toward both religion and education.

In fact, results of ongoing research involving Turkish university students and adults indicated that although religious beliefs showed a weak negative association with the parental education of the respondents, no association was observed with their own level of education, as in Sweden (E.O. Imamoğlu, 1996). In this new research, the religious beliefs index consisted of such beliefs as, "beliefs in a religion help one understand the meaning of life"; "beliefs in a religion enable people to be good citizens"; "religious faith contributes to good mental health"; and the negatively loaded beliefs of "religion makes people escape from reality" and "religious beliefs lead to unscientific thinking." Results of this ongoing research indicated the religious beliefs index to be positively associated with feeling inter-related ($r = 0.12$, $p < 0.03$) consistent with the present findings but negatively associated with individuation ($r = -0.37$, p 0.0001). In other words, the Turkish religious people appear to have "interrelated, normatively patterned out" selves ($r = 0.33$) (E.O. Imamoğlu, in press), being more likely to adhere to normatively patterned modes of thinking ($r = 0.46$), authoritarianism ($r = 0.57$), traditional value orientations ($r = 0.66$), traditional attitudes toward gender ($r = 0.57$), and conservative political ideologies ($r = 0.79$) and being less likely to maintain self-serving, unconstructive, negativistic modes of thinking ($r = -0.26$) and having lower needs for cognition ($r = -0.23$), all significant at the 0.0001 level. Others have also reported religiosity to be associated with narrowness of perspective, reflected in dogmatism, authoritarianism, and prejudices (Beit-Hallahmi & Argyle, 1997).

We can conclude that, in spite of some cultural and gender-related variations, religiosity generally appears to be associated with some positive outcomes. In thinking about the possible reasons for this trend, we may note that the religious elderly appear to maintain closer social contacts and to feel more interrelated and thereby may be more likely to benefit from social support. The related literature points to the beneficial effects of social support (Taylor, 1986). For example, an extensive longitudinal study indicated that people with many social and community ties were less likely to die during the study period than were people with fewer such ties (Berkman & Syme, 1979). Second, the religious elderly may be more likely to refrain from problem health behaviors, such as smoking, drinking, and lack of exercise. The adverse health effects of such behaviors have been well documented (Taylor, 1986). Third, the meaning system provided by religions may enable the elderly to have a more accepting and positive outlook toward life. For example, religious beliefs and prayers may induce a peace of mind, involving positive emotional experiences, such as relaxation, optimism, hope, self-confidence, forgiveness, self-control, empowerment, and sense of purpose, which in turn may activate the immune system (Beit-Hallahmi & Argyle, 1997; Dull & Skokan, 1995). Thus, the positive effects of religion may be associated with beliefs that provide peace of mind and meaning to human existence, commandments that may lead to a more disciplined life, and encouragement for a stable family and social support. In spite of such positive outcomes, however, religiosity appears to be associated with a narrow cognitive perspective and a passive adherence to normative modes of thinking and behavior, rather than an active search for meaning, at least in Turkey as implied by my ongoing research (E.O. Imamoğlu, 1996). Thus, the elderly appear to be religious in a conventional rather than a spiritual sense. Understanding religion in terms of spiritual growth, I feel, would require one to take an active interest in understanding the products of creation, including one's self, as well as microenvironments and macroenvironments. Instead, in Turkey, religiosity appears to be associated with a controlling, normative frame of reference and a low need for cognition. This is quite ironic in view of the fact that the Koran consistently emphasizes the importance of deep, reflective thinking. One hopes, in the near future, as more liberal and scientifically minded people engage in deep reflection on issues concerning the essence of religion and the meaning of life, true benefits of a genuine spiritual growth may be achieved.

ACKNOWLEDGMENTS

I thank Rikard and Marianne Küller, who undertook the Swedish study and made their data available for cross-cultural comparisons; and Vacit Imamoğlu, who collaborated in the Turkish study.
The research grant provided by the Middle East Technical University (AFP 86.02.01.01) is gratefully acknowledged. Thanks are due also to the Swedish Institute and Lund Institute of Technology for their support and to several research assistants, but particularly to T. Laike from the latter institution for his competent handling of the earlier computer analyses and to D. Kökdemir from the former institution for his assistance in follow-up analyses.
Address correspondence to Dr. E. Olcay Imamoğlu, Department of Psychology, Middle East Technical University, 06531 Ankara, Turkey.

REFERENCES

Bacanlı, H., Ahokas, M., & Best, D.L. (1994). Stereotypes of old adults in Turkey and Finland. In A. Gouvy, F.J.R. van de Vijver, P. Boski, & P. Schmitz (Eds.), *Journeys into cross-cultural psychology* (pp. 307–319). Lisse: Swets & Zeitlinger.

Beit-Hallahmi, B., & Argyle, M. (1997). *The psychology of religious behavior, belief and experience*. London: Routledge.

Berkman, L.F., & Syme, S.L. (1979). Social networks, host resistance, and mortality: A nine-year follow-up study of Alameda County residents. *American Journal of Epidemiology, 109*, 186–204.

Chamberlain, K., & Zika, S. (1988). Religiosity, life meaning, and well-being: Some relationships in a sample of women. *Journal for the Scientific Study of Religion, 27*, 411–420.

Dittmann-Kohli, F. (1989, July, International Society for the Study of Behavioral Development). *Possibilities and constraints for meaning giving in old age*. Paper presented at the ISSBD meeting, Jyvaskyla, Finland.

Dull, V.T., & Sloan, L.A. (1995). A cognitive model of religion's influence on health. *Journal of Social Issues, 51*, 49–64.

Erikson, E.H. (1968). *Identity: Youth and crisis.* New York: W.W. Norton.

Goldbrunner, J. (1962). *Individuation: A study of the depth psychology* of Carl Gustav Jung. New York: Pantheon.

Hood, R.W., Jr., & Morris, R.J. (1983). Toward a theory of death transcendence. *Journal for the scientific study of religion, 22*, 353–365.

Imamoğlu, E.O. (1987). An interdependence model of human development. In Ç. Kagıtçıbası (Ed.), *Growth and progress in cross cultural psychology* (pp. 138–145). Lisse: Swets and Zeitlinger.

Imamoğlu, E.O. (1995). *East meets West: Individualism versus collectivism in a model and scale of balanced differentiation and integration.* Unpublished manuscript, Middle East Technical University.

Imamoğlu, E.O. (1996). *Views of life.* Ongoing research, Middle East Technical University.

Imamoğlu, E.O. (in press). Individualism and collectivism in a model and scale of balanced differentiation and integration. *Journal of Psychology.*

Imamoğlu, E.O., & Imamoğlu, V. (1992a). Housing and living environments of the Turkish elderly. *Journal of Environmental Psychology, 12*, 35–43.

Imamoğlu, E.O., & Imamoğlu, V. (1992b). Life situations and attitudes of the Turkish elderly toward institutional living within a cross-cultural perspective. *Journal of Gerontology: Psychological Sciences, 47*(2), 102–108.

Imamoğlu, E. O., Küller, R., Imamoğlu, V., & Küller, M. (1993). The social psychological worlds of Swedes and Turks in and around retirement. *Journal of Cross-Cultural Psychology, 24*(1), 26–41.

Imamoğlu, V. (1992). *Traditional dwellings in Kayseri.* Ankara: Halk Bankası.

Imamoğlu, V. (1995). A synthesis of Muslim faith and secularity: The Anatolian case. *Architecture and Behavior, 11*(3–4), 227–234.

Küller, R. (1988). Housing for the elderly in Sweden. In D. Canter, M. Krampen, & D. Stea (Eds.), *Environmental policy, assessment and communication: Ethnoscapes* (Vol. 2, pp. 199–224). Avebury: Aldershot.

Lowenthal, K.M. (1993). Religion, stress and distress. *Religion Today, 8*, 14–16.

Levin, J.S. (1996). Religion and health: Is there an association, is it valid, and is it causal? *Social Science and Medicine, 38*, 1475–1482.

Serageldin, I. (1989). Faith and the environment: An inquiry into Islamic principles and the built environment. In I. Serageldin (Ed.), *Space for freedom* (pp. 213–225). London: Butterworth Architecture.

Sunar, D. (1988). Attitudes of Turkish students toward elderly relatives. *Journal of Cross-Cultural Gerontology, 3*, 41–52.

Taylor, S.E. (1986). Health psychology. New York: Random House.

Thomas, L. (1992). Identity, ideology and medicine: Health attitudes and behavior among Hindu religious renunciates. *Social Science and Medicine, 34*, 499-505.

Thomas, L.E. (1994). Reflections on death by spiritually mature elders. *Omega, 29*, 177–185.

Thomas, L.E., & Chambers, K. O. (1989). Phenomenology of life satisfaction among elderly men: Quantitative and qualitative views. *Psychology and Aging, 4*(3), 284–289.

Willits, F.K., & Crider, D.M. (1988). Religion and well-being = Man and women in the middle years. *Review of Religious Research, 29*, 281–294.

Witter, R.A., Stock, W.A., Okun, M.A., & Haring, M.J. (1985). Religion and subjective well-being in adulthood = A quantitative synthesis. *Review of Religious Research, 26*, 332–342.

PART FOUR

Glimpses of Gendered Spirituality

Spirituality: A Continually Evolving Component in Women's Identity Development

Patricia C. Burke

Quantitative methodology and the positivist paradigm from which social science theories were historically formulated have resulted in a scarcity of the study of religion and spirituality in the body of literature that addresses adulthood and aging. According to Thomas and Eisenhandler (1994), "What has been largely ignored by the field is the place that religious beliefs and practices hold in the lives of the aging individual" (p. xviii).

In the 1980s, with the emergence of life history or biographical methodologies and hermeneutics as credible research methodologies, psychologists joined other social scientists and historians in the gathering of qualitative data (Freeman, 1984; Gergen & Gergen, 1986; Manheimer, 1989; Mishler, 1986; Polkinghorne, 1988; Sarbin, 1986). At the same time, feminist social scientists joined the ranks of those pressing for a research methodology that would illuminate the lived experiences of women (Gergen, 1988; Geiger, 1986; Inglessi, 1990; Joy, 1995; Stivers, 1993). With changing methodological approaches, new categories for research have arisen to help clarify the developmental processes of individuals throughout the life span. Among these "new" categories is the role of religion and spirituality in the developmental or aging process.

METHODOLOGY

The chapter is the product of a qualitative research methodology that sought to understand the meaning of the life experiences of 40 women between the ages of 31 and 70. The original research questions revolved around the nature of the identity development in midlife women, a phenomenon that has been seriously neglected in spite of the wealth of literature evolving out of the women's movement in the 1960s and 1970s.

For the purposes of this study, identity was defined as a product of a meaning-making process, as described by Kegan (1982): "an adult's struggle to recognize herself in the midst of conflicting and changing feelings" (p. 16). As a result of a person's continual interaction with her environment, she forms a cognitive representation of herself in relation to both those in her immediate social world and society at large. This cognitive portrait of the self—one's personal identity—serves as an organizer of all the information to which a person is exposed that relates to self-knowledge. The organization of self-knowledge, however, is a life-long process in which an individual continually creates and recreates an identity that adapts as new events, thoughts, and life interpretations are presented. Unlike earlier suggestions by Erikson (1968) regarding identity clarification as an adolescent development task and by Manheimer (1989), who points out that the search for meaning has been "reidentified or displaced into old age" (p. 232), identity development is considered by many psychologists as an ongoing, meaning-making phenomenon that continues throughout the lifespan (Kegan, 1982; Riegel, 1975, 1976; Waterman & Archer, 1990).

Since narrative psychologists (Polkinghorne, 1988; Sarbin, 1986) have suggested that individuals attempt to make sense out of their lives by creating a narrative, I determined that the best way to understand these personal stories was a storytelling approach. Therefore, the primary method of data collection was an open-ended interview in the form of a personal narrative. The narratives, once transcribed, were coded, analyzed and synthesized into major theoretical categories using grounded theory procedures initially advanced by Glaser and Strauss (1967) and refined over the years by Strauss and Corbin (1990). The grounded theory methodology provides tools through which a researcher systematically organizes the data into a workable format so that conceptual categories can be identified and ultimately molded into a theoretical framework.

WOMEN OF THE STUDY

The core participants in this study were between 35 and 50 years of age, with smaller samples of women younger than 35 and older than 50 included for the purpose of contrasting midlife with other stages of life. Although the majority of the women do not fit into the later stage of life, it is appropriate to explore the stages that precede the later life stage. Manheimer (1989) remarked, "What one concludes about old age will have serious implications for how the previous stages of life are understood" (p. 232). The opposite is also true.

The criteria selected for the initial women interviewed were few because I anticipated that, as the interviewing progressed, the ideas generated would determine the subsequent interviews. Because the primary purpose of the study was to generate new research categories regarding women's identity, it was necessary to include among the participants women who represented a wide age span, varied childhood orientations, different cultural and racial backgrounds, and work and career directions. Unlike studies designed to prove or disprove hypotheses, where a sampling of quite similar participants is selected, difference was emphasized in the selection of this sample.

The total sample of 40 women encompassed the age span of 31 to 70 and included 32 White and 8 Black women. All of the women were currently married or previously had been; 30 were married at the time of the interview, and 10 were divorced or separated. All but 1 woman had at least one child. Educational backgrounds were diverse: 4 had no college degree, 14 had a 4-year degree, 13 had a master's degree, and 9 had a professional degree, a PhD. or MD. Twenty-three of the women were in nontraditional careers for women, in other words, engineering, law, medicine, law enforcement, architecture, and top management or administration. Seventeen were in traditionally female occupations, such as teaching, counseling, human resources, homemaking, and nursing.

The religious backgrounds of the 40 women were as varied as their occupations. As shown below in Table 7.1, all but 7 of the 40 women mentioned a childhood religious affiliation or indoctrination. In other words, they were brought up by parents who embraced and taught their children a particular set of religious beliefs. Many of the women also attended parochial schools.

Twenty-four women still considered themselves a part of a religious organization at the time of the interview but not necessarily the same religious affiliation that they "inherited" from their parents. Being affiliated with a religious institution did not mean the women were active participants. This was especially true of some of the Catholic women who described themselves as being "Irish Catholic," "Polish Catholic," or "Italian Catholic." Being Catholic was perceived as a component of one's ethnicity. Only one of the four Jewish women had a formal association with a Jewish organization.

Some of the participants who were not actively involved in a religious institution as adults were engaged in a spiritual search that stemmed from the contradictions they felt between their childhood belief system and the one they had acquired as adults. Table 7.2 summarizes the adulthood religious affiliation and participation of the women as adults. The "spirituality" category includes women who considered themselves spiritual but not associated with a formal religious institution.

TABLE 7.1   Childhood Religious Affiliation and Socialization of Participants

Affiliation/socialization	Number of women
Protestant	12
Catholic	17
Jewish	4
None mentioned	7

TABLE 7.2   **Adult Religious Affiliation and Spiritual Orientation of Participants**

Affiliation/orientation*	Number of women
Protestant	13
Catholic	10
Jewish	1
None	7
Spirituality	9

*Some form of involvement in or tie to a religious institution (church or synogogue).

The "none" category includes women who considered themselves spiritual but not associated with a formal religious institution. Others in this category did not mention religion or spirituality during their interviews or discounted it as an important element of their lives.

The following sections describe how the women in this study experienced religious and spiritual elements throughout their life span. To portray these experiences adequately in some instances requires lengthy quotes. Confidentiality of the women's lives have been protected by the use of pseudonyms.

SUMMARY OF FINDINGS REGARDING RELIGION AND SPIRITUALITY

The religious or spiritual element of women's lives presented itself in a variety of ways in this study. Five categories emerged from the narratives that reflect how the participants themselves perceived their religious or spiritual orientation at the time of the interview. These concepts should not be considered clearly delineated stages or levels of religious or spiritual growth but instead a religious orientation. This orientation is based on how the women described themselves in relation to values and religious beliefs that guided their life decisions, participation in religious organizations, and what they taught their children regarding religion and spirituality.

In the assignment of women to an orientation, I was assisted in some cases by the women themselves, who made it quite clear how their religious beliefs had influenced them. Others were in the process of defining their beliefs, and still others simply did not mention the topic. Because the methodology was designed to identify new categories regarding women's identity development, direct questions regarding religious beliefs were not asked unless the women first introduced the topic. Therefore, some of the women who were labeled "none" could possibly have beliefs that did not emerge because they chose to focus on other aspects of their lives as their narratives unfolded or, at least, did not perceive their beliefs as

TABLE 7.3   Participants' Perception of Religious Orientation

	By race	
Religious orientation	White (N = 32)	Black (N = 8)
Institutional[a]	8	0
Family/Religion[b]	8	0
Service to Others[c]	3	1
Spirituality[d]	6	7
None[e]	7	0

[a]Involvement in a religious organization.
[b]Family and religion were viewed as one, inseparable concept.
[c]Religious values dictated behavior, which included active involvement in a religious institution, in a capacity beyond "going to church," for example, community service.
[d]A focus on God as a power that directs people's lives; a relationship with a higher being.
[e]No mention of religious beliefs/involvement or spirituality.

significant in their developmental process. Table 7.3 summarizes the categories that emerged from these narratives. It must be noted, however, that these categories are not mutually exclusive; that is, some of the women could fit into more than one category but were placed in the one that seemed to be the most accurate representation of the women at the time they related their personal narratives.

To gain a clearer picture of the women's lifelong process, see Table 7.4, which illustrates the change, or lack of change, in the individual woman's religious affiliation or orientation over the years. This Table may also be referenced throughout the remainder of this chapter to identify participants' ages and race.

RELIGION—A PIECE OF LIFE

For some women, religion was simply another "piece" of their lives, similar to work, family, and volunteer work—something in which they were involved or an institution to which they belonged. For example, these women spoke of "going to church" or "being Catholic." Cara, age 44, represented this religious emphasis:

> We'd go to church every Sunday but that was it. It [religion] wasn't really discussed any other time during the week. We followed the ritual of it, but the family was not a real spiritual unit as it were . . . I still don't seem like a really spiritual person . . . but I believe in Christian values.

Cara discussed how she taught her children Christian values, which translated into a "do unto others" philosophy. These values dictated how a person might

TABLE 7.4 Summary of Personal and Religious Orientation Data by Participant

Participant	Age	Race	Childhood religious affiliation	Adult religious affiliation	Religious orientation/ perception
Barbara	31	B	Protestant	Protestant	Spirituality
Stacey	32	W	Catholic	Catholic	Institutional
Sally	32	W	Catholic	Protestant	Service to others
Janene	34	W	None	None	None
Renee	35	W	Catholic	Catholic	Institutional
Mindy	35	W	Jewish	None	Family/religion
Colleen	36	W	Protestant	Protestant	Spirituality
Olivia	36	W	None	Protestant	Family/religion
Randi	36	W	Catholic	Catholic	Family/religion
Gail	38	B	None	None	Spirituality
Sandy	38	W	Jewish	None	Family/religion
Karen	38	W	None	None	None
Bell	39	B	Protestant	Protestant	Spirituality
Kelly	39	W	Catholic	Catholic	Institutional
Laura	39	W	Catholic	None	Spirituality
Leslie	40	W	Catholic	Catholic	Institutional
Diana	41	W	Catholic	None	None
Rachel	41	W	Protestant	Protestant	Family/religion
Ginger	42	W	Protestant	Protestant	Family/religion
Faye	42	W	Catholic	None	Institutional
Lena	42	B	Catholic	Catholic	Spirituality
Nadine	43	W	Protestant	None	Institutional
Cara	44	W	Catholic	Catholic	Institutional
Haley	44	B	Protestant	Protestant	Spirituality
Belinda	44	B	Protestant	Protestant	Spirituality
Amanda	45	W	None	None	None
Holly	45	W	Catholic	None	Spirituality
Pauline	46	W	Protestant	Protestant	Spirituality
Rhonda	47	W	Catholic	None	None
Vera	47	W	Catholic	Catholic	Service to others
Wilma	48	B	None	None	Spirituality
Terri	48	W	Protestant	Protestant	Family/religion
Merry	48	MW	Protestant	Protestant	Family/religion
Wendy	49	W	Jewish	None	None
Pam	49	W	Catholic	Catholic	Institutional
Helen	50	W	Catholic	Catholic	Service to others
Heather	58	W	Catholic	None	None
Tommi	59	B	None	None	Service to others
Rose	68	W	Jewish	Jewish	Spirituality
Gloria	70	W	Protestant	Protestant	Spirituality

"treat people," "care for others," and "really do more than you have to do" on the job and in life in general.

Leslie, a corporate finance manager age 40, espoused a similar philosophy. She was raised a Catholic but had spent a period of time "re-exploring" those early teachings, after which she and her husband decided to teach their children a "more basic value system than 'if you are this, you are good, and if you are this, you are bad.' " At the time of the interview, Leslie still considered herself a Catholic, but was not an active participant.

In Table 7.3, this category is labeled "institutional" and includes eight of the participants. This label does not indicate that a woman was attending a church; she was, however, still espousing the religion of a specific church. Interestingly, all of the eight were White women who were at one time associated with the Catholic church.

FAMILY AND RELIGION

Family and religion surfaced as a theoretical category that merged two seemingly separate realms of life. According to Randi, a full-time homemaker and mother of four, "religion sort of makes you family oriented . . . it's part of what you need to be a family and to hold the family together." Randi, a practicing Catholic, had given up a career to stay home with her children because she wanted her children to be raised in the same way she was raised, wanted to "convey that [the importance of religion and family] to my children."

Although "going to church" was not discussed by Renee, a corporate lawyer, she repeatedly referred to her extended family which is "very Catholic, very Italian, very traditional." Merry, a research pathologist, was adamant that her values centered around her family and religion. She insisted that her husband become a Lutheran before they married, and at the time of the interview they were faithfully attending and quite involved in weekly activities in the Lutheran church. Religion had been part of her value system since she was a child:

> My mother is extremely religious and my father is in a quiet way . . . Religious, that's kind of a strange word, but I always valued church; I loved going to church and I always liked Lent because we got to go to church an extra day, you know. This type thing. So, it was kind of part of me. Now, I don't know why, and I'm still that way. I love going to church on Sunday morning; it's a neat thing to do.

As shown in Table 7.3, all eight of the participants who fell into the "Family and Religion" category were White. One was Jewish, one was Catholic, and the remaining six were Protestants.

SERVICE TO OTHERS

Another religious emphasis surfaced in the form of service to others. Religious values dictated behavior, which included active involvement in a religious institution, in a capacity beyond "going to church." Because of her religious upbringing, which included attending a church or synagogue, a woman participated in an organization that operated from religious values. For example, Helen, whose heavy involvement in community activities resulted in being chosen a "Mother of the Year" recipient, spent most of her time at work as a bereavement counselor in a mortuary, counseling those who had suffered the loss of a family member or close friend, and, in her leisure time, working with other Catholics in caring for the homeless. Similarly, Tommi, a higher education administrator, felt it was her social obligation to "pay back" what she had received in this world, and she considered this her religion: "I believe in tithing by giving my time, my energies, and my abilities." Tommi was not formally associated with a church. Four of the participants fell into this category (see Table 7.3), but this does not mean that women in other categories were not also involved in service. Service was not, however, the primary focus of their religion.

SPIRITUALITY

The most "spiritual" group of women went beyond any of the emphases mentioned previously to a point where God represented continuity, an underlying theme or a continuous thread in their lives since childhood. As a result of the women's words, I defined spirituality as a focus on God as a power that directs people's lives. It is a relationship with a higher being, not the act of doing something to fulfill a religious commitment. Through this relationship, the women transcended the activities of daily living and reached a peaceful state where life's experiences were more cohesive or coherent. This definition of spirituality is supported by Eisenhandler (1994): ". . . spirituality is often associated with the idea of transcendence; a spiritual experience or set of experiences is understood to transform the individual's relationship to God or to a divine force and to intensify the person's engagement with life by deepening of appreciation for its struggles and joys" (p. 136).

God was casually and frequently mentioned throughout the interviews of those participants considered "spiritual," which included 13 women (see Table 7.3). They did not speak of "going to church" or of "religion." Their focus was on God as a being more powerful than they who guides their every decision and, in some cases, has a life plan for them. Some of the women in this category were in the midst of a spiritual quest or search for meaning.

Barbara, the youngest of the women interviewed (age 31), felt her spirituality was instilled in her by her grandmother when Barbara was a very young child but is something that she and her husband now "just know is important."

I think it's because I know how important God is in my life. My husband agrees so our life is what all we can do to spread the message of God's love . . . I am who I am and I am where I am because of my beliefs in God. Things that people attribute to luck or fate, I attribute to a plan mapped out for me by God.

Bell (age 39), a corrections officer, grew up with a father who "preached" Christian values and a mother "who prayed about everything." In adulthood, prayer became a natural source of strength when she was facing obstacles at work or at home. Likewise, Wilma, an executive director of a nonprofit organization, felt God was instrumental in leading her to a job that was the "right fit" for her. Lena (age 42), a corporate training specialist, spoke of how she loved to read the Bible and how she frequently asked God to give her faith. Her spiritual side gave her "comfort." Belinda (age 44), whose life had been sprinkled with numerous crises and uncertainties, prayed to God for guidance for all decisions she made as a single mother with tremendous responsibilities at home and in her job as an inner-city teacher: "I think prayer is constant and I think that God is within you and that as long as you carry consideration and love for other people, that he is working within your life."

Because she felt that God takes care of her, Belinda tried to give to others what she received: "There is a God; he takes care of me . . . even the things that happen to me I've always come out okay . . . and I want to give back just a little of what he's given me in my life and every once in a while to just hug a kid and listen to them."

All of the women just mentioned in the "spiritual" category are Black, although there were six White women who were included in this category (see Table 7.3). Some of their stories are given in later sections. The overwhelming influence of God in the lives of the Black women in this study led me to ask Haley (age 44), an administrator at a medical school, why Black women appear to be more spiritual than White women are. Her answer was,

I don't necessarily think we are more spiritual but I think spirituality is closer to reality. To me, it's like God sitting over on the other end of the couch. I could sit here in this chair and rock and talk to God like God is sitting in this room with me. God's not a way off yonder somewhere. God is very close. God is very, very close. All I have to do is just be ready to talk to God . . . You know what that goes back to? You know when you're little and you are cleaning up and your mother says, 'now, you have to dust under the bed because even if I don't see it, God sees it.' So I thought God was up under the bed with the dust bunny. It was just that real to me. I'd go to see if I could catch God under the bed. When I say God is there, it's not a God up in heaven or God away off down the street. God is everywhere.

Regardless of the function of religion in the women's lives, whether focused on the institution, family and religion, service to others, or God as a powerful being, to slightly more than half of the women, religion or spirituality was connected in some way to their identity or search for meaning. The remainder of this chapter, therefore, will focus on the role of religion and spirituality in the identity development process in midlife women.

SPIRITUALITY AND IDENTITY DEVELOPMENT

In this study, spirituality was considered as an outcome of the adult identity process. As discussed before, it became a key concept in this study because of the contrast between the Black women, all whom spoke very naturally of their spiritual lives, and the majority of the White women, who mentioned their religious affiliation or church synagogue participation instead of a relationship with God.

The presence of spirituality in Black women can be partially explained by looking at the theoretical tenets on which this study was built, a dialectical process in which conflict or contradiction in one's life triggers a search for stability or continuity (Riegel, 1975, 1976). Because of adverse social conditions under which Black women have lived, they are more likely to encounter discontinuity in the form of discrimination or from being different from the dominant group in society. Because our society has always been dominated by White males, and Black people have traditionally been a downtrodden group, the search for and belief in a power greater than the one encountered daily was the only hope for many Blacks. Consequently, this dependence on God became, over time, instilled in the Black culture.

The Black women in this study spoke of how religion was a vital part of the all-Black communities where they lived as children. According to Levin, Taylor, and Chatters (1994), "participation in religious communities provides members with a framework for deriving meaning from their life experiences and with structured opportunities to interact with others who are alike with respect to values, beliefs, and attitudes" (p. 137). Haley, the medical school administrator mentioned earlier, gave an example of how participation in religious activities in the Black communities in the South was "confirming": "Some of the fondest memories I have of my childhood is . . . walking to church together and sitting in church together . . . We all went to church together and even in my church community at that time, there were a lot of opportunities for expression, something I see very much missing in Black communities today."

She described how "very warm, very loved, very supported and very encouraged" she felt within this community and, in contrast, how horrified she was when she first encountered a White person outside her safe community who called her a "nigger." Those "small isolated incidents" happened only when "outside my community."

Levin et al (1994) also described how the leadership position that Black women assume within the family puts tremendous stress on them, that is somewhat alleviated by having a "religious orientation." Although Levin was speaking primarily of religion as a support system, in this study, the Black women spoke more of God as a support "person."

There were very few White women among the 32 in this study that appeared to have the depth of faith in God that these Black women had. The most notable distinction between the Black and White participants in this category revolved around continuity. The Black women discussed a spirituality that had been with them since childhood, whereas the White women frequently reached this state through a life crisis or through the resolution of contradictions stemming from their childhood religious teachings.

One of the narratives revealed a woman struggling to reclaim her spirituality. This was Rose, a 68-year-old Jewish woman. During the interview, as she recalled important people and events from her life, it was obvious that a constant theme had been her faith and the friends with whom she shared this faith:

> . . . through that [Zionist] organization [following World War II] . . . I developed the core of friends who are with me today . . . I would say that that's when a certain stability entered my life . . . we all had common interests . . . I would say that became my stability at that time. I didn't flounder in those years because I was so imbued with Zionism . . . those were magical times for me because I had never really had that.

In her late 60s, Rose's life revolved totally around her faith: "I feel to my core my Judaism . . . I would call myself a spiritual Jew." To reach this point, however, Rose went through a difficult midlife transition in her 40s that included the beginning of a college education at age 46. She studied several years and eventually wrote a book on 12 Polish Jews who survived the Holocaust during World War II.

Gloria, who was 70 years old at the time of the interview, discussed her spiritual development as an outcome of a midlife transition that was initiated by a divorce when she was 43 years old. During the early years of her marriage, she was active in the children's education program of a church that had been established by her husband's ancestors. She described how she went to church because it was her "husband's church" and her mother-in-law expected it. During her marriage, she dedicated her life to her four children. After her divorce, Gloria began a search for meaning. In her 50s, she found what she felt she had been searching for all her life: "a group I could really belong to." Her religious involvement began more as a social activity, but in her 60s, after years of a difficult second marriage, Gloria said, "I put as much of my life as I can into God's hands," trying not to be "herself," which was a "controlling" person. At age 69, after she separated from her second husband, Gloria described a new relationship with God in which she "personally dedicated" her life to God, "asked him to help her to do his will, to his glory." At age 70, she said, "I'm still on that track." Her identity stemmed from her role as a Christian woman.

Pauline, an Episcopalian priest who was 46 years old, described herself as "one of the baptized, somebody called by God to a full life." She stated that "the spiritual journey for me has meant I'm free to just be and continually be in deeper trust." Her faith in God was the source of her feeling of wholeness and peacefulness, but this had not always been the case. Pauline experienced an extremely long and traumatic life transition that culminated with her decision to become a priest. It was through analysis of Pauline's narrative that the role of religion and spirituality in midlife transitions became especially clear.

THE ROLE OF RELIGION AND SPIRITUALITY IN LIFE TRANSITIONS

There were at least 10 women in this study for whom religion or spirituality played a role in a difficult life transition. Most were in their mid to late 30s when the transition began. An attempt to resolve contradictions between religious beliefs instilled in them in childhood and their adult images of God triggered or played a large role in the transition. They were struggling to make sense out of previous life experiences and to find continuity and meaning in the midst of conflict. Therefore, spiritual development and the identity development processes became closely entwined in these midlife quests. Excerpts from the narratives of 3 of these women are given below. These vignettes include Laura, a 39-year-old artist, Lena, a 42-year-old corporate training specialist, and Pauline, a 46-year-old Episcopalian priest.

LAURA—RESOLVING RELIGIOUS CONTRADICTIONS THROUGH ARTWORK

Laura, a 39-year-old sculptor and painter had, in adulthood, reacted strongly to her religious upbringing in which she was taught to fear God. She wanted to believe that he was a benevolent God and had spent much of her adult life trying to understand the contradiction between her early religious orientation and what her life experiences taught her was the "truth."

... you can't grow up Roman Catholic and not feel guilty. The first thing they tell you, the very first thing you learn in religion is: who made you? God made you. Why didn't he make you so you would be happy with him in heaven? And your body is evil, especially if you are a woman ... Eve was the one who caused the downfall of the whole human race, and growing up with nuns especially, they are very, very obvious about that.

I can still remember the story the nun told us about how Jesus would come down and strike you dead if you did something horrible, and I could not coincide the vengeful, horrible God that these nuns were talking about and the concept of a God that I was evolving out of, taking in the other half: the good, the provider, the creator of the world; there were too many conflicts . . .

These early teachings resurfaced as a contradiction after her son nearly died of injuries from a car accident. As she sat in his hospital room, she had time to meditate, and the questions that she needed to answer before moving on with her life began to crystallize:

I could remember wanting very much to do some art, and I was at the point where I couldn't pull myself out of the . . . just the pain, the trauma, whatever, uh . . . watching your child suffer; struggle is very, very painful and . . . instead I centered on thinking . . . in terms of properties, emotions, or what have you of women and the experience of a woman, as a nurturer, as a teacher, as a mender . . . like what is the condition of a woman?

The contradiction between her thoughts as she watched her child suffer, sitting beside him for months on end as he slowly regained the use of his faculties, and what she had been taught as a child triggered a search for truth. "What is the condition of a woman?" was the question that encompassed Laura's uncertainties regarding whether women were evil, like Eve in Genesis, or good as she felt she was as a mother. Mothers are "nurturers, teachers, menders and they suffer much." Her words reveal a search for truth regarding the nature of God, womankind, and herself as a woman and a mother, in particular.

If you asked me to define a God I don't think I could . . . and yet every time I'm in a real jam, like when my son was in the hospital, I prayed. I don't know to whom; I just believe that there was nothing else to be done but to pray, and you know, if it worked, it worked, and it seemed to have worked. So again, I wouldn't deny it.
. . . what I found was that once I was not involved in formal, organized religion, it was much easier to see people as good, uh, because somehow within the church there was always, I felt that I always owed people something when I was in the Roman Catholic church, that I had to do something, give them something, or I wasn't being a good Catholic. You can't give anything to anyone except if it comes from inside. You have to want to do it . . . so I find that it's a lot easier to treat people fairly, to treat them kindly, to be more giving so long as I don't feel an obligation to do it.

After her son returned home from the hospital, Laura resumed her drawing and sculpting. At that point, her art took a different form.

But, with my experience with my son, I just started thinking in terms of the birthing, the nurturing aspect of what is female and what is so beautiful about that, and so painful about that, and how the pain enhances the joy really, because you can't have joy without pain, you just can't . . . the pain is just as important I think as the joy. And I think, having gone through that experience with my son, I am much more aware of the joyfulness, and I appreciate it that much more, and as part of my artistic expression, I just keep wanting to find a way to get it out. I'm finding that all my metaphors are female now suddenly.

Making sense of life through art, then, became the core theme in Laura's life. It gave her continuity, a sense of purpose, and a means for resolving religious issues dating back to childhood. It helped her bring all of life's pieces together, and, as the whole became clearer, her personal philosophy of life began to take form, as is evidenced through what she said she was teaching her children:

We are not religious; we don't practice any particular religion, but I saw to it, since we do live in a Christian country, my own kids were introduced to the Bible and things like that, but I always figured that religion is something that you acquire in the process of a lifetime. And you evolve what you need from it . . . . I keep telling my kids, it's more important to live your lives in such a way that you hurt no one than it is to go to church and pray and turn around and beat the heck out of the kid next door, or what not, or cheat on a test, or whatever. To be a good person is more important.

Laura's search for truth was still in progress when I completed the last interview with her. Spirituality was, at age 39, a continually evolving piece of her life.

LENA-IN A QUEST FOR CONTENTMENT

Lena grew up in the South during the 1950s and was part of a "strong, cohesive, Black community" where religion was a given. She attended an all-Black Catholic church and school and felt generally positive about the experience, but as an adult seldom attended the Catholic church or her husband's religious (Quaker) services. She described herself, however, as a deeply spiritual person:

Sometimes I read the Bible a lot; sometimes the Bible frustrates me because I don't understand it, or I'll read the Old Testament and say, 'I don't know if I believe this,' but still it doesn't seem to alter my faith. I don't go to church every Sunday . . . . I actually believe people were created good and we make choices that we want to do so. I don't know, my spirituality is just sort of my own way of thinking, of living. . . . I don't go to the Catholic church very much. But, if you were to ask me, 'what is you religion?' I would certainly say, "Catholic."

When I interviewed Lena, she was working as a corporate training specialist and had just attended a work-sponsored, career development class where she had been surprised to discover that her "spiritual life" was the most important thing to her. In contrast, a colleague's test revealed that power was the most important to him. It was not a surprise to me, the interviewer, however, because throughout her narrative she referred to herself as a "very spiritual" person.

At age 36, Lena had begun what she called a "quest," which was a search for peace. The quest coincided with her second marriage because she saw in her husband a calmness that she did not feel, especially regarding issues of discrimination.

One of the things that attracted me to my husband was his serenity, and I would ask him questions, and his answers were so clear, so simple, so obvious, and I would say, "but how did you know that?" . . . my husband is Quaker, and Quakers like to meditate about life. But I guess I was so curious about this serenity. He always seemed to be so peaceful and calm within, so maybe that was what I was looking for, the calmness and that was what sent me on my quest to think about things . . . and it [the quest] just took a spiritual path.

In Lena's mind, spirituality and formal religion were separated. She remained a Catholic because she had always "just been inundated with Catholicism and religion," but, she was questioning many of the teachings of the Catholic church. Early in childhood, she concluded that priests and nuns were "not infallible" and, in adulthood, her God was not like the one she learned about as a child. As a result of her own spiritual path, she was exposing her daughter to a broader, more humanitarian religion: " . . . the important thing is not that she belongs to an organized religion; the important thing is that she be a kind, confident, kind, gentle person. And treat other people in a respectful manner. That's true and very, very important for me, and she does; I think she does . . . ."

Her spirituality, not her religious affiliation, helped her deal with life's contradictions and problems, such as prejudice, which "creeps into your thought process whether you want it or not."

Lena, at age 42, was still seeking peace and the calmness that she believed would eventually come from her spiritual quest. She was aware that her spiritual development was still in process. Regarding her search for the qualities she observed in her husband, Lena said: "I don't think I'm there. I don't know if I will ever get there . . . . I hope I will get there."

The two women just discussed were obviously still in the middle of their spiritual search. Each was conscious of the search but unsure of what the outcome would be. The next vignette reveals at least a temporary end point to a midlife search for meaning.

PAULINE—CREATING A NEW BEING

Pauline experienced deep trauma, both in childhood and in adulthood, because of child abuse and later psychological abuse from her husband. She changed her life's direction quite dramatically, when she was in her mid-30s. She was "in transition" for at least 10 years, probably longer. Her search for meaning, which became in her words a "pathway to priesthood," began when she was just a child, but she was unaware of the source until midlife.

At age 27, during a crisis period when she was diagnosed as having cancer only to discover after surgery that there was no cancer, Pauline began what she referred to as a discernment process, which was her church's term for a life assessment and determination of what to do with the rest of one's life. The discernment process, as defined by Pauline, was "an internal kind of purpose for my life which I think was a theological piece. For what purpose was I created and what was I going to do with what I had been given?" The process began with a feeling of restlessness:

I was bored. It was kind of: "What am I going to do for the rest of my life?" I was open to that question of what I was going to do; I just didn't know which direction and I remember standing in my office one afternoon, and there was a social worker serving as my director of volunteers who turned around and said to me, "when are you going to do what you were called to do?" I could put us in the same position, in the same room, with the same light, that's how incisive a moment it was for me. Within 24–48 hours, the priest with whom I was working said, "you know there's a new Christian educator coming from Columbia going to Yale, why don't you go down and take a class with him and see if you want to be a Christian educator." And also, my marriage was not in good shape, that was about 10 years into my marriage and things were really not good between us . . . .

Her physician husband was abusing drugs and was not willing to change to save their marriage. He had frequent, severe mood swings.

I think at some level I was plotting my escape. I was beginning to make some shifts that I was not going to live like that for the rest of my life. So this intense discernment with friend and colleague, but also I had a dream. I saw myself vested and celebrating as a priest, and I didn't think I was asking that question and it scared me to death, and I wouldn't tell anybody about it for years, for I thought they would think I was crazy. I had no models. I knew that the Episcopal Church was beginning to ordain women, but I didn't think, I'm not sure I believed I was capable of doing everything that was required to get there.

At this point, several conscious forces were driving Pauline's search. Her marriage was stifling and unfulfilling, she was bored with volunteer work, and she wanted to do something worthwhile during her lifetime, but there were some obvious barriers confronting her. Her husband was not supportive. She had three children for whom she was the sole caretaker because her husband was not involved with the family. Later, as she reflected on those times, she knew that there were also some subconscious barriers. She did not see herself as the type of woman who could handle the conflictual nature of a woman priest in a male-dominated institution; she had always been submissive and nonassertive. Some subconscious force drove her to take the first step to escape her oppressive life. "And the first day I went to classes, 50% of the student body were females [in 1982] . . . .But I was at home when I got to seminary, full engagement of my brain, my heart, of my spirit. I loved it, loved it, loved it, all of it."

Pauline discovered a purpose for her life but had to work through many layers of repressed anger and feelings of powerlessness before she could move to fulfill her purpose. This was accomplished over a 7-year period through education (a master's in theology); the ordination process which included psychiatric and peer evaluations; and therapy. Through one of her feminist classes, she determined that "it was okay to break a promise if the promise was death dealing for me . . . ." She was speaking of her marriage and her hesitation to leave a husband who abused her. "I was living in a really abusive marriage and I think at some psychic subconscious level I was reaching for a power that was even greater than the power I lived with, and that [her husband] might feel free to wrestle with me, but if God were on my side, then maybe I had a powerful piece of support."

Pauline struggled for at least 15 years to overcome a childhood socialization that instilled in her the idea that women must sacrifice their own dreams to allow their husbands and children to accomplish their goals. To make this drastic change in paradigm she had to get permission from someone. She had never received permission as a child to do what she wanted to do and her abusive husband reinforced her childhood thoughts. She finally received this permission from the scriptures and other women who had been through similar situations.

Pauline finished her seminary degree and was ordained in 1987. She was continually validated by her parish and other women priests, but her marriage was still oppressive:

I just wasn't good enough. I never measured up and as soon as I would change to kind of accommodate him, the mood would change and it was never enough, and one of

my therapists said at one point, "Pauline, if you weren't such a willow, you would
have broken a long time ago. You bend and bend and bend and bend to everyone
else's needs. When are you going to take care of yourself?"

I really got it when one other woman who had been ordained longer than I have
turned around to me and said, "do you believe the gospels are true?" All the time I
could feel my gut just in a knot and she said, "well, you know, Jesus promises abundant life for everybody, do you think that's true?" I said, "well, I think it's true, but
some have a better chance at abundance than others, that kind of thing." She said,
"well, people who live on wafers starve to death." and that hit me right between the
eyes that I had been living on crumbs and if I didn't believe the gospel was true for
me, but was true for everybody else, what was that all about?

After 3 years of therapy, Pauline gained the courage to leave her husband.
During the therapy, she began to understand herself better:

I was also emerging into some new creation and I had to get some feedback that was
going to validate that in a way that could hold me accountable again.

By this time, he [her husband] earned a lot of money, I had a beautiful home, I had
gardens that I loved, an in-ground pool, a screened-in porch . . . mom car, station
wagon, so the externals were certainly set up to provide security and a certain style
of life, but it was deadly for me, just deadly. And all those pieces eventually gave me
the courage to leave.

Pauline's life is a vivid example of how a woman moves from silence and
a diffused identity to a clear, solid sense of who she is and what her place in
the world is. It is obvious that Pauline moved through a step-wise process,
perhaps stages of development, and yet the boundaries are blurred. Her development as a unique, independent person and her spiritual development
processes were so tightly interwoven that they emerged as a single, meaning-making process.

At the end of the interview with Pauline, she mentioned, nearly as an af-
terthought, a spiritual element that she felt had been with her from childhood:

. . . my earliest memory as a child is that I was seated on a swing that was hung from
a tree behind somebody else's house, and the sunlight was coming through the trees,
and you know the creak of one of those rope swings on a tree, and I knew I was
blessed by God. I have a real clear piece that God was there and I was fine. Now it
may have been one of the few safe places for me, I don't know. But I was lost and I
was safe and I was doing something that I enjoyed, which was swinging on that
swing and that was a holy place for me, and why I can't tell you, but it was. I have a
clear memory of that.

The only thing that she could find that was continuous (from her early childhood) was her belief in God, that she was blessed by God. As she reconstructed her life, she traced this theme through to the end, to where she was at age 46:

I see myself as one of the baptized, somebody called to God to a full life and it's a life that I'm accountable for here, but it's going to go on long beyond me, and I'm a human person who's been gifted . . . . I'm creating a life. It's certainly been on the edge. It's a continually evolving piece.

Pauline's narrative illustrates how identity development and spirituality can be intertwined. In midlife, her identity was synonymous with her spirituality, but her life was still evolving.

DISCUSSION AND CONCLUSIONS

In this study of identity development in midlife women, some form of a religious or spiritual theme arose from the narratives of approximately half of the 40 participants. The theme emerged because the unstructured, narrative approach used for collecting data encouraged participants to select and interpret life events that were important to them. The concept of being religious or spiritual arose naturally during the women's storytelling because it had been a continuous, cohesive element in their every day lives or it had become a source of contradiction that had to be resolved. There were an additional 8 to 10 women who mentioned briefly attending a Catholic school or going to church, but it was no longer important enough in their lives to merit more than a cursory statement in their storytelling. All the women who considered religion or spirituality as an important life theme had a religious orientation in childhood that later served as a foundation for the development of religious beliefs, or at least a starting point for formulating their own belief system.

An important observation from this collection of life stories, then, is that in those women for whom religion was a major factor in their midlife development, a religious or spiritual seed had been planted early in life. Because of diverse childhood, adolescent, and young adult experiences, the outgrowth from the seed took various forms. Religion may be perceived in midlife as a negative or counterproductive life force or as a positive, enriching force. It may represent continuity and stability because it has always been with them, as was true of so many of the Black women, or it may be a discontinuous force that rises to the surface in midlife, stimulating a search for truth or meaning. It is during such a quest that religion and identity become inseparable.

Some valuable insight was gained from this study regarding the relationship between spirituality and identity development in midlife. Based on the narratives of the participants, the achievement of a mature or integrated identity is a developmental task that surfaces around age 35 and culminates in the mid to late 40s. An integrated identity is an outcome of a meaning-making process that makes a person feel "whole." Through the counter forces of continuity, coming from values such as education, religion and work ethic, and discontinuity, contradictions that "force" re-evaluation of one's life philosophy and personal identity, an individual in midlife resolves many of life's uncertainties and creates a new, more integrated identity. For nearly one third of the participants in this study, the re-evaluation in midlife included a spiritual element.

A formal religious orientation in childhood, then, can serve later in life either as a form of continuity or a form of discontinuity. Whether or not it becomes an element in one's integrated identity depends on an individual's specific set of life experiences and his or her cognitive ability to connect seemingly isolated events to form a pattern or theme. For example, being a part of a religious affiliation may result in a connection between a personal identity and a group identity, as was evident in the narrative of Rose, the 68-year-old Jewish woman discussed earlier. She said, "I didn't flounder in those years because I was so imbued with Zionism." She had belonged to a Zionist organization for more than 40 years, and her spirituality stemmed from her identity as a Jewish woman, but she was in her late 40s or early 50s before she recognized the centrality of Zionism in her life.

Several of the Black women in the study spoke of being raised in a Black community and attending Black churches where they felt "safe" and "warm." Their personal identity in adulthood was tied to that group identity from childhood. The fact that continuity promoted a sense of well-being to these Black women is supported by other research on the role of religion in the lives of Black people and especially Black women (Taylor et al., 1987; Chatters, Levin & Taylor, 1992; Levin & Taylor, 1993). This study, however, went further and illustrated the depth of spirituality in Black women's lives. From their words, it is evident that they shared an active, personal relationship with God: "my prayers were answered," "God has directed my life," "God calls everybody to do certain things," "I am who I am . . . because of my beliefs in God," and "there is a God; he takes care of me."

If religion serves as a form of continuity in an individual's developmental process, then, it may evolve to a higher form of belief—spirituality or a dependence on God as a guiding force —contributing to the "wholeness" that is indicative of an integrated identity. Not only does spirituality serve as a support system and as a guide for making important life decisions, but also it gives individuals a peace that is seldom found in the fast-paced society that the participants of this study were experiencing. As Pauline, the priest, described it, a spiritual relationship results in a state of contentment, a feeling of being safe in spite of the daily problems that one encounters.

Because the participants in this study represented a broad range of ages, from age 31 to 70, it was possible to observe some patterns that can serve as a foundation for future research. Based on this small sample, my thesis is that some women who have a spiritual seed planted in childhood evolve from a point early in their life span, where religion is only a "piece" of their lives, to a place in midlife where a personal relationship with God, actualized through prayer, encompasses every area of life. This spiritual relationship is a thread that ties together life's many pieces and helps the women cope with life's troubles. An important element in this transition is the presence of conflict, crisis, or another form of suffering that forces an encounter with one's past and ultimately a resolution of contradictions.

In midlife, therefore, as individuals resolve many of life's contradictions and come to accept conflict and suffering as natural occurrences in one's life, they feel as if they are beginning life again. In the perception of many women in this study who were in their 40s, they were finally, in midlife, ready to "create" their lives or were just beginning to live a "full" life. It can be assumed from what we know about the nature of continuity in life span development that the rest of their lives will be spent perfecting the mold of the persons they are becoming.

Based on a small sample of women over age 50, it appears that beyond midlife the relationship with God, for those women who have a religious or spiritual focus, becomes more reciprocal. The spiritual relationship supports the women's needs, but the women, in turn, attempt to repay or "glorify" God through their work with other people. Because they can finally make sense of their own life experiences and understand the importance of God in their own developmental process, they want to help others achieve the state of contentment that they have reached.

IMPLICATIONS FOR FURTHER RESEARCH

A number of questions remain unanswered regarding the role of religion and spirituality in the identity development process of women: How many women who reach the point where religion or spirituality is a piece of their lives go on in midlife to a deeper relationship with God? How many of these continue on to an increasingly complementary relationship with God in later life? Is the personal relationship with God of greater importance to Black women and, if so, is it related to their subordinate position in society and their generally difficult lives? This leads to an underlying question that links spirituality even more closely to identity: If conflict, contradiction, life crises truly lead to a more integrated identity in midlife, as this study suggests, then does it also lead to a deeper level of spirituality? The idea that suffering leads to spiritual growth, is indeed a major theme in the Judeo-Christian Scriptures and one that requires a collaborative effort of social scientists and theologians to unveil the mysteries surrounding the life-long search for meaning and the role of religion and spirituality in the aging process.

Several concepts emerged from this study that have implications beyond the topic of religion, spirituality, and identity in midlife women's developmental process. The first is directed to therapists, counselors and social workers who have the opportunity to develop and implement interventions that would help people in the later stages of life reflect on and revive religious or spiritual seeds that were planted in their childhood. The aim would be to identify a theme that had been continuous throughout their lives that would help them cope with such issues as social isolation, physiological changes and questions of meaning.

The second implication from this study relates to the need for research on men and women who have early life religious experiences but have not by midlife shown any signs of integrating these religious or spiritual seeds back into their identity. What happens to people when they reach their later years and face their inevitable death, if they have turned their backs on their religious upbringing during young or middle adulthood? Is there ever a resurfacing of these themes late in life, and, if so, what brings about the change?

The final implication is related to a broadening of the research to a life span development perspective. The theoretical concepts that emerged from this study need to be explored for both males and females throughout the life span. The narrative methodology used to gather data should be used to understand further the impact of early-life religious or spiritual experience on all stages of adulthood. We need to trace more diligently the evolution of these threads of continuity throughout the life span, looking at the effects of such factors as gender, race or ethnic origin, individual life events and crises, social change, and religious affiliation on the spiritual development process. As mentioned previously in this chapter, any knowledge we have of earlier life stages should be beneficial in understanding the final stage of life.

REFERENCES

Chatters, M., Levin, J.S., & Taylor, R.J. (1992). Antecedents and dimensions of religious involvement among older Black adults. *Journal of Gerontology: Social Sciences, 47*(6), S269–S278.

Corbin, J., & Strauss, A. (1990). Grounded theory research: Procedures, canons, and evaluative criteria. *Qualitative Sociology, 13*(1), 3–21.

Eisenhandler, S.A. (1994). A social milieu for spirituality in the lives of older adults. In L.E. Thomas & S.A. Eisenhandler (Eds.), *Aging and the religious dimension* (pp. 133–145). Westport, CT: Auburn.

Freeman, M. (1984). "History, narrative, and life span developmental knowledge. *Human Development, 27,* 1–19.

Geiger, S. (1986). Women's life histories: Method and content. Signs: *Journal of Women in Culture and Society, 11*(2), 334–351.

Gergen, K.J., & Gergen, M.M. (1986). Narrative form and the construction of psychological science. In T.R. Sarbin (Ed.), *Narrative psychology: The storied nature of human conduct* (pp. 22–45). New York: Praeger.

Gergen, M.M. (1988). Toward a feminist metatheory and methodology in the social sciences. In M.M. Gergen (Ed.), *Feminist thought and the structure of knowledge* (pp. 87–104). New York: New York University Press.

Glaser, B., & Srauss A. (1967). *The discovery of grounded theory: Strategies for qualitative research.* Chicago: Aldine.

Inglessi, C. (1990). *Advocating a biographical approach in feminist research: a personal experience.* A working paper, Wellesley College, Center for Research on Women. Wellesley, MA.

Joy, M. (1995). God and gender: Some reflections on women's invocations of the divine. In U. King (Ed.), *Religion and gender* (pp. 121–143). Cambridge: Blackwell.

Kegan, R. (1982). *The Evolving self: Problem and process in human development.* Cambridge, MA: Harvard University Press.

Levin, J.S., & Taylor, R.J. (1993). Gender and age differences in religiosity among Black Americans. *Gerontologist, 33*(1), 16–23.

Levin, J.S., Taylor, R.J., & Chatters, L.M. (1994). Race and gender differences in religiosity among older adults: Findings from four national surveys. *Journal of Gerontology 49*(3),137–145.

Manheimer, R.J. (1989). The narrative quest in qualitative gerontology. *Journal of Aging Studies 3*(3), 231–252.

Mishler, E.G. (1986). The analysis of interview-narratives. In T. R. Sarbin (Ed.) *Narrative Psychology: The storied nature of human conduct.* (pp. 233–255). New York: Praeger.

Polkinghorne, D.E. (1985). *Methodology for the human sciences: Systems of inquiry.* Albany: State University of New York Press.

Polkinghorne, D.E. (1988). *Narrative knowing and the human sciences.* Albany: State University of New York Press.

Riegel, K.F. (1975). Toward a dialectical theory of development. *Human Development, 18,* 50-64.

Riegel, K.F. (1976). The dialectics of human development. *American Psychologist, 30,* 689-700.

Sarbin, T.R. (1986). The narrative as a root metaphor for psychology. In T.R. Sarbin (Ed.), *Narrative psychology: The storied nature of human conduct* (pp. 3–21). New York: Praeger.

Stivers, C. (1993). Reflections on the role of personal narrative in social science. *Signs, Journal of Women in Culture and Society, 18*(2), 408–425.

Strauss, A., & Corbin, J. (1990). *Basics of qualitative research: Grounded theory procedures and techniques.* Newbury Park, CA: Sage.

Taylor, R.J., Thornton, M.C., & Chatters, L.M. (1987). Black American's perceptions of the sociohistorical role of the church. *Journal of Black Studies, 18*(2), 123–138.

Thomas, L.E., & Eisenhandler, S. (1994). Introduction: A human science perspective on aging and the religious dimension. In L.E. Thomas & S. Eisenhandler (Eds.) *Aging and the religious dimension* (pp. xvii–xxi). Westport, CT: Auburn.

Waterman, A.S. & S.L. Archer (1990). A life span perspective on identity formation: developments in form, function and process. In P.B. Baltes et al (Eds.) *Life-span development and behavior* (Vol. 10, pp. 29–57). Hillsdale, NJ: Lawrence Erlbaum.

Surprised by Joy and Burdened by Age: The Journal and Letters of John Casteel

Susan H. McFadden

In the Introduction to his as yet unpublished "Journal of the Last Years," John Casteel dismissed the "golden years syndrome," saying that it falsely assures aging persons that "what made life possible, not to say gratifying and worth living, up until now, can continue to do so now that they are old."[1] For some fortunate ones, this may be true. Income reduction, health crises, and the deaths of loved ones, however, represent the hard realities of aging for most older adults. For them, the "facts" of aging accumulated by gerontologists offer little comfort and no answers to their deepest questions. What older people want and need—what John Casteel himself wanted and needed— is "the truth about the inner dimensions of my life, and my prospect as a human being who comes daily nearer to the end of my existence."

The Journal, completed in 1987, when he was 84 years old and living in an Indiana retirement community, reflected John's conviction that the way to learn about the interior of aging was to examine the immediate, personal experience of older persons themselves. Ever sensitive to what Thomas Cole called "the complexity and ambiguity of aging in an emerging postmodern culture" (Cole, 1992, p. 251), he offered his own experience and astute observations of others as testimony to the core ontological issues of later life. Although he had had a long and distinguished career teaching in universities and seminaries and had written five books and many book reviews, and essays, he could find no one willing to publish the Journal.

Editors told him it was "too pessimistic" and thus confirmed his perceptions about the hold of the "golden years" illusion on persons unable to face their own fears and anxieties about old age. Their one-sided reading of the Journal saw only its depictions of the burdens of age. Either they completely dismissed his writings about the joys of later life, or, more likely, they were unable to hold the two images in creative tension. Perhaps, also, they felt uneasy about his central question—"what, then, does it all come down to?"—or perhaps they could not accept his answer in the Christian promise of life eternal. Whatever the reason, John Casteel's wisdom is presently unavailable to the increasing number of people yearning for insights into the meanings of aging and the ways spirituality and religious faith function in the face of diminishment and death.

Acting as the conduit through which his thoughts on aging can be made known to others, I write this chapter in order to introduce readers to John Casteel. Because I do not intend to peer at his letters and journal through an analytical instrument, this chapter can only be loosely called a "case study." John can no longer offer his own report on matters of the aging body, mind, and spirit. Therefore, I will be the reporter, my sources being the letters he wrote to me, his journal, and my conversations with his children and several others who knew him through letters.

The maturing of gerontology has produced in recent years an increasing openness to consideration of religion and spirituality in later life. Well-designed empirical studies have received support from federal funding agencies, and prestigious gerontological journals have published the results. In addition, with the vibrant growth of qualitative gerontology, we now have many scholarly papers on the power of metaphor and narrative to disclose the inner experience of aging. I do not need to replow that ground. Rather, I want to examine the experience of narrative exchange in letter writing and to report on the perspectives on aging contained in the metaphors and narratives of John's journal. Moreover, because at the time we exchanged letters, I was editing *Aging, Spirituality, and Religion: A Handbook* (Kimble, McFadden, Ellor, & Seeber, 1995), I often asked him direct questions about late-life religiosity and spirituality. Because I believe his to be a valid and important perspective on religion and spirituality, I offer insights from his letters and journal.

The chapter begins with a brief description of John Casteel's life and career and tells how I became acquainted with him. It also introduces him as "a Christian gentleman," a designation that probably sounds old-fashioned but nevertheless accurately describes a gentle and complex man of profound faith. Next is a consideration of the joys and burdens of old age, held together in wisdom about the need to remain involved in the world while recognizing limitations on that involvement. John's awareness of the losses and loneliness of old age was tempered by his deep commitment to community and, ultimately, by his own ability to give and receive love, especially through the exchange of letters. Finally, the chapter focuses on his analysis of the spirituality and religiosity of old people living in continuum-of-care facilities. This section shows how John explored the spiritual interior of the aging experience and shed light on meanings that are obscured and distorted by cheery paeans to the golden years.

INTRODUCTION TO JOHN CASTEEL

Born in Randolph, Nebraska, on a wintry day in 1903, John Casteel's life eventually led him to jobs on both coasts. He never really let go of the sturdy, pioneer piety of the midwest, however. He received his bachelor's degree from Nebraska Wesleyan University and his Ph.D. in speech from Northwestern University. He taught speech at the University of Oregon for several years, and then, in 1942, he moved his family east, where he took a position as Associate Professor of Speech at Union Theological Seminary. In the early 1950s, the became Professor of Speech and Liturgics at Colgate-Rochester Theological Seminary; in 1956, he returned to Union to establish one of the country's first seminary programs in field education. Raised a Methodist and ordained a Congregationalist, John served two churches while on the faculty at Union. At other times in his life, he eagerly accepted opportunities to be a guest preacher. Arrival at the retirement community in Muncie, Indiana, did not curb his appetite for preaching; he initiated and led a weekly vespers service there for 9 years, quitting only when he felt he had said all he could to the residents there.

John's years at Union were spent in the company of two of the greatest theologians of the 20th century—Paul Tillich and Reinhold Niebuhr. I cannot say how they influenced him, although Niebuhr's vivid image of the "children of light and the children of darkness" appears in his early books as a way of talking about the place of religion in modern societies. The increasingly secular and privatized lives of people in the 1950s led John to write about the need to rediscover prayer (Casteel, 1955, 1957a) and the possibilities for "growth in grace" available in small groups (Casteel, 1957b, 1967). He saw clearly the difficulties people had in creating and sustaining a sense of community and even when writing about prayer, he noted its communal elements.

In addition, he believed the emerging consumer society of the 1950s, in which so much time was devoted to earning and then spending money, did damage to the soul and prevented spiritual growth. Such growth had to be nurtured, he wrote, through the private discipline of daily prayer, reflection, and meditation and through the occasional retreat taken with other persons (Casteel, 1959). His studies of the writings of Evelyn Underhill exerted a lifelong influence on his thinking about the ways retreats offer renewal to individuals and to communities. Many of the ideas he articulated in his writings of the 1950s appeared again in his writings about aging and older people. As he grew to be old, he grieved the loss of communion, community, and companionship experienced by so many elders. Saddened by the lack of interest in spiritual growth evidenced by his fellow residents of the retirement facility, he created his own spiritual support group through letter writing.

My introduction to John came a year and a half before he died just a few months short of his 90th birthday. I had been asked to present a paper on "Spirituality and a Good Old Age" at a conference at Ball State University. The program I received prior to my arrival in Muncie noted that a man named John Casteel would offer a response to my paper. The night before the conference, still not knowing who he was, I attended a dinner for participants, where I met John and learned that his near blindness had not prevented him from painstakingly reading my paper and composing a reply.

Soon after I arrived home, I received a four-page, typed letter from John in which he added further thoughts on my paper. Mixing humor and storytelling, John's letter seemed too much a treasure for me to part with. Although I am not in the habit of saving letters, I saved this one, and the next, and the next, until I had a file full of missives from a man who was willing to face squarely the trials of aging and to question easy assumptions about the spiritual lives of old people. In return, I wrote one letter for every three of his; he repeatedly urged me not to feel obligated to reply to each of his letters, saying that he felt happy in being free to write to me.

Letter writing was important to John throughout his life. In *Rediscovering Prayer* (1955, pp. 220–221), he spoke of being enriched and strengthened in his journey to God through the art of letter writing:

> Nothing can be quite so satisfying as a means of genuine communication between two persons as a thoughtfully written letter . . . The individual seeking to nurture his life of devotion will find a new wealth of insight and encouragement open to him through the faithful exchange of letters with those few persons who can become his "soul friends."

I later learned that at the end of his life, he was corresponding regularly with more than 50 persons, sometimes writing as many as eight or nine letters in 1 day. These were typed, often four or more pages long. He had maintained ties through letter writing with some of these people for more than 50 years. Some were former students and colleagues; others were persons he had never met. These people represented a wide range of ages and backgrounds. In one essay in the Journal, he marked "the contours of growing old" by quoting from recent letters from persons 40, 50, 60, 65, 76, and 95.

Early in 1993, John underwent surgery to repair a detached retina; a week later, he suffered a stroke that left him paralyzed on the left side. The next letter I received, dated January 26, needed to be deciphered. He explained, "I am lrarning to walk and I typr in thre olg hung-and-peck way. Ans I (hav-ing time to reflect anew on Spitiyualt for the aged." In response to a friend who asked what he did with his despair, John wrote that he replied, "Bear it." He said he had plenty of it.

A Christian Gentlemen

In one essay in the Journal titled "Sweetness and Dark," John reflected on the old-fashioned notion of being a gentlemen. Old age, he said, confronts people with two courses: to "become sweeter ladies and gentlemen and better Christians; or to become bitter and crabbed individuals and worse Christians." The choice is experienced throughout life but at life's end becomes "more insistent, more crucial." People seldom are aware of becoming sweeter; those who are crabbed and bitter, however, often take pride in their temper. Quoting Matthew Arnold, who spoke of "sweetness and light" as the highest qualities of personal character, John remarked how modern cultures opposed that type of character. This is all the more reason, he said, for older people to "go on struggling as valiantly as we can against the spirit of contention and embitterment which, like acid rain, threatens to descend on our society like the dark."

How did this man, who could enumerate so clearly his losses, manage to avoid becoming bitter? The answer for him lay in Christianity, a religion he described as having a great advantage in "how little we have to believe." At the center of Christianity lies the idea and experience of love. This, however, can be a problem for the old because, as he put it in his first letter to me, "love grows more slender and its expression less supple." Nevertheless, a lifetime of nurturing a relationship with the holy through prayer, loving relationships with others, appreciation of the world's beauty, and honest self-examination could result in an old age in which hope triumphs over despair and comfort is assured in the face of loneliness and tribulation.

The source of this hope and comfort lay in John's religious practice and his core religious beliefs. His practice was centered on prayer, a practice and idea he had reflected on and written about throughout his life. In his first letter to me, he wrote, "None of the attempts to prove the 'power of prayer,' or to reduce it to a method or system or discipline, seem to me to be very helpful or even plausible. One prays. Or one doesn't." He did. Much influenced by his early religious training and a friendship with the Quaker writer Douglas Steere that began in 1935, John began each day with the simple pattern of the "morning watch." Little could he have imagined in 1955, when he wrote his book about prayer, that more than 30 years later he would be a resident in a retirement community in Muncie, Indiana, still finding solace in this practice. In his journal, he described how he devoted half an hour twice each day to

> reading the Bible or some appropriate book; reflecting on and putting in order, the day ahead; offering one of the great collects—"Almighty God, unto whom all hearts are open . . . ," "God, who dividest the day from the darkness . . . ," "Almighty God, give us grace to cast away . . . "; and then the waiting in silence at whose heart is the petition, "Pray thyself in me."

In this time of quiet, reflection, and aloneness, he found companionship and even community, for his prayers often focused specially on individuals. (He once told me that I was on his "Friday list," both as one prayed for and as one written to.) Not only did John experience companionship and community in these times of prayer, but most especially he also knew "enfolding communion with the over-towering and everlasting THOU." This is, he said, he was beginning to see, "is the special privilege given to me as I grow old."

Knowing how much he appreciated the work of Evelyn Underhill and others who wrote so intuitively about mysticism, I once asked him about his own sense of the mystical. He replied that he recognized within himself a disposition to believe in a realm of Reality beyond the immanent, but he did not think that made him a mystic. He admitted that he believed that the main directions of his life had been determined somehow by the Spirit, and he agreed with Underhill about the joy of "standing back from our life and seeing the Spirit gently, relentlessly pressing us home to our goal."

What was this goal? Herein lay the answer to the question, "What, then, does it all come to?" He recorded his answer in the last two entries of the *Journal* and noted its origin in his experience of growing old. The answer had two parts. The first was represented symbolically in the Second Law of Thermodynamics: everything eventually "runs down and falls into a state of total disorganization." The old know well the workings of the Second Law. John insisted, however, that human beings are not only victims of the Second Law but also its agents through their willful exploitation and destruction of creation and the disorder they spread throughout the planet. Old people do not escape this dreadful agency. All human beings sin by turning God's creation order back into chaos. John Casteel believed that the life and death of Jesus Christ represented a powerful way of understanding fully the consequences of this disorder, because Jesus's life represented the very archetype of order. Because he proclaimed the highest form of order—the kingdom of God—Jesus was crucified and died. This would not be the final word, however, and so in the last entry of the Journal John described the second part of his answer: the resurrection.

In the symbol of the resurrection, John found a way to escape the verdict of the Second Law. The resurrection confirmed for him a confidence "in a life of spirit beyond this life on earth in the body." How could one know about such a thing, however? The heart of knowing lies in the living experience of communion in spirit, an experience that is partly manifested in relationship with other persons. John found this to be particularly true in his friendships ordered through the exchange of letters. He learned from these friends, especially those older than himself, that there is "no correlation between the condition of the body, its health or decline, and the power and beauty of the spirit." He concluded his essay with a simple statement about the foundation of his hope:

I expect, therefore, before long, to fall before the Second Law. My dust will return to dust. But I expect, also, to be transmuted from the dust of death into the life of the spirit, where spirit with spirit meets in communion and love.

Six years after he completed the Journal, this Christian gentlemen's spirit departed from a weary material existence on the afternoon of October 10, 1993. His daughter reported that death was quiet and peaceful. That morning he had sung favorite hymns with his nurses. One can easily imagine the sweetness of that moment.

ON BEING OLD: WISDOM ABOUT JOYS AND BURDENS

After many years of neglect, psychologists have begun to study wisdom. However wisdom is approached, John exemplified it. The work of cognitive psychologists Paul Baltes and colleagues describes John's wisdom: "good judgment and advice in important but uncertain matters of life" (Baltes & Staudinger, 1993, p. 77). The work of Gisela Labouvie-Vief, Fredda Blanchard-Fields, and others also sheds light on the contours of John's wisdom. They assert that wisdom derives from an integration of cognition and affect (Blanchard-Fields & Norris, 1995; Labouvie-Vief, 1990). In Jung's words, "where wisdom reigns there is no conflict between thinking and feeling" (Jung, 1963, pp. 248–249).

Although Western societies have traditionally polarized the intellect and the emotions, wise people neither ignore their emotional responses to life's uncertainties when they offer their judgments and advice nor expect that the experience of life, especially later life, will be unidimensional in its power to elicit emotion. Moreover, the wise individual is able to retain "a detached and yet active concern with life itself, in the face of death itself" (Erikson, 1976, p. 26). John's active concern radiated from his letters and journal; his detachment lay in his understanding that he could not impose his wisdom on others but only gently suggest a way of responding to life's uncertainties.

John often experienced the ache of loneliness in old age, especially because he lived in a community where few others seemed willing or able to remain intellectually engaged with the world. At the same time, in knowing the joys and comforts of receiving a letter from a friend, he never lost confidence in the power of community to nourish the human spirit. He recognized the intense desire for companionship among older people and yet knew how often they feared becoming a burden to others. He often noted that old age confers the ability to imagine new possibilities while robbing individuals of the capacity to realize these possibilities. He grieved the losses wrought by retirement from the meaningful involvements of a profession but also recognized that such losses freed individuals from the imposed obligations of work.

In other words, John chronicled the diminishments and narrowing of life in old age but held out hope for certain gains and compensations. In particular, he wrote to me, freedom from the preoccupations and responsibilities that have obscured spiritual growth releases people to "invite the gestures of rebirth." Although life narrows in heartbreaking ways, it can also produce astonishing and joyful surprises by springing back resiliently to wider dimensions. That an old person could be "surprised by joy" seemed to John to be a gift of grace, not unlike the experience of C. S. Lewis (1955) who, as a young man, was surprised by his conversion to Christianity. John remained confident of the "possibility that an encounter with the Presence of God can come to us right now in the midst of our much constricted life in retirement." Sadly, however, his experiences in the retirement community led him to conclude that many old people fortify themselves against such possibilities; they neither turn their grief over diminishment into joy in simplification, nor do they seize opportunities for spiritual growth. Often, they simply acquiesce.

SPIRITUALITY AND RELIGION IN THE RETIREMENT COMMUNITY

Unlike gerontologists who avoid critical assessments of older people's behavior in order to avoid supporting cultural biases and victim blaming, John, at 89, had no such inhibitions. He understood the temptations to become enveloped in bitterness; he saw how some elders proudly accumulate their many complaints like medals on a uniform; he noted the tendency of others to counter loneliness by angrily withdrawing from social engagement. He also observed the lack of fit between some persons' religiosity and the demands made by the contingencies of later life.

Always aware of the futility and foolishness of trying to speak for all old people, he nevertheless offered his candid observations of religious practice in the retirement community where he lived for 14 years. These observations resulted from his efforts to communicate with his fellow travelers about spiritual and religious matters through his vespers sermons, the columns he wrote for the facility's newsletter, and informal contacts. His comments were not offered in the spirit of judgment and condemnation but more compassionately out of concern that developmental, biobehavioral, institutional, and cultural forces often work against spiritual growth in very late life.

One of the central reasons why some older adults slip away from the spiritual moorings of earlier years is because those moorings were built with cheap materials and not maintained; they could not withstand the storms of old age. Although an individual may have been religiously active in earlier years, the later years raise acute existential questions that cannot be effectively answered on the basis of a faith that has not matured. Using Allport's (1966) terminology, it may be that those of an extrinsic religious orientation are more likely to retire from religion and give spirituality no large place in their thoughts or activities.

In addition to his concerns about persons who had not matured in their religiosity by asking the hard questions earlier in life, John also felt great sympathy for people whose religious beliefs and practices proved to be ineffective when coping with the shocks of loss in late life. His experience of living 14 years in a continuum-of-care facility exposed him to types of late-life suffering that may be hidden from healthier older persons living in the community. All this led him to write in one letter,

> Whatever spiritual resources we may bring to our last years may not be enough to see us through to the end. In a way, spirituality for the aged makes the double demand that (1) we have had some kind of religious life before we grow old, but (2) we somehow gain or are given significant new resources for our old age. The real problem may be how a person can begin to grow into a religious life of depth and significance in the earlier years that will also have continuity in the late years.

Another reason why the salience of religion may fade for persons living in institutional settings results from inexorably waning energies, due in part to the naturally occurring slowing of central nervous system processes that thwart initiative and engagement with the world. The sameness of daily life in an institutional environment and the lack of control people have over decisions dissipates energy. When old people living in regimented institutional settings become habituated to their environments, a certain dullness of spirit sets in, making them increasingly passive. Their lack of energy may prevent even the quiet moments of prayer and reflection that could fortify the soul in the face of suffering.

A third cause of dissipation of religious practice in old age is institutional. Churches and synagogues may have little to offer older people, especially those not living within the community. John believed that many churches pay attention only to maintaining people's current levels of religious experience and faith rather than encouraging spiritual growth. In other words, churches do little to prepare people spiritually for the rigors of old age. Clergy and religious institutions that intentionally develop older adult ministries with the goal of assisting and supporting elders in their spiritual journeys are still the exception. Already overworked local pastors may have little time and no training to deal with the spiritual concerns of elders living in long-term care settings, most of which offer no chaplaincy services.

The cultural reasons for a lack of spiritual engagement among older people living in a retirement community arose in several of our letters written in the autumn of 1992, when we focused on the celebration of Christmas. I wanted to know how Christmas was experienced within his setting and whether within that experience there might be possibilities for spiritual growth or even rebirth. It occurred to me that stripped of the glitter and glitz, the holiday season might produce an opportunity for deeper reflection upon its real meanings. John, however, had another perspective.

Christmas, he said, is not a very "spirited" time in the retirement community. He was offended by a former activities director's efforts to stage a "happy party" in which residents sat on Santa Claus's knee and told their wishes. To counter this inanity, he initiated a Christmas Eve service with carols and readings of the prophecies and Gospel stories. Christmas day, he said, ends the season rather than beginning it, as he felt it should. "For us, by sundown of Christmas day, we're 'bushed' by the whole thing. Perhaps this is a parable of our religious experience as we grow old!" He also felt that the "empty" mood of the night and day exposes the shallowness and transiency of the season as celebrated in the culture. Rather than offering an opportunity for authentic spiritual insight, the Christmas experience stripped of its wrappings shows itself to be an empty box.

All of this does not have to be the final word on the Christmas experience, however. Although John expressed profound skepticism about a materialistic culture and its destruction of the spiritual meanings central to the nativity narrative, he continued to believe in the possibility of "new birth" and growth in the spirit. For some persons, the disorganization and contraction of life in the later years can produce a reorganization at a deeper level of spiritual insight. Even those who have failed to nurture a lifelong spiritual attitude, those weakened by illness and the general dissipation of energy, and those for whom religious institutions and the culture at large have produced roadblocks to spiritual journeying can receive the gift of grace. John believed that grace can be expressed in loving human relationships intentionally focused on spiritual growth. Guided by this hope, he sketched out ideas for the Disciplined Order for Older People.

THE DISCIPLINED ORDER FOR OLDER PEOPLE

John began discussing the "Order" a month after our exchange of letters about Christmas. He imagined the kind of encouragement, support, and enrichment that might be possible for elders bound together in a common spiritual discipline. In other words, he sought a way for elders to be in communion with one another, creating community even if they could not be in direct contact with one another. He proposed the formation of loosely organized networks of older people in which each individual would be in a letter-writing relationship with at least one other person in the network. All involved would commit to making spiritual growth and maturing consciously intentional in the later years. Although each person would have some freedom to compose his or her personal spiritual discipline in line with circumstances and needs, all would have the opportunity to share in resources that could be in the form of books or tapes. He also thought these groups of elders might meet occasionally for retreats.

Ideas about the creation of caring communities of older persons who support one another in spiritual growth are beginning to surface(e.g., Thibault, 1995). Interest is also growing in the design of intergenerational communities to support the spiritual growth of all residents. Throughout the developed world, there is a felt need for community development based on small interpersonal groupings. The old high-rise public housing units of the 1960s are being demolished along with the failed social policy that supported them. Architects are designing neighborhoods that encourage an ease of interaction not currently experienced in most suburban subdivisions. Continuum-of-care facilities are struggling with finding cost-effective ways of designing living environments that encourage the formation of supportive relationships. John knew about these developments but was concerned that today's elders might not live long enough to enjoy their benefits.

Many adults today recall being linked in childhood with "pen pals" in other countries. The program was intended to generate international understanding through children's exchange of letters about their own lives. John thought the same could be done for older people; now, the goal would be mutuality nourished in letter writing about the spiritual challenges of remaining open to joy while also grieving accumulating burdens. Just as most fourth graders who receive names of pen pals lack the will and resources to nurture the relationship, John recognized that only a small proportion of older persons would be interested in the "Disciplined Order." For those older people willing to risk entering into this kind of supportive exchange of letters, however, the rewards could be great.

CONCLUSIONS

John possessed all the qualities of a spiritual director once enumerated by his friend Gerald May. He had a deep spiritual commitment of his own, experience and knowledge, humility, and the "capacity to be caring, sensitive, open, and flexible with another person" (May, 1979, p. 158). Although John conceived of the "Order" being made up of older adults serving as spiritual directors to one another, his own life and extensive correspondence suggests intergenerational possibilities for such spiritual linkages. Older persons could offer considerable guidance, support, and love not only for their peers, but also for persons preparing to be old by deepening their relationships to the holy and all of creation.

John believed that spirituality is essentially an experience of giving and receiving love: love of God and love of others. This perspective on spirituality differs radically from much contemporary talk about spirituality that, being split from religion, begins and ends with the self. Because such a spirituality seeks no engagement with a community and historical tradition and makes no commitment to passing insight to future generations, it offers little to old people struggling, often alone, to find meaning in personal diminishment and death.

John's last letter to me, written in late summer 1993, demonstrated his approach to meaning-making although he did not speak of it directly. Instead, he related a humorous story about a train trip he took across Wisconsin in the 1930s; inquire about a journey I had recently taken with my daughter; commented on a recent article on higher education; and advised me to take good care of myself in anticipation of a new academic year. By the time he wrote this letter, he had given up his apartment and had given away his books; he was living in the health center, where, fortunately, he still had access to his typewriter. Surely this image of an infirm old man patiently typing a letter with one finger would not be featured in a glossy brochure touting the joys of the golden years. John knew a different kind of joy; he had written often of the experience of grace that produced surprising joy even admidst the burdens of age. In his writings and in his very example of living, John Casteel demonstrated possibilities for revaluing old age through openness to the spiritual domain of life, an experience dependent on communion with others and blessed by communion with God.

NOTES

1. With the exception of quotes from letters written to me, all quotes from John Casteel's writing come from the unpublished *Journal*.

REFERENCES

Allport, G.W. (1966). The religious context of prejudice. *Journal for the Scientific Study of Religion, 5*, 447–457.
Baltes, P.B., & Staudinger, U.M. (1993). The search for a psychology of wisdom. *Current Directions in Psychological Science, 2*, 75–80.
Blanchard-Fields, F., & Norris, L. (1995). The development of wisdom. In M.A. Kimble, S.H. McFadden, J.W. Ellor, & J.J. Seeber (Eds.), *Aging, spirituality, and religion: A handbook* (pp. 102–118). Minneapolis: Fortress Press.
Casteel, J.L. (1955). *Rediscovering prayer*. New York: Associated Press.
Casteel, J.L. (1957a). *The promise of prayer*. New York: Associated Press.

Casteel, J.L. (Ed.). (1957b). *Spiritual renewal through personal groups*. New York: Associated Press.

Casteel, J.L. (1959). *Renewal in retreats*. New York: Associated Press.

Casteel, J.L. (Ed.). (1967). *The creative role of interpersonal groups in the church today*. New York: Associated Press.

Cole, T.R. (1992). *The journey of life: A cultural history of aging in America*. New York: Cambridge University Press.

Erikson, E.H. (1976). Reflections on Dr. Borg's life cycle. In E.H. Erikson (Ed.), *Adulthood* (pp. 1–32). New York: W.W. Norton.

Jung, C.G. (1963). Mysterium coniunctionis: An inquiry into the separation and synthesis of psychic opposites in alchemy. In H. Read, M. Fordham, & G. Adler (Eds.) and R.F.C. Hull (Trans.), *The collected works of C.G. Jung* (Vol. 14). New York: Bollingen Foundation.

Kimble, M.A., McFadden, S.H., Ellor, J.W., & Seeber, J.J. (Eds.). (1995). *Aging, spirituality, and religion: A handbook*. Minneapolis: Fortress Press.

Labouvie-Vief, G. (1980). Wisdom as integrated thought: Historical and developmental perspectives. In R.J. Sternberg (Ed.), *Wisdom: Its nature, origins, and development* (pp. 52–83). New York: Cambridge University Press.

Lewis, C.S. (1955). *Surprised by joy: The shape of my early life*. London: Geoffrey Bles.

May, G.G. (1979). *Pilgrimage home: The conduct of contemplative practice in groups*. New York: Paulist Press.

Thibault, J.M. (1995). Congregation as a spiritual care community. In M.A. Kimble, S.H. McFadden, J.W. Ellor, & J.J. Seeber (Eds.), *Aging, spirituality, and religion: A handbook* (pp. 350–361). Minneapolis: Fortress Press.

PART FIVE

Is There a Distinctive Spirituality of Late Life?

Religion As a Quest and the Search for Meaning in Later Life

Andrew Futterman, James J. Dillon,
François Garand III, and Joshua Haugh

The main purpose of this chapter is to examine the nature and validity of "religion as a quest" in later life (Batson, Schoenrade, & Ventis, 1993), that particular orientation to religion that purportedly involves an honest questioning of religious tradition and a search for meaning and purpose in life. Using both quantitative and qualitative data derived from a longitudinal study of religious involvement, coping, and health, we address two specific questions: (1) What constitutes the quest religious orientation? Do older adults who demonstrate a quest orientation really ask questions about the meaning and purpose of life, as Batson et al. suppose, or do they merely doubt the validity of religious traditions to which they have been exposed? (2) Can an older adult be committed to a particular religious doctrine and tradition and concurrently question that doctrine and search for other religious meanings? In other words, is the quest religious orientation in which religion is a "search" compatible with an intrinsic orientation in which religion is an "end-in-itself," or are "quest" and "ends" religious orientations incompatible and more accurately considered to be opposite ends of a single dimension of religious involvement?

RELIGIOUS ORIENTATIONS OR WAYS OF BEING RELIGIOUS

Sociological and epidemiological research on religious involvement in adulthood has identified several dimensions of religious activity. For example, in *Religion and Society in Tension*, Glock and Stark (1965) define religious involvement as consisting of five dimensions: religious belief, knowledge, feelings, practice, and consequences. Recent epidemiological studies of religion in later adulthood also demonstrate multiple dimensions of religious activity; in general, these studies demonstrate that attitudinal and belief dimensions are empirically distinct from the frequency of both organizational and nonorganizational religious practice (Chatters, Levin, & Taylor, 1992; Krause, 1995).

Although sociological and epidemiological researchers demonstrate that different religious dimensions are empirically distinct and demonstrate divergent relationships with other aspects of the social environment and physical health, researchers also find that most measures of religious involvement are highly intercorrelated (see Gorsuch, 1984, for discussion). Thus, an individual who goes to church more frequently also typically prays more often, has stronger beliefs in God, and knows more about the denominational creed. Depending on one's research purpose, religious involvement as currently assessed may thus be conceptualized and measured either as multidimensional, unique aspects that vary in relationship to one another and other characteristics or as a single overarching construct, for example, religious commitment (Futterman & Koenig, 1995; Gorsuch, 1984).

The one area where the empirical literature on religious involvement has demonstrated independence among religion measures is among different orientations to religion. Historically, orientations to religion have been a primary focus of research in the psychology of religion. Orientations have been conceptualized in terms of religious "motivations" or "attitudes" (Allport, 1950; Allport & Ross, 1967) and "ways of being religious" (Batson et al., 1993) and focus on the reasons or functions of religion in an individual's life. There appear to be important theoretical distinctions between the concepts "orientations," "motivations," "attitudes," and "ways of being religious." Whereas attitudes refer to specific judgments about the significance of religious beliefs or behaviors, motivations refer to more general reasons for religious behavior. By contrast, orientations and ways of being religious are more general descriptions of a style or pattern of action without necessarily involving a particular causal, motivational theory of action. Involved in each of these concepts is the implicit assumption that religious behavior is enacted for different reasons or serves different functions across individuals and contexts.

In keeping with this functionalist point of view, Allport (1950) developed the framework of "intrinsic" and "extrinsic" religious orientations. Intrinsic religious orientation involves religion as a "meaning-endowing framework in terms of which all of life is understood"; extrinsic religious orientation involves a "religion of comfort and social convention, a self-serving, instrumental approach shaped to suit oneself" (Donahue, 1985, p. 400). Intrinsic religiousness was initially conceived as a "mature" orientation to religion in which a person's religious commitment is the primary motive prompting social behavior. By contrast, extrinsic religiousness was initially conceived as an "immature" orientation to religion in which religion is a way of achieving other nonreligious, selfish ends, such as comfort and social support. A similar framework to that of Allport's intrinsic–extrinsic religiousness—committed vs. consensual religiousness—was developed by Spilka and colleagues (Spilka, Stout, Minton, & Sizemore, 1977) and is reviewed by Batson et al. (1993).

A significant body of research has been conducted within the intrinsic-extrinsic framework using various scales developed to these make these two dimensions operational (Allport & Ross, 1967; see Donahue, 1985, for review; Feagin, 1964; Hoge, 1972). The intrinsic scales tend to comprise items that assess intensity of traditional religious beliefs, concepts, behaviors, and so on. Such scales have often been criticized for being heterogeneous and ill designed to tap the "intrinsic-ness" of religious involvement apart from more superficial commitment to religious doctrine and tradition (Donahue, 1985; Gorsuch, 1994; Kirkpatrick & Hood, 1990). Extrinsic scales comprise items that assess the use of religion to obtain support and comfort and to fulfill other nonreligious needs. Although Allport originally conceived of intrinsic and extrinsic religiousness as opposite ends of a single dimension, most research suggests that these scales represent independent dimensions or demonstrate modest positive correlations (Donahue, 1985).

In a series of studies, Batson and colleagues (Batson et al., 1989; Batson et al., 1993; Batson & Schoenrade, 1991a) have criticized the intrinsic-extrinsic framework. With respect to the specification of the intrinsic religious orientation, in particular, they note that Allport did not adequately differentiate the questioning, open-minded form of religious commitment that characterizes some deeply religious individuals from the more rigid, unquestioning form of religious commitment which characterizes other deeply religious individuals. In order to distinguish these two types of potentially intrinsic individuals, Batson and colleagues introduced a third type of religious orientation, conceived initially as a searching, "interactive" dimension of religious activity in which the religious person actively questions and remains open to new interpretation of his or her religious beliefs (Batson & Ventis, 1982). Three "ways of being religious" were thus described in this new framework—religion as an end, means, and a quest or interaction—and a new six-item Quest Scale was developed to operationalize the interactional or quest dimension (Batson & Ventis, 1982).

The ends-means-quest framework has also spawned considerable research. Studies with younger participants established that the Quest Scale largely defined a third quest dimension (Batson, 1976; Batson, Naifeh, & Pate, 1978; Batson et al., 1993), whereas intrinsic and extrinsic scales defined the end and means religious dimensions, respectively. Moreover, correlations among ends-means-and quest measures are typically low, indicating relative independence of dimensions (Donahue, 1985). Thus, available data suggest that it is entirely possible, for example, for the same young adult to question (score high on quest) and believe deeply (score high on ends) at the same time. On the other hand, more complex relationships among the three dimensions may exist. For example, Watson, Morris, and Hood (1989) describe overlap among subgroups of Quest items and both ends and means dimensions. Although psychometric work using the Quest Scale has described the nature of the quest dimension in young adult samples, similar empirical work has not been conducted with older participants. In the next sections, we briefly describe data derived from our sample of Worcester elders relating to both the nature of quest religiousness in later life and the relationship between quest religiousness and means and ends religious orientations.

RELIGION AS A QUEST IN LATER LIFE: ANALYSIS OF QUANTITATIVE DATA

SAMPLE CHARACTERISTICS

In 1993 to 1994, we began a longitudinal study of religious involvement, coping, and health involving community-dwelling older adults living in Worcester, Massachusetts. It may be useful to describe Worcester in order for the reader to better understand the characteristics of this sample. Worcester is a medium-sized city of 160,000 people approximately 60 miles from Boston, Providence, and Hartford. Worcester was founded in the early 1700s as a trading post along the Blackstone River, which runs north from Narragansett Bay in Rhode Island. Worcester grew rapidly to become an industrial city of paper, furniture, footware, abrasive, and wire manufacturing, and by the mid-1800s, it included a large working population of French Canadian, Irish, German, Slavic, Greek, Armenian, Russian, and Swedish immigrants. By 1880, the city was (and still is) the second largest city in New England. Today, Worcester has become a city dominated by the computer, medical, biotechnology, educational, and financial services industries and boasts 10 colleges, a medical school, many large hospitals, and a biotech research park, but few of the industries of the last century remain.

Although many industries left Worcester some time ago, there is an old joke in central Massachusetts that people never leave Worcester. In fact, the joke may be true. Worcester has among the lowest "outmigration" rates of any city in New England (Cuba, 1989; Horner, 1991), a fact corroborated by the mean length of time our sample has lived in Worcester—66 years. Indeed, one quarter of our participants lived in Worcester for more than 74 years, frequently in the same house in which they were young adults.

Table 9.1 includes descriptive data relating to the present sample. The interested reader is referred to Dillon and Futterman (in press) for a more complete description of the sampling, interviewing procedures, and background characteristics of the sample. Data described in this chapter were derived from a sample of 342 older adults. This sample comprised two subsamples: a random sample of 262 older adults and a "snowball" sample of 80 African American older adults. For the

TABLE 9.1   Demographic Characteristics of Worcester Older Adult Samples*

	Random sample (n = 262)	African American sample (n = 80)	Total sample (n = 342)
Age (*M, SD*)	75.1 (6.9)	69.3 (7.3)	72.3 (7.1)
Sex (%)			
Female	59.4	64.0	62.0
Male	40.6	36.0	38.0
Marital status (% in category)			
Married	51.0	43.0	48.0
Divorced/separated	6.8	19.5	10.9
Never married	4.9	5.6	5.0
Widowed	37.2	31.9	36.1
Education (% in category)			
8th grade	9.1	12.7	9.4
Some HS	11.0	15.5	11.9
HS diploma	27.8	28.2	27.9
Some college	26.6	21.1	25.4
College degree	14.5	7.0	13.0
Adv. degree	11.0	15.5	12.0

*Adapted from Dillon, J., & Futterman, A. (in press). Faith, doubt, and well-being in later life. *Journal of Aging and Identity.*

random sample, participants had to be living in Worcester in 1993 to 1994, more than 65 years of age, and able to complete the interview. Participants meeting these criteria were randomly selected from the 1993 annual Worcester city census.

Since Worcester has only a small population of African American older adults, a second "snowball" sample of 80 African American elders was developed. For this sample, we identified potential African American older adult participants by gathering names from the 10 African American participants who were included in the random sample of 262 older adults. We then interviewed each of the identified sequentially. Response rate in the random sample was 68%; response rate in the "snowball" African American sample was 90%.

In general, the combined sample can be described as predominantly female, married for a long time to the same spouse, and of moderate income and education. Differences in background characteristics between random and "snowball" African American samples are few. A small difference in age (the African American sample is slightly younger than the random sample is) is worth noting, as are small differences in gender and marital status (the African American sample is proportionately more female and not currently married). In general, however, similarities between the random and African American samples reflect the fact that the small number of African American older adults living in Worcester are highly assimilated in the community.

More than 98% of the sample reported some denominational affiliation. Assessment of denominational affiliation used procedures and classification schemes developed in the National Election Study (Kellstedt & Green, 1993; Smith, 1990). Individuals were placed in one of six denominational families: Mainline Protestant (e.g., Episcopal, United Church of Christ, etc.), Black Protestant (e.g., African Methodist Episcopal), Evangelical Protestant (e.g., most Baptist denominations), Roman Catholic (and including Eastern Rite), Jewish, and Other (e.g., most predominantly Muslim, Buddhist, and Hindu denominations in the current sample). In keeping with the ethnic and denominational composition of New England, denominational composition of the sample is predominantly Catholic (47%). There are significant numbers of Mainline Protestants (24%), Black Protestants (12%), Jews (8%), Evangelical Protestants (8%), and Other (2%).

THE NATURE OF QUEST RELIGIOUSNESS

The first question we address relates to the nature of quest religiousness in later life. We administered the revised version of the Quest Scale (Batson & Schoenrade, 1991b). The revised scale enlarged and modified the original scale in order to increase scale reliability and validity. Table 9.2 includes the 12 items of the revised Quest Scale, mean levels of endorsement, and item to total scale correlations. Internal consistency for the 12-item scale in our sample of 342 older adults is good (Cronbach $\alpha = 0.75$) and is comparable to what Batson and Schoenrade (1991a) report in younger adults (Cronbach $\alpha = 0.78$). The reversed scored items "I find my religious doubts upsetting" and "I do not expect my religious convictions to change over the next few years" were most divergent from other items in this sample, indicating participants may have had difficulties interpreting the wording of items written in the "opposite direction." Without these two items, scale reliability would have improved significantly (without these two items improved from 0.72 to 0.76).

Older adults in the current sample reported moderate levels of quest religiousness (M item score = 4.67, SD = 1.56, range 1 to 9) comparable to levels reported by Batson and Schoenrade (1991a) in younger adults (M item score 5.02, SD = 1.14). Participants tended to endorse most strongly items suggesting openness to change in religious outlook (items 9 and 11) and to endorse least strongly items suggesting past lack of interest in religion (items 1 and 4). Our findings, together with those of Batson and Schoenrade (1991a, 1991b), provide support for the view that the revised Quest Scale reliably measures some attribute—quest religiousness—in younger and older adults. What precisely is measured by the Quest Scale?

TABLE 9.2 Batson and Schoenrade's (1991a) Revised Quest Scale (Items Arranged by Intended Subdimensions*)

Items	M	(SD)	Item—Total r	Alpha excl. item
Readiness to face existential questions without reducing their complexity				
1. I was not very interested in religion until I began to ask questions about the meaning and purpose of my life.	3.71	(2.98)	0.56	0.70
2. I have been driven to ask religious questions out of a growing awareness of the tensions in my world and in my relation to my world.	5.02	(3.00)	0.58	0.69
3. My life experiences have led me to rethink my religious convictions.	4.46	(3.22)	0.63	0.69
4. God wasn't very important for me until I began to ask questions about the meaning of my own life.	3.75	(3.10)	0.59	0.69
Self-criticism and perception of religious doubt as positive				
5. It might be said that I value my religious doubts and uncertainties.	5.29	(2.82)	0.61	0.69
6. For me, doubting is an important part of what it means to be religious.	5.14	(3.07)	0.60	0.69
7. (-) I find religious doubts upsetting.	3.64	(3.04)	0.18	0.77
8. Questions are far more central to my religious experience than are answers.	5.08	(2.74)	0.54	0.70
Openness to changing religious beliefs				
9. As I grow and change, I expect my religion also to grow and change.	6.21	(2.88)	0.45	0.72
10. I am constantly questioning my religious beliefs.	3.90	(2.99)	0.66	0.68
11. (-) I do not expect my religious convictions to change in the next few years.	6.94	(2.13)	0.21	0.74
12. There are many religious issues on which my views are still changing.	5.14	(3.07)	0.63	0.69

Note: A minus sign preceding an item indicates that it is reversed in scoring. Each item is responded to on a nine-point scale, ranging from strongly disagree (1) to strongly agree (9).
*Intended subdimensions from Batson and Schoenrade, 1991a.

Adapted from Dillon, J., & Futterman, A. (in press). Faith, doubt, and well-being in later life. *Journal of Aging and Identity*.

In order to address this question, we present both quantitative, for example factor analytic, and qualitative interview data in the next sections.

FACTOR ANALYSIS OF THE QUEST SCALE

Table 9.3 reproduces the factor loadings for items in the 12-item Quest Scale in our older adult sample. We have added to this table the Quest Scale item factor loadings obtained by Batson and Schoenrade (1991a) from their younger adult

TABLE 9.3   Factor Loadings for Revised Quest Scale Items in Older and Younger Samples

	Factor		
Item	*1*	*2*	*3*
1. I was not very interested . . .	0.07 (0.18)	**0.77** (0.63)	0.10 (0.03)
2. I have been driven to ask . . .	0.28 (0.26)	**0.57** (0.18)	0.23 (0.06)
3. My life experiences have led me to rethink . . .	0.43 (0.54)	**0.52** (0.11)	0.14 (0.06)
4. God wasn't very important for me until . . .	0.10 (0.11)	**0.80** (0.85)	0.04 (0.05)
5. It might be said that I value my religious doubts . . .	**0.81** (0.50)	0.02 (0.15)	0.02 (0.48)
6. For me, doubting is an important part . . .	0.76 (0.33)	0.05 (0.18)	0.01 (0.56)
7. (-)I find religious doubts upsetting.	0.07 (0.03)	0.19 (0.04)	**0.67** (0.57)
8. Questions are far more central . . .	**0.49** (0.25)	0.22 (0.28)	0.32 (0.26)
9. As I grow and change, I expect my religion . . .	0.22 (0.42)	0.31 (0.20)	**0.40** (0.10)
10. I am constantly questioning my religious beliefs . . .	**0.67** (0.73)	0.27 (0.20)	0.03 (0.21)
11. (-)I do not expect my religious convictions to change . . .	0.05 (0.43)	0.14 (0.07)	0.75 (0.11)
12. There are many religious issues on which my views . . .	**0.57** (0.51)	0.33 (0.01)	0.21 (0.18)

Correlations for the older sample are based on a sample size of 342.

Correlations in parentheses are from Batson and Schoenrade (1991a).

Bold typeface denotes highest factor loading for an item.

A minus sign preceding an item indicates that it is reversed in scoring.

Adapted from Dillon, J., & Futterman, A. (in press). Faith, doubt, and well-being in later life. *Journal of Aging and Identity*.

samples. All loadings reflect principal component analyses with Varimax rotation to enhance interpretability of extracted factors. Three principal components are extracted in the current analysis explaining approximately 62% of the total variance of the 12 Quest items. The first principal component accounts for 25% of the variance, the second 21%, and the third 16%. The second principal component or factor corresponds exactly to Batson and Schoenrade's (1991a) intended subdimension "Readiness to face existential questions without reducing their complexity" (Question) and includes items such as "God wasn't very important for me until I began to ask questions about the meaning of my own life." The first and third components are less distinct but correspond most closely to "Self-criticism and perception of religious doubt as positive" (Doubt) and "Openness to change" (Change), respectively. The Doubt subdimension is best exemplified by items such as "It might be said that I value my religious doubts and uncertainties," whereas the Change subdimension is best exemplified by items such as "I do not expect my religious convictions to change in the next few years" (reversed score). With respect to the Doubt and Change factors, several items load on the opposite factor from that intended by Batson and Schoenrade (e.g., items 10 and 12 load on Doubt but were intended to reflect Change, whereas items 7 and 8 load on Change but were intended to reflect Doubt). This suggests that although Question is a distinct factor corresponding to Batson and Schoenrade's curious, intellectual search for meaning within a religious tradition, Doubt and Change factors as initially conceived by Batson and Schoenrade may overlap significantly at the item level in an older sample.

Notwithstanding difficulties in interpretation resulting from item overlap, principal component analysis clearly demonstrates multidimensionality of the Quest Scale. Individuals who score high on the Quest scale, therefore, may be endorsing different groups of items within the scale—one group of items reflecting questioning of religious meanings, and a second group reflecting religious doubt and willingness to change religious beliefs. Individuals who score high on the Quest Scale may potentially demonstrate different forms of quest religiousness depending on which groups of items they endorse. We turn now to qualitative data that provide more detail about differences in the types of quest religiousness demonstrated by individuals who score high on the Quest Scale.

QUALITATIVE DIFFERENCES AMONG INDIVIDUALS WHO SCORE HIGH ON THE QUEST SCALE

Although the revised 12-item Quest Scale appears to demonstrate adequate reliability in both younger and older samples, the preceding discussion supports the view that Quest Scale may measure at least two different types of quest: The first type, a curious, intellectual questioning of religious beliefs in which the complexity of existential questions is not reduced; and the second type, a doubting of belief and a willingness to change religious traditions. In order to assess the possibility that there may be different types of quest, we interviewed the 20 individuals from the 342 individuals initially assessed who scored highest on the revised Quest Scale, 12 women and 8 men, about the nature of their religious beliefs and doubts, their religious activities and denominational affiliation, and their religious development. Specific questions in these interviews included the following:

1. Are you on a "spiritual journey"?
2. What is life's purpose?
3. Does God have a plan for us?
4. How open are you to new religious experiences?
5. Have you had any exposure to religious faiths other than your own?
6. Do you ever question the religious beliefs you have been taught or the religious people who have been your teachers? What do you question?
7. How did you come to believe and doubt?

These interviews were taped and transcribed and read by two project interviewers. Interviewers were asked to describe themes or patterns that emerged in each interview. Across the 20 interviews, two patterns or types of quest religiousness are discernible that roughly correspond to the Questioning factor and to a blend of the Doubt/Change factor described previously. In the first type of quest, individuals ask existential questions motivated by a sense of wonderment and awe, and in the second type, individuals doubt the validity of religious beliefs and rituals largely in reaction to negative experiences they have had in their particular religious community. Francis and Lucinda are examples of the first type of proactive, open-ended quest; James and Peter are two examples of the second type of reactive, negativistic quest. All four individuals are Roman Catholic and have been living in Worcester for at least 40 years.

PROACTIVE, OPEN-ENDED QUEST

Francis is a 71-year-old retired machinist. Happily married for more than 40 years, Francis lives in the same house in which he and his wife raised four children. Francis completed high school and presently takes courses at the nearby community college. He is active in many social organizations and has been a weekly participant in church services for as long as he can remember. Francis is generally healthy, although he reports frequent bouts of "arthritis and bursitis" in his hips and legs that do not interfere with his daily functioning. Other relevant data include the following: Francis reports a substantial amount of available social support and names 20 different people on the Arizona Social Support Interview Schedule (ASSIS) (Barrera, 1981); he reports few depressive symptoms (his Center for Epidemiological Studies—Depression (CES-D) score is 6 (Radloff, 1977); and he scores in the upper quartile of Intrinsic and lower-middle quartile of Extrinsic Religious Orientation Scales (ROC) (Allport & Ross, 1967).

Francis admits to frequently asking questions about the existence of God, or as he puts it a "higher force in the universe." In fact, he admits to questioning "how just about everything came into existence." In response to the question "Is there anything you doubt," he states, "I'll put it down in one sentence: I know there has to be one supreme being who created the whole universe . . . I have to think that it must be a God, but there's . . . Nobody's found that truth yet, of how the world got made, the universe . . . how did the other millions of galaxies come into being? Must have been a supreme being or some other force that I don't know. That's why I am in doubt." Almost without prompting, Francis shared with the interviewer a list of "mysteries" that he puzzles over on a "daily basis." For example, Francis states,

> Stars and the millions of galaxies . . . Was it God who made all that stuff . . . it's mysterious how the whole thing got started. And then sometimes I go beyond that. Who made God? If God created all this, how did he come into being? Who knows? In other words, everything had to start . . . everything had a beginning, an origin. We don't know. Mystifying!

For Francis, the Bible points to right questions and offers a "good start" toward answering his many existential questions, but the biblical answers are not sufficiently convincing or comprehensive. For example, Francis explains, "Religion talks about the earth that we're in. Genesis. God made the oceans, and the sun, but that's all. Those are the basic things. Doesn't mention anything about beyond. Stars and millions of galaxies." Francis turns to science and scientists, magazines, television, and literature for answers to many of nature's mysteries. He comments, "I enjoy coming up with answers, even if they're not right!" and implies that all knowledge is provisional when he says

> No one has proved anything except what we've learned through association . . . scholars, historians, religious people . . . they all say there's an origin for everything. There's an origin for all materialistic things. An origin for you and me . . . but how did the original factors take place? How did the stars get up there? What's the origin of that? What was the force that created the stars, and what is the force that created that force? The power . . . was it a God or supreme being? Or did it just happen? Nobody knows and nobody will give you an answer.

For Francis, religious involvement is enhanced by asking questions of existential meaning and purpose, and he views his participation in religious rituals and prayer as a way of focusing on the "right" questions, as a way of deepening his faith. Religious belief and religious questioning are but two sides of the same coin for Francis, as he said in the interview, "I can't imagine not asking questions."

Lucinda, a 78-year-old widow and mother of four, has been a weekly participant at the same church for more than 30 years. One of seven siblings, Lucinda reports frequent contacts with her siblings and children, many of whom are still living in Worcester. During her young adulthood, Lucinda was primarily a housewife. Although she finished high school and had some inclination to go to work as a secretary, Lucinda chose instead to stay at home with her children. Her husband of 43 years, a businessman in the city, died 6 years ago. Lucinda states that her health is generally good. She has diabetes (for which she takes medication) and has had cataracts removed from both eyes; nonetheless, she states she "is able to shop and clean for herself." Although Lucinda doesn't drive, she takes free transportation provided by the church, enabling her to attend religious services regularly and to participate in a weekly meditation group at her church. She describes a fairly large social support network (16 people, 12 of whom are family members) on the ASSIS, reports few depressive symptoms (score of 7) on the CES-D, and, like Francis, is in the upper quartile on the Intrinsic ROC but is in the lower-middle quartile on the Extrinsic ROC.

Lucinda reports spending a great deal of time by herself, quietly contemplating her past experience, her future, and the world around her. She states, "I'm not one who needs to have the radio on, and I don't come in the house and turn on the TV. I don't mind having quiet, silence . . . I'm trying to get rid of all the outside stuff and meditate." Lucinda spends time, wondering "about the nature and powers of God," like Francis, "about the forces of nature" and "the origin of the universe." Unlike Francis, however, Lucinda seems more open ended and less driven to find answers in the way she contemplates and questions. For example, in answer to the question, "Does God have a plan," Lucinda seemed somewhat confused and responded,

> I'm not sure He has a plan anymore than I'm sure that God is responsible for things . . . such as someone's death. God is responsible for this or that . . . I don't know. Cause He can't . . . I don't know that it's a "He" either . . . and I don't think it's a person, and I don't think it's up there, necessarily or any particular place. But I don't think God decides everything.

Lucinda seems to pose questions to herself, and the question almost seem to "float" for a while, becoming the focus of her thought, without any answer or, for that matter, pressure for an answer coming forward.

Lucinda, like Francis, is fascinated by science. In the middle of the interview, in answer to no apparent question, Lucinda described an article she had just finished about scientific approaches to demonstrating the existence of God. In reference to the article, she said, "There's this physicist, I think, who wants to prove there's a God. Fantastic idea! But what can you do . . . it seems sort of silly. No?" On the other hand, Lucinda is most interested in what science is able to discover and recognizes certain limits. In describing an article about an archeological finding she read some time ago, Lucinda remarked, "They know the world is really old, but how old? I think they may go back and say 10,000 years or 50,000 or whatever, but they won't find the starting point. That's it . . . that's the problem." For Lucinda, religion offers a solution to problems of "starting points", and like Francis, Lucinda seems to enjoy wondering about the beginnings of things.

Lucinda also finds special comfort in wondering about what comes after life on earth. She volunteers the following story about her husband's death in order to explain her wonderment about an afterlife:

> Before my husband died . . . oh boy . . . First place, I don't think there's any hell or purgatory. And I thought that . . . I don't think that heaven's a place. I don't think it's up there, I don't think it's . . . I don't know. But I felt that he had a place to go after he died. But I wasn't sure. I wanted to be sure . . . I just felt it couldn't be a house or anything.

At this point, Lucinda laughs with embarrassment and adds, "Maybe a spirit world. . . . After my husband died, I didn't change my mind so much as I just started thinking about it more. I just don't know now."

Common to both Francis and Lucinda is the belief that a life without questioning is tantamount to what Francis calls "blind faith." He comments that he doesn't "take things for granted" and say "this is the way it is." Instead, he asks "Why should I wonder about things?" and replies to himself, "Sometimes those who ask questions are happier than those who don't. The ones who don't ask, don't worry. They've got it decided." Both describe a lifetime of wonderment, with past valleys of doubt and distress. Neither Francis nor Lucinda can imagine living without asking questions, however, even when the answers are not entirely satisfying. The process of questioning for both Francis and Lucinda appears to be its own reward.

REACTIVE, NEGATIVISTIC QUEST

For both Francis and Lucinda, faith in and questioning of religious belief go together; participation in religious services simultaneously deepens their faith and increases their wonderment. Their proactive, open-ended search for meaning and purpose in life is readily contrasted with the more reactive, negativistic form of questioning James and Peter demonstrate toward religious belief and ritual. For James and Peter, religious involvement in their church community has been more stressful. Although they readily endorse specific core religious beliefs (e.g., the belief in the Holy Trinity) and readily admit they obtain many social and emotional rewards from church activity, they doubt the validity of certain religious claims, question the necessity of specific religious rituals, and frequently have had negative interactions with clergy or other church personnel. These negative interactions often led to periods of withdrawal from their church community and religious inactivity.

James, an 83-year-old father of five, is a retired businessman. Married for 60 years, he has lived in Worcester for 42 years. James completed 3 years of college after serving in the Army in Europe during World War II. He is very active in many social and civic organizations, including the Knights of Columbus, the Scouts, and his local VFW lodge. James grudgingly goes to church "with his wife," usually on a weekly or biweekly basis. James' social networks are extensive; he reports many family, business, and personal contacts (he named 20 different people on the ASSIS; only 9 were family). Although James' health is good (he reports no chronic or acute illness), he complains of several depressive symptoms (a score of 16 on the CES-D) and reports being "sometimes lazy and bored" since retiring.

When asked if there is anything he questions, James responded, "I divide it two ways. I think the God part and the spiritual part—I think that's pretty good. I think that's on an even keel. But the way it's administered is not." James shared several negative experiences to account for his uneasiness with what he calls the Roman Catholic Church's "administration." The earliest experience occurred when James attended Catholic grammar school.

> When I was a kid, I went to Catholic school, and boy were they tough. They used to beat you to pieces . . . those nuns . . . for nothing and nobody would believe this. If you were late, you'd get hit. If you didn't know your homework, you'd get hit. They say they don't do it now. Of course they don't, but they did when I was a kid.

James describes resentment from early in his schooling toward particular individuals and what he perceives as the "rigid" authority of the Church. For example, James describes a second experience as further support for his resentment. James was a member of the Boy's Club and attended activities there daily after school. He explains that the club's swimming and boxing teams contributed to his "developing a healthy life style" and even goes on to say "To tell you the truth the reasons I'm sitting in front of you right now and I'm 83 years old and in good shape is that I never drank and I never smoked and I thank the Boy's Club." The Boy's

Club, a Protestant organization, was not, however, "exactly in good grace with the nuns and brothers of the Catholic school." James recalled the day a nun at the school discovered he had joined the club:

> We had a membership card and we put it in our pocket here. I was in school. I was sitting there one day, and the nun come down and she saw the card and she pulled it out and she pulled it off my neck. But it had a heavy string and it cut the back of my neck right around here and she said," I told you not to go to the Boy's Club . . . I told you, woe betide the boy who goes to the Boy's Club. It's a Protestant organization and they make you eat meat on Friday." So like a dumb-dumb, I said, "No Sister, they don't give you nothing to eat at the Boy's Club, we go after meals." Well that was the worst thing I ever could have said. She pulled me out of my seat and brought me up and she had a stick, and she whacked me on the legs and said, "When I say something, I don't want to be corrected!" And she pushed me back in my seat.

James went on, "Anyway, it's not like we all never ate meat on Fridays. Hell, I even saw a Sister sneak a hotdog once."

Although such early incidents prompted James to distrust particular individuals in the Church and to question the validity of what he was taught in Catholic school, two events later in his adulthood prompted what James describes as his "real problems" with the "whole" Church. Both events typify for James "the lack of compassion for ordinary members" and the "money-oriented" nature of the Church. The first event occurred months before James' marriage and the second more recently, after his wife had a massive stroke.

Some months prior to his wedding, James and his wife-to-be went to their parish to arrange for a wedding date. The priest with whom they spoke admonished James' wife, saying "Your father is not much of a contributor to the church . . . . You can get married in the church, but you will get married downstairs in the church, and that is good enough for you." James winced when he described the priest's words and said, "Even now those words hurt." James continued,

> Now my wife felt very bad. She was a very nice girl, hard worker, she says, "I contribute to home because we got seven kids in my house." "Well," the priest says, "that makes no difference. I see your father goes around in a new car and all. Your family don't give, and that's that." My wife said, "That ain't true, we don't even own a car, and my father don't drive!"

Fortunately, James and his wife found another church for their wedding, but "that left a bad omen for me," James remembers.

The second experience in which the Church's lack of compassion and its money-oriented nature became clear to James occurred after his wife suffered a massive stroke that left her in a coma. For nearly 7 years, James visited her in a nursing home. During much of this time, James recalls "debating in his mind" whether or not to remove her respirator and feeding tubes and just end his wife's and his own "long struggle." Toward the end of this long ordeal, Frank bought a headstone in preparation for his wife's death. On purchasing the headstone, the salesman informed him that he had to pay "an extra $160 for a foundation for the stone" if he wished his wife to be buried in the parish cemetery. James agreed. After several weeks, James describes going down to the cemetery plot and discovering that the foundation had not been laid. So he returned to the salesman to insist the plot be readied for his wife's now imminent death. He describes his conversation with the salesman as follows: "I say, 'Listen, it is quite a while now. No foundation, no stone yet.' The salesman says, 'Well, I got news for you. In order for you to get into that cemetery you better pay the $160 or no stone will go in at all. The Church don't know you're watching us. What they usually do is just put sand there and put the stone on it.'" James describes being astonished, he explained, "She was going to be buried next to her sisters [in that cemetery] . . . everything was gonna be all right . . . and I would pay the $160. But I never forgot it. These guys [the priests] are talking money and they don't care about me. I don't think that's right . . . they talk out of both sides of their mouths." After relating this difficult experience, James said, "When I was a kid, I used to believe . . . you know I was going to church and I always went to church. I wouldn't miss it no matter where I was, but after this stuff, I just tapered off. I don't take nothing at face value . . . after this stuff."

The second high scorer on the Quest Scale, Peter, is 76 years old, a recently retired mechanical engineer who ran his own business in Worcester for more than 40 years. Peter is a married father of four who, like James, has been very active in the community, serving on the boards of several civic organizations and service agencies. Peter is also generally healthy (although he had a very mild heart attack 18 years ago), goes to church weekly with his wife, and remains very socially active (describing 17 nonfamily contacts on the ASSIS). He reports some depressive symptomatology (a score of 13 on the CES-D) but otherwise describes a "fulfilling life."

In many respects, Peter's testimony parallels that of James. Peter also describes several early negative experiences in church (in Michigan where he was raised) as well as more recent negative interactions with priests surrounding significant family events such as marriages, births, illness, and death. More surprising, however, is the way Peter echoes James' resentment of the Church over matters of money and rigidity of doctrine. Peter explains,

> It seems that sometimes the Church goes too far money-wise. I always give a check
> to them because they're trying to buy an elevator here, a garden there, you know . . .
> and I always give them a check. And now they sent me a letter and they said how
> about another check. Well, you know we're retired. I know its hard for folks to take

the stairs . . . you know the handicapped older folks who come to church. But give me a break! They got money for everything . . . last year expenses for bingo were $35,000! How can it cost $35,000 for bingo, and yet they're at my door every other week! Maybe cut down on something so you can build a rectory proper!

Although Peter is not quite so angry at the Church as James, he nonetheless shares James' sense that church could be more responsive to members' emotional needs. Peter views the Church as doctrinally "rigid" on significant moral issues, and it is this rigidity rather than negative interactions with particular clergy that prompts Peter to view the Church as insensitive and unresponsive. For example, Peter describes an incident "soon after his wife's nervous breakdown' when he became most disappointed with the Church. An active member of the Church at that time, he went to church to find solace and strength. Instead, Peter states, "All I heard was the Church says this on abortion, the Church says that on women priests. They never ask women what they think. They [the priests] do the talking. And we just sit there and believe what they say." Peter continues, "I don't think they necessarily know the first thing about how people live day to day." For Peter, the Church can't be responsive to members emotional needs because it is "locked into certain ways of doing things."

Notwithstanding their doubts and resentment, both James and Peter state that they continue to go to church frequently. James says, for example, "I go but not all the time. I go mostly to see friends and see how things are going with their families. It's mostly social for me." Similarly, Peter reports that "My life still includes people at church . . . my friends and neighbors . . . we all go to see one another." In addition, Peter describes other social functions that for him only the Church can fulfill: "When it comes to a marriage or a funeral, where else are you going to go?" On the occasion of a marriage or first communion, Peter states, "I sit in my seat, look around at my children and nieces and nephews and think how wonderful things are . . . At the same time, I try not to let the priest ruin the moment with his comments. I sometimes have to tune him out." Indeed, for many individuals who demonstrate this more reactive, negativistic form of quest, like James and Peter, religious involvement clearly involves a compartmentalization of the social and intellectual or belief aspects of religion: On the one hand, going to church for social reasons or because of family obligation is acceptable and, indeed, enjoyable. On the other hand, going to church triggers doubt and resentment and requires what James calls "putting up with some of the other [bad] things."

In light of the both quantitative (e.g., factor analytic) and qualitative analyses, it should be clear that the quest orientation, at least as it is assessed by the Batson and Schoenrade (1991a) revised Quest Scale, may be an agglomeration of different modes of interacting with one's religious traditions. More specifically, we would argue, based on these quantitative and qualitative data, that at least two distinct types of quest religiousness can be discerned in later life—a proactive, open-ended "readiness to face existential questions" and a reactive, negativistic, "doubting" of religious doctrine and institution. What is the relationship between these forms of quest religiousness and other religious orientations, for example, means and ends religiousness? In the next section we examine these relationships in greater detail.

RELATIONSHIP AMONG QUEST, ENDS, AND MEANS: QUANTITATIVE ANALYSES

Previous studies suggest that the Quest Scale measures an independent dimension of religious orientation from that of means and ends religiousness (Batson & Schoenrade, 1991a, 1991b). In the present older sample, the full Quest Scale is largely independent of measures of ends religiousness (rs equal 0.03, –0.07, 0.08, –0.05 with Intrinsic ROC [Allport & Ross, 1967], Internal, External, Orthodoxy scales [Batson & Schoenrade, 1991b], respectively. Full Quest Scale scores demonstrate significant but low correlations with measures of means religiousness (e.g., Extrinsic Scale scores, r equals 0.24). Correlations between measures of quest, ends, and means religiousness are also typically less than 0.30 in younger adults (Batson et al., 1993).

On the other hand, both factor and qualitative analyses described above suggest multidimensionality of the Quest Scale, i.e., that at least two different types of quest religiousness are assessed by scale. Indeed, Watson et al. (1989) argue that the apparent independence of quest and ends religiousness may be a statistical artifact resulting from such Quest Scale multidimensionality. Watson et al. hypothesized that the Quest Scale comprises "polarizing" dimensions that, when taken together in a single scale, cancel out relationships between quest and measures of ends religiousness. In keeping with this view, we found that whereas the Doubt factor described previously is negatively correlated with ends measures (e.g., r with Intrinsic ROC is –0.19), the Question factor is positively correlated with ends measures (e.g., r with Intrinsic ROC is 0.17). Taken together in a single scale, these Quest factors "cancel each other out", yielding in this case overall independence between the Quest Scale and ends religiousness.

By contrast, it should be noted that Quest factors do not "cancel out" relationships between Quest and means religiousness: The two factors demonstrate low positive correlations with measures of means religiousness (rs between the Doubt and Question factors and Extrinsic ROC are 0.29 and 0.14, respectively).

Although factor analytic results provide some sense of the degree of relationship between quest, means, and ends orientations, how do we account for these relationships theologically and psychologically? For example, how is it that some individuals report concurrently a deep faith as well as substantial doubt in religious doctrine? Religion researchers (other than Batson and colleagues) have not attended to this question. In the following section, we turn again to the interviews of individuals who score high on the Quest Scale and examine their comments from both a theological and a psychological perspective.

THEOLOGICAL AND PSYCHOLOGICAL ACCOUNTS OF RELATIONSHIP AMONG QUEST, ENDS, AND MEANS RELIGIOUSNESS: QUALITATIVE ANALYSIS

If we look at individuals like Francis and Lucinda, exemplars of the active, open-ended quest, we see that questions and doubts about their faith serve to add something of positive value to their religious commitment. Although it may at first appear contradictory for individuals to have a deep religious commitment and at the same time doubt and question their faith, within many religious traditions, this duality is not a contradiction at all. For example, in the Roman Catholic tradition, there is a long history of considering faith in the context of doubt. The Jesuit theologian, Hans Kung (1981), notes that certain aspects of reality pose questions to human beings the world over. Specifically, human beings question two things. First, they question whether there is any ground, any support, to what at many times appears to be fundamentally uncertain reality. Second, Kung says, human beings question whether there is any meaning or purpose to their lives. So for Kung, it is an ineluctable aspect of human experience to confront over and over again the radical uncertainty and possible meaninglessness of existence. It is this aspect of reality that provides atheism with sufficient reason to maintain that reality has no primal ground, no support, no goal at all. For Kung, it is in the face of these questions and doubts that the faith act is made. Religious commitment, for Kung, rests on a constantly renewed affirmative response to the ever-present question about fundamental reality. He writes,

> It has been shown therefore that man cannot evade a free, although not arbitrary, decision, not only in regard to reality as such but also in regard to a primal ground, primal support and primal goal of reality. Since reality and its primal ground, primal support and primal goal are not imposed on us with conclusive evidence, there remains scope for man's freedom. Man must decide without intellectual constraint but also without rational proof. Both atheism and belief in God are therefore ventures, they are also risks. (Kung, 1981, p. 570).

Faith and doubt, for Kung and for people like Francis and Lucinda, both logically and theologically stand together.

In the Protestant tradition, such figures as Tillich (1957) and Niebuhr (1963) present a similar conception of religiousness as a response to certain fundamental questions and doubts. In the faith act, one utters a resounding "yes" to the gnawing presence of doubt. This aspect of the faith act leads Tillich to claim that doubt is a necessary consequence of the risk of faith. "Courage," he writes, "as an element of faith is the daring self-affirmation of one's own being in spite of the powers of 'nonbeing' which are the heritage of everything finite"; that is, the heritage of the world we know (p. 17). So if doubt appears, Tillich cautions, it should not be considered as the negation of faith but as an element that was and always will be present in the act of faith itself.

Similarly, in Niebuhr's (1963) "relational" conception of religiousness, he sees faith taking form in our earliest relationships with caregivers in infancy. Faith, for Niebuhr, grows through our experience of "trust" and "mistrust" with those people who are closest to us toward a larger search for an overarching trust in a center of value and power to whom we relate and who relates to us in a way that imbues our lives with meaning and purpose. Niebuhr writes,

> Our primordial interpretation of the radical action by which we are is made in faith as trust or distrust. Between these two there seems to be no middle term. The inscrutable power by which we are is either for us or against us. If it is neutral, heedless of the affirmations or denials of the creatures by each other, it is against us, to be distrusted as profoundly as if it were actively inimical. For then it has cast us into being as aliens, as beings that do not fit. (p. 119)

As with any relationship, with faith cast as trust or mistrust the possibility always presents itself that the other may let us down, betraying us. For Niebuhr, it is in spite of this very real and painful possibility that we believe. Faith and doubt, for Niebuhr, are intimately interwoven.

The intimate relationship between faith and doubt is not spoken of only in Christian traditions. Among Jewish theologians Buber (1958), for example, presents a similar "relational" account of religiousness. He describes a twofold attitudes toward relationships in human beings: the "I-It" and the "I-Thou" attitude. In looking at a tree, for example, we can classify it in a species and study it as a type in its structure and mode of life. We can chop it down, plant more trees, and so on. In this "I-It" attitude, Buber says, "the tree remains my object, occupies space and time, and has its nature and constitution" (p. 7). The tree can, however, become a different sort of object, a "Thou." This can come about, Buber says, when, " . . . in considering the tree I become bound up in relation to it. The tree is now no longer It. I have been seized by the power of exclusiveness" (p. 7). For Buber, human beings are naturally thrust into a world of It relationships and reside there indefinitely. It is only through "will and grace," in other words, a faith act, that one can transcend the It world and see the Thou. Buber writes, "Men do not find God if they stay in the world. They do not find Him if they leave the world. He who goes out with his whole being to meet his Thou and carries to it all being that is in the world, finds Him who cannot be sought" (p. 79). In the face of the sense that there very likely may not be a Thou to be found, in other words, against doubt, Buber notes, human beings seek the Thou anyway, that is, they believe.

Against this background of theological work on the relationship between belief and doubt, commitment and quest, we note that in the context of the development of emotional relationships, psychologists have long focused on a similar tension between holding on and letting go, between trusting and mistrusting. For example, Erikson (1963) posits the initial stage of emotional interaction with others as being constituted by this tension between basic trust and basic mistrust. For Erikson, trust involves a faith that another will provide, and mistrust involves the recognition that this will not occur. The resolution of the tension between trust and mistrust, for example, the ability to recognize accurately when faith is appropriate, is essential for meaningful social interaction. For example, Erikson states that later in life "man brings to these [social] institutions the remnants of his infantile mentality and his youthful fervor, and he receives from them—as long as they manage to maintain their actuality—a reinforcement of his infantile gains." (p. 250). In fact, when Erikson speaks here of "institutions," he is speaking specifically of conflict between basic trust and basic mistrust as it plays out in the context of adult religious involvement. He continues,

All religions have in common the periodical childlike surrender to a Provider or providers who dispense earthly fortune as well as spiritual health; some demonstration of man's smallness by way of reduced posture and humble gesture; the admission in prayer and song of misdeeds, of misthoughts, and of evil intentions; fervent appeal for inner unification by divine guidance; and finally, the insight that individual trust must become a common faith, individual mistrust a commonly formulated evil, while the individual's restoration must become part of the ritual practice of many, and must become a sign of trustworthiness in the community. (p. 250)

It is not surprising, therefore, that quest and ends religious orientations, or religious doubt and commitment, can coexist for some and not for others. From the Eriksonian point of view, the resolution of the conflict between basic trust and basic mistrust plays a significant role in determining the way an individual demonstrates his or her faith. For those who successfully resolve the basic trust and mistrust conflict, doubt is not threatening and can coexist with faith; for those who less successfully resolve the basic trust and mistrust conflict, doubt and faith cannot coexist.

Francis and Lucinda illustrate faith coexisting with doubt; the second type of quest religiousness—doubt and faith in opposition—is well illustrated by the reactive, negativistic form of quest religiousness demonstrated by James and Peter. Both report many instances in which their trust in others, particularly in the Church hierarchy, was "betrayed," and they describe their quest as a result of these "betrayals." Certainly these individuals display a degree of religious involvement—they attend religious services with their spouses, participate in activities at church or synagogue, talk about religious matters with friends—and frequently they even endorse core religious principles. As opposed to the first type of quest religiousness, in which religious doubts deepen and constitute the individual's attachment to a religious community and a set of beliefs, among individuals who demonstrate this second type of quest, religious doubts are mixed with anger and resentment and prompt feelings of alienation. In a sense, their mistrust of religion makes traditional faith impossible.

Although the reactive, negativistic form of quest appears to diminish the possibility that traditional religion provides a framework for existential meaning, it does not stop these individuals from asking existential questions and coming up with more personal, nontraditional answers. For example, both James and Peter endorsed core Catholic beliefs, for example, belief in Jesus, in the Trinity, and so on, but then went on to interpret these beliefs, frequently qualifying their comments with phrases like "but that's not what I was taught in school." They clearly found meaning in religious doctrine and clearly expressed a sense of "spirituality" but tailored their interpretation of traditional doctrine to the particulars of their lives, often explicitly disregarding past religious teaching in the process.

Neither proactive nor reactive forms of quest appear incompatible with a means orientation. For both types of high Quest individuals, questions and doubts about faith do not preclude involvement in religion as a way of meeting other significant social and emotional needs. Francis, Lucinda, James, and Peter spontaneously reported participating in Church activities as a way of meeting friends, and all regarded religious ritual as the sine qua non for marking the significance of births, weddings, deaths, and other life transitions. Religious involvement, notwithstanding even James' and Peter's anger and alienation, is still a source of personal meaning, social integration, support, and comfort.

CONCLUSIONS

In this chapter we examine "religion as a quest" in part to counter a caricature of religion as unthinking, dogmatic, adherence to doctrine. Religion is typically studied by psychologists and sociologists of religion in terms of extent of religious commitment alone, as though more commitment means more religion. In fact, there are other important orientations or "ways of being religious," important for both theological and psychological reasons. In this chapter we presented data pertaining to the nature of late-life religious quest and the relationship between quest, ends, and means orientations. Although much remains to be empirically demonstrated regarding religion as a quest, several conclusions are appropriate.

First, although the revised Quest Scale demonstrates adequate reliability (in terms of classical test theory) in our older adult sample, it also demonstrates multidimensionality. Two factors emerge in our analyses of the Quest Scale: one factor reflects quest as an open-minded "search for meaning" in life, and the second factor reflects a more negative, doubting form of quest. In this latter form, quest appears as a reaction to particular clergy or church policies and is associated with significant life experiences. These two forms of quest demonstrate different relationships to measures of ends religiousness and religious commitment. On the one hand, the open-minded search form of quest is associated with greater commitment; on the other hand, the doubting form of quest is associated with diminished commitment.

Second, if you are to take any single message from this chapter, we hope that you consider carefully the complexity of the relationship between religious belief and doubt. In simple terms, we demonstrate that knowing the depth of an individual's religious commitment tells us little of the extent of his or her doubt, and vice versa. For many, deep belief goes hand in hand with thoughtful reflection, a search for meaning, and doubt.

ACKNOWLEDMENTS

The study described in this chapter was supported by grant #AG11438 from the National Institute of Aging to the first author. The authors wish to acknowledge Genine Swanzey and John Gibson Fay for their help in collecting and transcribing interviews for this project. Portions of this chapter were presented at the annual meeting of the Gerontological Society of America , November, 1996, Los Angeles, CA. Direct correspondence to Andrew Futterman at the Department of Psychology, Holy Cross College, Worcester, MA. or to the following email address: afutterm@holycross.edu.

REFERENCES

Allport, G. (1950). *The individual and his religion*. New York: Macmillan.
Allport, G.W., & Ross, J.M. (1967). Personal religious orientation and prejudice. *Journal of Personality and Social Psychology*, 5, 432–443.

Barrera, M. (1981). Social support in the adjustment of pregnant adolescents: Assessment issues. In B.H. Gottlieb (Ed.), *Social networks and social support* (pp. 69–96). Beverly Hills, CA.: Sage.

Batson, C.D. (1976). Religion as prosocial: Agent or double agent? *Journal for the Scientific Study of Religion, 15*, 29–45.

Batson, C.D., Naifeh, S. J., & Pate, S. (1978). Social desirability, religious orientation, and racial prejudice. *Journal for the Scientific Study of Religion, 17*, 31–41.

Batson, C.D., Oleson, K.C., Weeks, J.L., Healy, S.P., Reeves, P.J., Jennings, P., & Brown, T. (1989). Religious prosocial motivation: Is it altruistic or egoistic? *Journal of Personality and Social Psychology, 57*, 873–884.

Batson, C.D., & Schoenrade, P.A. (1991a). Measuring religion as quest: I. Validity concerns. *Journal for the Scientific Study of Religion, 30*, 416–429.

Batson, C.D., & Schoenrade, P.A. (1991b). Measuring religion as quest: II. Reliability concerns. *Journal for the Scientific Study of Religion, 30*, 430–447.

Batson, C.D., Schoenrade, P., & Ventis, W. L. (1993). *Religion and the individual: A social-psychological perspective.* New York: Oxford University Press.

Batson, C.D., & Ventis, W.L. (1982). *The religious experience.* New York: Oxford University Press.

Buber, M. (1958). *I and thou.* New York: Charles Scribner's Sons.

Chatters, L.M., Levin, J.S., & Taylor, R.J. (1992). Antecedents and consequences of religious involvement among older Black adults. *Journal of Gerontology, 47* (Suppl.), S269–S278.

Cuban, L. (1991). Models of migration decision making reexamined: The destination and search of older migrants to Cape Cod. *Gerontologist, 31*, 204–209.

Dillon, J. & Futterman, A. (in press). Faith, doubt, and well-being in later life. *Journal of Aging and Identity.*

Donahue, M.J. (1985). Intrinsic and extrinsic religiousness: Review and meta-analysis. *Journal of Personality and Social Psychology, 48*, 400–419.

Erikson, E. (1963). *Childhood and society* (2nd ed.). New York: Norton.

Feagin, J.R. (1964). Prejudice and religious types: A focused study of southern fundamentalists. *Journal for the Scientific Study of Religion, 4*, 3–13.

Futterman, A., Dillon, J.J., Garand, F.I., & Haugh, J. (1997). *Of ends, means, and quest: Religious orientations in later life.* Manuscript submitted for publication.

Futterman, A., & Koenig, H. (1995). *Measuring religiosity in later life: What can gerontology learn from the sociology and psychology of religion?* Paper presented at the Conference on Methodological Advances in the Study of Religion, Health, and Aging), Bethesda, MD.

Glock, C.Y., & Stark, R. (1965). *Religion and society in tension.* Chicago: Rand-McNally.

Gorsuch, R. (1994). Toward motivational theories of intrinsic religious commitment. *Journal for the Scientific Study of Religion, 33*, 315–325.

Gorsuch, R.L. (1984). Measurement: The boon and bane of investigating religion. *American Psychologist, 39,* 228–236.

Hoge, D. (1972). A validated intrinsic religious motivation scale. *Journal for the Scientific Study of Religion, 11,* 369–376.

Horner, E.R. (1991). *Massachusetts municipal profiles, 1991–1992.* Palo Alto, CA: Information Publications.

Kellstedt, L.A., & Green, J.C. (1993). Knowing God's Many People: Denominational preference and political behavior. In D.C. Lege & L.A. Kellstedt (Eds), *Rediscovering the religious factor in American politics* (pp. 53–71). Armonk, NY: M.E. Sharp.

Kirkpatrick, L.A., & Hood, R.W. (1990). Intrinsic-extrinsic religious orientation: The boon or bane of contemporary psychology of religion? *Journal for the Scientific Study of Religion, 29,* 442–462.

Krause, N. (1995). Religiosity and self-esteem among older adults. *Journal of Gerontology: Series B: Psychological Sciences and Social Sciences, 50B (5),* P236–P246.

Kung, H. (1981). *Does God exist?: An answer for today.* New York: Vintage.

Niebuhr, H.R. (1963). *The responsible self: An essay in Christian moral philosophy.* New York: Harper & Row.

Radloff, L.S. (1977). The CES-D scale: A self-report depression scale for research in the general population. *Applied Psychological Measurement, 1,* 385–401.

Spilka, B., Stout, L., Minton, B., & Sizemore, D. (1977). Death and personal faith: A psychometric investigation. *Journal for the Scientific Study of Religion, 16,* 169–178.

Tillich, P. (1957). *Dynamics of faith.* New York: Harper & Row.

Watson, P.J., Morris, R.J., & Hood, R.W. (1989). Interactional factor correlations with means and end religiousness. *Journal for the Scientific Study of Religion, 28,* 337–347.

Late-Life Transcendence: A New Developmental Perspective on Aging

Lars Tornstam

The theory of gerotranscendence was developed by Tornstam (1989, 1994). The 1989 article describes the theoretical basis of the theory; whereas the 1994 article gives empirical support of its validity. In this chapter, a closer look at the qualitative content of gerotranscendence will be presented. First, however, we need to give a brief summary of the basic characteristics of the theory.

Drawing on my own studies as well as on theories and observations of others (Chapman, 1988; Chinen, 1985, 1986, 1989a, 1989b; Erickson, 1950, 1982; Grothjan, 1982; Gutman, 1976; Holliday & Chandler, 1986; Jung, 1930; Kramer & Woodruff, 1986; Peck, 1968; Rosenmayr, 1987; Storr, 1988), I have suggested that human aging, the very process of living into old age, is characterized by a general potential towards gerotranscendence. Simply put, gerotranscendence is a shift in metaperspective from a materialistic and pragmatic view of the world to a more cosmic and transcendent one, normally accompanied by an increase in life satisfaction. Gerotranscendence is defined as qualitatively different from both "ego-integrity" (Erikson, 1950) and "disengagement" (Cumming, Newell, Dean, & McCaffrey, 1960; Cumming & Henry, 1961) because it implies a shift in metaperspective.

As in Jung's theory of the individuation process, gerotranscendence is regarded as the final stage in a natural progression towards maturation and wisdom. It defines a reality somewhat different from the "normal" midlife reality that we often tend to project on old age. Neugarten and associates (1964) wrote about the contemplative nature of the inner lives of old people, and Clark and Anderson (1967) described how older people turn away from the competitive values of midlife. Many theories, however, have been based on the assumption that "good aging" equals continuity and preserving midlife ideals, activities, and definitions of reality (e.g., Havens, 1968; Rosow, 1967). The theory of gerotranscendence takes a perspective that emphasizes change and development.

The term gerotranscendence has been chosen because most of the changes described in what follows involve various ways in which elderly people break through old boundaries, moving on to a new stage in life. Thus, in this context, the word transcendence is used in this simple sense, not in the religious, metaphysical sense.

METHOD

The qualitative analysis presented in this article is based on interviews with 50 people between 52 and 97 years of age. After having listened to a lecture on gerotranscendence, these people (out of 500) recognized the phenomena described by the theory in their personal development and were willing to be interviewed.

The interviews were semistructured, in other words, some theoretically generated themes were discussed, but the conversations had an open format. For each theme, the goal was for the interviewer to guide the conversation as little as possible.

The interviews, lasting from 1 to 3 hours, were tape-recorded and transcribed, in other words, they were listened to several times, and their essential parts were identified and written down. Each transcription consists of about 25 pages of text. The resulting total of 1,250 pages constitutes the empirical basis for the present analysis.

Each interview began with an open theme; the respondent simply was asked to tell about changes in attitude toward life, oneself, and relationships with others during life. This was followed by specific themes generated by the theory. The analysis as well as the following presentation are organized in terms of some major categories obtained during the open-ended interviews. The open theme generated three main dimensions of gerotranscendental change: the cosmic dimension, the self, and the social and the personal relations.

It is interesting to note that Achenbaum & Orwoll (1991) obtained similar dimensions in a psychogerontological analysis of the book of Job. Job's struggle toward wisdom is described as developmental changes in the transpersonal, intrapersonal, and interpersonal dimensions. I became acquainted with the work of Achenbaum & Orwoll after I had finished my own analysis.

The organization of the presentation starts with a full comparison of two respondents who have reached different positions on the way toward gerotranscendence. Next comes closer descriptions of the main dimensions of gerotranscendental change, followed by a section on obstacles and shortcuts on the way to gerotranscendence.

GEROTRANSCENDENCE AND ITS OPPOSITE

Among the 50 respondents, some had come a long way toward gerotranscendence whereas others had not; it is my impression that some people came to the lecture and agreed to be interviewed not because they had experienced such a development, but because they felt that it might be possible. Thus, the present material offers the possibility to clarify the qualitative content of gerotranscendence by comparing a gerotranscendent and a non-gerotranscendent individual.

EVA—WHO HAS COME A LONG WAY TOWARD GEROTRANSCENDENCE

Eva, formerly a nurse, was 69 years old at the time of the interview. Although not from a poor family, she had a difficult childhood; her upbringing was strict and brutal. She had been married and had three adult children. She experienced a deep crisis in connection with her divorce a number of years ago. She said, "I don't think a person should ask for crises, but I think that we learn something from the crises we go through."

In answering the open question about whether she has changed her attitude toward life and herself, she described a rather radical change in perspective:

Using an earlier analogy, I used to feel that I was out on a river being carried away by the stream without being able to control it. Even if I wanted to go ashore I couldn't control it; I was carried away both from pleasant and unpleasant things. But today I feel like the river. I feel like I'm the river. I feel that I'm part of the flow that contains both the pleasant and the unpleasant things.

In contrast to her earlier experience of being a powerless object being thrown back and forth in the "river of life," Eva now perceives herself as a part of the flow of life itself. The boundary between herself as an object and the universal life has been transcended. Eva came back to this type of change several times during the interview. Now, she said, she feels that she "participates in a wider circle, in humanity."

Her perception of time has also changed. Eva now sees time as circular, rather than linear. She realizes now that she, in fact, has always lived in a circular time frame without understanding it. According to Eva, this is particularly true of women:

I mean, she gives birth after 9 months, she has her monthly periods, she hangs out her wardrobe in the spring and brings it in in the fall and so on. There are a lot of examples of circularity in women's lives.

Eva's circular time also implies that "one always lives with the past and the future" as she puts it. One lives in different times simultaneously. In other words, the boundary that we normally draw between past, present, and future has been transcended by Eva. She also has strong links with her ancestors, "because I [literally] live very much in the time of my ancestors' generations, too." About her feelings of kinship with earlier generations she said, "That's immortality. The genetic chain that coils." In this coiling genetic chain, Eva sees a form of eternal life. It is only natural that she does not fear death. "No, it's quite a natural part of life."

In her formulation of "immortality in the coiling genetic chain," Eva in a way combines science and faith (or mysticism), a unification of scientific genetics and the immortality of mysticism and faith. The boundary between science and mysticism is transcended. Eva pointed out that she is not at all religious. Nevertheless, she has come to accept science and faith as equal: "Some people stick with a natural science theory, and other people stick with a religious theory. One theory is just as good as the other. Some things are unanswered."

With this complete change in her attitude toward life, Eva has also noticed that the sources of joy in life have changed:

Well, earlier it may have been things like a visit to the theater, a dinner, a trip. I wanted certain things to happen that I was a little excited about. [. . .] My best times [now are] when I sit on the kitchen porch and simply exist, the swallows flying above my head like arrows. Or a spring day like this when I can go to my nettle patch and pick nettles for soup.

It is not only the definitions of "the cosmic dimension" that have changed for Eva. Her perception of who she is and who she wants to be has also changed. She has discovered sides of herself that she is now trying to change:

[. . .] I wanted to keep things to myself. I wanted my inner space, my integrity. I used to think that integrity depended on keeping as much as possible secret, on not giving yourself away. Also in my relationship to my husband I thought I wanted something that was my own. I think that has changed a lot. Feeling that my integrity doesn't depend on that. It would have helped my marriage a lot if I'd realized that earlier.

Opening up her enclosed self to the outer world, Eva has achieved an ability to watch herself from the outside. Describing her change she said about her old self that "I couldn't see myself from the outside." Now watching her old self from the outside she can see a good deal of self-infatuation:

It was all narcissism. I remember as a girl, lying on the beach touching myself, touching and kissing my skin. Playing with a friend's hair. I mean, it was all narcissism.

This has changed a lot. I'm not the slightest bit worried about my belly or bad skin or the wrinkles in my face. It means nothing to me, nothing at all.

In this statement, Eva demonstrates not only her new insights into herself but also that she has transcended conventions about the body. She does not deny that her body is changing. It does not scare her. She has no need to separate body and mind in the way that many aging people do, in other words, to look at the aging body with disgust, claiming the unchangeability of the mind or the self. Separating body and mind has almost become the norm for the aging human being as well as for the gerontologist. In her book *The Ageless Self*, Kaufman (1986) has introduced this separation of body and mind as part of the normal aging process. The self does not age, only the body. In this perspective, then, Eva's aging is not normal. In her, changes occur in both body and mind. There is a self developing in an aging body. Eva not only accepts but also enjoys this development.

In relation to other people, Eva has also become a different person. She is more open to other people today. At the same time, she has become more restrictive in her choice of friends and company. She has abandoned the big circle of friends: "I think it's more fun to . . . I go to an older woman that I know, sit and talk to her. I get much more out of this than going to parties and being with a lot of people where you really don't talk so much with people."

Being with a lot of people used to involve a good deal of make believe and disguise that Eva has now abandoned: "I somehow walked around and played "The discreet charm of the bourgeoisie," and I did it well. [. . .] I adjusted a great deal to the roles people expected me to play. I have been a very well-behaved little middle-class girl, but I'm not anymore."

Having found the courage to be herself, Eva today dares to say and do things that she did not dare to earlier out of fear of breaking the rules and embarrassing herself. "I'm old enough and wise enough to dare to do dumb things," Eva said.

When asked if it has become easier with age to make wise decisions and give good advice to other people, however, Eva answered, "Well, it's easier to make both dumb and wise decisions, but there is one thing that I find easier today. That is to refrain from giving good advice."

For Eva, the previously clear difference between good and bad advice has been transcended. Eva thinks that deciding what is good and what is bad is not as easy as it used to be, particularly where other people are concerned.

Eva is happy and satisfied with her life today. She radiates satisfaction with life.

GRETA—WHO SEEMS TO BE STUCK IN HER DEVELOPMENT

A person who does not radiate any real satisfaction with life is Greta. Greta is a former school teacher, 72 years of age at the time of the interview. She grew up in a quiet and safe middle-class environment, but her mother died when she was only 13 years old. Greta has been a widow for many years and has two adult sons. She also had a daughter, but the girl died at 15 years of age. Her husband, who was very domineering, died when the children were in their first school years.

Thus, like Eva, Greta has gone through difficulties in her life, but she does not seem to have been able to turn them into something positive. The crises in her life have been compounded. Answering the open question about whether she may have changed her attitude toward life and herself, she told about how meaningless life became after she retired:

I thought that, as a senior citizen I would be active, have adventures, but this just hasn't happened. It's like my feet have been knocked out from under me. I'm surprised that I gave up that easy. I quickly feel into a life as a senior that is rather pointless for me. [. . .] I miss my work a lot. I miss the satisfaction of working.

Greta has not experienced any considerable changes in perspective when it comes to her perception of herself and the surrounding world. Rather, she seems to cling firmly to middle-age ideals and definitions of reality. She evaluates herself within these frames of reference and arrives at discouraging conclusions: "When I watch myself it's mostly disappointing. Now I'm rather disinterested, unfortunately. I feel that I've used up my supply of . . . , I'm afraid I have used up my supply of interest in other people and things like that."

As Greta told her story, it sounded as if she had given up. Her interests and perspectives had not changed much, they had just ceased.

About her relationships to other people, Greta said, "I've had an enormous social network but it's also . . . , I think I have [. . .] I'm not interested anymore. Disengaged and disinterested."

Perhaps the cause of her disinterest is that she is still stuck in the patterns of middle-age life. Measured in terms of middle-age performance ideals, Greta is not worth much, nor are other senior citizens. Greta got to the point when she said, "I'm not fond of seniors but, of course, I don't need to be." It is evident that Greta includes herself in the category of people that she does not like. Greta is not satisfied with her life.

The comparison between Eva and Greta might lead to the conclusion that Eva had succeeded in attaining, in the terminology of Erikson (1986), ego integrity in the face of despair, whereas Greta has not. There is more to it, however. Instead of just attaining a balance between ego integrity and despair, Eva transcends such opposites.

For example, Eva's whole perspective has changed from floating powerlessly in "the river of life" to being the river itself. She is not just balancing the possible despair of being even more powerless in old age, she transcends it. Eva has also transcended the conventional way of perceiving one's body. She has no need to separate body and mind. Again, this means more than just balancing or coping with an ageless self in an aging body. Instead, she transcends the duality of the two.

THE DIMENSIONS OF GEROTRANSCENDENCE

THE COSMIC DIMENSION

Time and Childhood

Earlier we saw that Eva had changed her definition of time. The change in the concept of time is one of the dimensions subsumed under the heading "the cosmic dimension." The interviewer introduced the time concept theme in the following way:

> Some people say that they have gradually come to a concept of time which is different from the one they had before. They say that, in early life and adulthood, they had a very clear idea of what is today and what belongs to yesterday, but that it has changed and they feel like they are able to be in two time periods at once. Their past may be present so strongly that they almost live in it, at the same time as they live in the present. Is this something that you recognize?

Only one third of the respondents answered "yes" to the specific question, but the majority offered reports on how childhood has come more alive in old age.

The fact that people, irrespective of any transcendence of time, begin to think more about childhood experiences and places is well illustrated by the 86-year-old woman who said "You go back to childhood almost daily. It comes without reflection. I talked to a good friend about this. [. . .] We both go back to the town where we grew up [in our thoughts]. [. . .] Childhood means much more than one thinks, I go back to it all the time."

A 79-year-old woman expressed a similar view, saying that it both pleases and scares her: "Now I'm almost 80 and now I dare to remember my childhood." She added, "The older you get, the more your remember of your childhood. There's a dangerous trap in this. I have heard about that all my life."

Thus, when she realized that recalling the experiences of childhood was beginning to mean a lot to her, she became frightened. She interpreted it as a negative sign of her own aging. She had not come up with this negative interpretation herself; she said, "I have heard about that all my life." Thus, the pleasure that this woman finds in recalling her childhood is offset by the negative interpretation of "returning to childhood" that she has internalized.

The Connection to Earlier Generations

The descriptions of transcendence of the time dimension and the importance of childhood in several cases drifted over to another theme, namely the relation to earlier generations of people. A 72-year-old man describes how the distance to the 17th century has decreased: "If we take the 17th century, it used to be (earlier, in my younger years) tremendously distant, but today I don't think that the 17th century is all that far away. It is somehow as if it has come nearer. And everything in history has come nearer."

A 65-year-old woman, during the conversation about time and childhood, told of an experience of kinship with earlier generations:

[. . .] I particularly remember one night, I looked out and saw the moon [. . .] suddenly I got the thought that it was the same moon and the same sun that the Greek philosophers describe, it was just as if . . . , you know, such a strange feeling that . . . , I can't explain . . . , a feeling of kinship . . . , yes, that's it.

We also recall that Eva perceived "the coiling genetic chain" as her immortality. In both cases, the feeling of kinship and affinity with earlier generations has been expressed in more general terms. In one case as a general kinship with previously living people, in the other case as a definition of immortality.

During the interview, the interviewer introduced the theme in a way that more directly related to the respondents' own ancestors:

Some people say that, during the course of life, they experience a change in how they feel in relation to their ancestors. It's a kind of increasing kinship with those who lived earlier, a feeling that you are a link in the chain of generations. Have you experienced this?

This theme provoked many reactions in the respondents. The most prominent were the many reports about the wakening interest in genealogy. Several respondents had begun to seek their roots in this tangible manner. When describing their feelings of increased kinship with earlier generations, respondents used expressions or metaphors showing that the kinship with ancestors has a very strong appeal. "It's the desire under the elms, you know," said a 65-year-old woman referring to an old classic. "Yes, yes, it is almost a religious feeling," said a 71-year-old man.

Life and Death

The theme concerning life and death was introduced in the following way:

> Some people experience changes during life in relation to the questions of life and death. Somebody who has feared death in his or her youth can get rid of the fear later in life. Others have always feared death, etc. How do you feel about this?

There were various reactions to this question, but a common denominator was that the respondents did not in general fear death. They might fear dying, that it will be extended and painful, but they do not fear being dead. Some have had this feeling all of their lives; others achieved it later in life.

A 58-year-old man formulated an attitude that was reflected in several interviews:

> [. . .] much of life may be preparation for dying. It is in the character of maturation. I think it comes completely by itself. I don't live in order to die, I want to live. But implicit in maturation is a greater and greater capacity for dying. Some kind of preparation. I think that eventually one dies quite naturally.

This attitude, and consequently a decreasing fear of death, had come gradually during life. A couple of respondents describe a more sudden disappearance of the fear of death in connection with "near death experiences." No matter how people have "come to terms" with death, our material indicates the great importance this seems to have for gerotranscendence and positive maturation in old age. None of the respondents who either feared death or avoided the question showed any signs of development towards gerotranscendence.

Mystery in Life

This theme, focusing on the acceptance of the mysteries of life, was introduced in the following way:

> Some people say that they have come to accept that there are things in life that cannot be explained with science or reason, things that must be left incomprehensible, part of the mystery of life. Do you recognize this?

Several respondents recognized this, and many pointed out that it had been a gradual change during life. An 85-year-old woman said, "I guess I have taken for granted [earlier] that science knows what it talks about. But now I have realized that there is an awful lot beyond the reach of human knowledge [and] especially senses, that we can't know anything about."

The same woman said that there may be "knowledge categories" that are quite different from those that we are used to.

A related thought was expressed by a 71-year-old man who thinks that what we can understand is limited by language. Language constrains us to a certain form of understanding, he says, and implies that transcending the barriers of language gives rise to new forms of understanding. He gives as examples music and painting, which may allow forms of understanding beyond those that can be expressed through language.

Transcendental Sources of Happiness

The respondent just quoted had discovered music as a "gateway" to new insights. Similar experiences were related by a 77-year-old man who kept them at a distance in front of the interviewer, however.

> [. . .] one is, of course, a little softer now than before in certain situations. Above all pretty music. The tears flow almost, well, my eyes get moist at least. There are other situations, too . . . , like drama and music. It wasn't like that before. But now it's a block that's breaking down. [. . .] you experience it as a sort of euphoria, feeling of happiness. It has come during the last few years.

Regarded superficially, it may seem as though the man has simply become more interested in music or has just become more sensitive. The real meaning of this new source of joy can go deeper, however. The respondent himself says that it is a block that is breaking down. The experience of music borders on something that has previously been sealed off. Now, however, this block is broken through— it is transcended.

When the interview touched on the joys of life and how these may have changed, there were many answers that can be seen as related to the previous example. The transcendent Eva and many others said that earlier it was the more spectacular events that gave joy in life but that now it is more a question of small and commonplace things. These are, as in the case of Eva, often events and experiences in nature.

Instead of assuming that such changes are adaptations to decreasing possibilities in life, one should ask whether the increasing interest in the small everyday experiences of nature does not have a deeper significance. A 58-year-old man describes what it may be about: "I see trees, buds, and I see it blossom, and I see how the leaves are coming—I see myself in the leaves."

The experience of nature evokes the feeling of being at one with the universe, which is called "at-one-ment" in the Eastern tradition. The increasing significance of these small everyday experiences of nature could therefore be interpreted as a way in which the barrier between the self and the universe is transcended.

Almost all respondents who have children and grandchildren stressed their importance. This well-known phenomenon, too, can be given an interpretation in terms of the concept of transcendence. Through children and grandchildren the time barrier between the present and the future, as well as the barrier between life and death, is transcended. "The coiling genetic chain" is present in the children and the grandchildren. This chain provides the opportunity to participate in life on earth in the future.

THE SELF

The theory of gerotranscendence assumes that the self is gradually changed and developed. In this regard, the theory contrasts sharply with theories that assume that the self, like the perception of the self, is constant and ageless. In our interviews, we have approached the question of the constancy or variability of the self and the perception of the self in aging using several conversation themes.

Self-Confrontation

The constancy of perception of the self is partly dependent on the degree to which we discover the hidden aspects of our personality, what Jung calls the shadow. This theme was introduced in the following way: "Some people say that, during the course of life, they have begun to discover sides of themselves that they hadn't known before, both positive and negative. Do you recognize any of this in yourself?"

Our respondents reported that they had discovered both positive and negative sides of themselves in their older years. An 85-year-old respondent discovered a literary talent. It can also be a question of previously unknown personal characteristics. One respondent discovered that she is actually a cheerful, lighthearted person; another respondent realized that she is more serious that she had once thought. Still another respondent said that what he had earlier considered positive carefulness in his personality was in fact an exaggerated pedantry.

The latter case is not about discovering new qualities in oneself but rather about redefining qualities that were already known. Another example of this redefinition of qualities is given by a 72-year-old man who used to think that his driving force was engagement and empathy but who now understands that it was pure performance anxiety that drove him.

The most common discovery or redefinition, however, is about relationships with other people. Respondents described egocentricity that they had been unaware of previously. The 69-year-old woman who earlier in life thought that she had an unselfish interest in her children has now discovered that it was really about something else: "I have been much too domineering. [. . .] I kind of forced myself on them in a way."

Along similar lines, another respondent said, "I talked very egotistically about how I was doing. It was me all the time. [. . .] I never listened to my children. Today I can listen."

Decrease in Self-Centeredness

In connection with the theme about self-confrontation, several respondents gave descriptions of how the perspective of the confined self had been transcended. In addition, this topic was introduced as a special theme using a somewhat different approach:

> Some people say that they have changed their view of themselves during life in such a way that they no longer see themselves as being as important as before. Is this something that you recognize?

Considering the indoctrination of the people of this generation with the theses of the Jante Law (first thesis: Don't think that you are important! (Sandemose, 1933)), it is not surprising that many reacted to this question by saying that they never felt important. The conflict between the egocentricity of early life and the self-denial of the Jante Law was also described. According to a 60-year-old woman, "Well, I guess I have always liked to be in the middle of things, I always talked a lot and expressed my opinion, but I never tried to be important."

The new insight during old age may, in the best case, be about realizing that one was not really as unimportant as the Jante Law described it and as one felt. A 62-year-old woman formulated this insight in the following way: "I always had low self-confidence. [. . .] always felt insufficient. It's only when looking back, in hindsight, that I can see that what I have achieved is not so bad."

Thus, for the people interviewed there has hardly been any inflated self-importance to transcend. Rather, it has been a question of struggling to establish a level of confidence that feels appropriate.

Self-Transcendence

The reactions to the self-confrontation theme illustrate, among other things, that people have come to see certain egotistical features in themselves and replaced them with a higher degree of altruism. This type of change—from egoism to altruism—has been called self-transcendence by Chinen (1989a). The wishes and needs of the self are transcended in favor of other people's needs and wishes.

In the interview this topic was introduced in the following way: If one thought in earlier life "I'll do this for myself," it has turned out later in life that one is more likely to do things for others. There has been a shift from doing things for oneself to doing things for others. Is this something that you recognize?"

Even if the respondents during the earlier part of the interview spontaneously related their previous egoism, this introduction usually generated another reaction. The transcendent Eva seems quite sincere when saying that she always gave the well-being of the family priority over her own wishes and needs. In fact, all women giving an opinion on this theme answered similarly. Among the male interviews there are descriptions that are closer to the type of change referred to in the theme. An 85-year-old man said,

> When I did things to improve myself [. . .] I did it for my own sake, because it gave me satisfaction, but also because it was to the benefit of the family. They were always in the picture. But I don't feel that way now. I must say that everything I do now is in order to help others.

Even if this man recognized the shift from egoism to altruism there is, also in this male report, a description of a lifelong altruism.

EGO-INTEGRITY

We tried to approach the eighth and last stage of development described in Erikson's (1950, 1985) psychological model of development using a theme introduced in the following way:

> Some older people say that they feel that their life has now become a whole—even if their earlier life may have been uneven and chaotic. They have the feeling that the pieces of life's puzzle have fallen into place and formed a coherent pattern. Is this something that you can recognize?

The stories told by our respondents were very similar to Erikson's description of the last and eighth stage of development. A 65-year-old woman said, "Earlier I thought that . . . , if it weren't like this, if I had had a little more money, then things may have been different. But now I think [. . .] this is my life after all, and it didn't turn out all that bad."

A 62-year-old man said that the feeling of wholeness and coherence in life, that has come lately, is not stable. When alone, he often experiences the ego-integrity that Erikson speaks about. Under the pressure that he sometimes experiences with other people, this feeling of wholeness disappears.

Many respondents told about the difficulty to achieve, or preserve, the experience of ego-integrity. In the case referred to above, tranquillity and solitude is a prerequisite for the appearance and, in the best case, consolidation of ego-integrity.

SOCIAL AND PERSONAL RELATIONSHIPS

A pilot assumption of the theory of gerotranscendence has been that what can be interpreted superficially as "social disengagement" can be understood as changes in point of view, shifts of emphasis, and redefinitions of the meaning of social relations. Guided by these assumptions, we have included the following themes in our interviews.

The Importance of Social Contacts During Different Phases of Life

Given the assumption that the nature and importance of social contacts can change character during the course of life, the following theme was introduced: "Some people say that their interest in other people changes character during the course of life. One becomes more selective and prefers deeper relationships with a few people rather than more superficial relationships with many people. Is this something that you recognize?"

Some respondents said that they had not changed in this regard, but an even greater number of respondents said that they had. "Those superficial things that were fun when I was younger are not fun in the same way anymore," said a 79-year-old woman. The changed need for glamorous social company is well illustrated by the following statement by an 86-year-old woman:

> I used to dance at the spring ball, I enjoyed it enormously. No, it's a tremendous difference. Now, a few friends are quite enough, that's for sure. So [now] I have a much greater need for solitude. It's striking. It's extremely sufficient to meet and . . . , just a few people, to sit down and talk. [. . .] One doesn't need so many.

The increased need for positive solitude, in contrast to loneliness, is evident in the previous quote, as in the reports of many other respondents. A 77-year-old man said, "I appreciate solitude more now. You know, you become fed up with company faster. And you feel that a lot of talking is just nonsense. [. . .] You long for home and a good book instead, or to put on a record."

It is clear in these and other interviews that we are not dealing with a kind of passive withdrawal, as a young observer might easily think. It is rather about changes in the importance of social relationships. We shed the company and activities that lack content; we become more selective, preferring literature or music, or a few friends. This is not because of a lack of possibilities but because of choice.

Sometimes, a professional life forces people into social patterns that they never asked for and that they can easily give up. An 85-year-old man showed his relief through a symbolic act: "As long as I was working I had to go to different things. Then I had both tails and a tuxedo. Tails were required at some dinners, at others a tuxedo. The day I retired I got rid of both the tails and the tuxedo."

This quote is not about a redefinition of the importance of social contacts. The man had always disliked the big parties, but only after his retirement could he reconcile interest and behavior.

Social Masks

An insight that increases with maturation is assumed to be that certain social interactions are merely role playing, where the role does not necessarily fit the actor very well. This theme was introduced in the following way: "Some people say that they have become more and more conscious about the fact that interaction with other people is a masquerade, role playing. Some have gotten the inclination to throw off their mask or role. Is this something that you recognize?"

The transcendent Eva said that she was good at playing "the discreet charm of the bourgeoisie" but that she had now changed behavior. She claimed explicitly that it is a question of maturation. Another 60-year-old woman said, "I don't think that older people need to wear masks. It's just so clear that everyone is allowed to be himself. I don't have anyone to answer to, it doesn't matter if they think I'm strange. [. . .] I think that's a great relief, you know."

Many respondents mentioned that the new capacity to "be one's self" is related to an increased self-confidence. Earlier, there was a tendency to fear not being accepted and to hide behind the kind of role offered by, for instance, work or motherhood. "It feels like I don't need to take on any role because I'm confident in myself," said a 69-year-old woman.

Some people who tell about the increasing inclination to "be one's self" still stress the necessity of playing roles in various situations. "Out in society, of course, we play our roles and wear our masks," said the transcendent Eva. Several respondents had similar thoughts. Roles are necessary for life to function and can be played easily, even when they are not genuine. Those respondents had discovered and accepted the difference between the self and necessary roles.

Emancipated Innocence

A frequent theme in many of the open theme reports was an almost roguish delight in breaking away from the role expectations that were earlier seen as compelling. A 68-year-old woman related, "Now I don't care a bit about what people think. [. . .] I dare go to out biking or walking in [X-town] wearing torn stockings. I couldn't do that before. [. . .] Sometimes I think, but I really can't do this, you know . . . but I do it anyway."

The delight in doing things that one did not earlier dare to do falls most closely into the theme that we, following Chinen (1989a), have called "emancipated innocence." It refers to a capacity to break away from certain social conventions. A new kind of innocence and spontaneity is added to adult judgment and rationality. This allows important feelings and questions to be expressed regardless of the barriers of social conventions.

A special quality of this new attitude seems to be that people can admit that they do not know about something without feeling embarrassed. Not only is it a question of not caring about making a fool of oneself, but it also involves the recognition that an admission of ignorance is far from foolish. A 60-year-old man said,

> Previously I had to read the newspaper in order to keep up with what was going on, in order to have something . . . well, people should not be able to attack me because I didn't know this or that. Today I read the newspaper only when I feel like it. [. . .] I no longer have the need to pretend to know more than I do.

This change is connected with other, parallel changes. A 72-year-old man associated with his new capacity of emancipated innocence with his decreasing interest in his own prestige: "Since I don't care about prestige anymore I don't feel it's such a big deal to make a fool of myself once in a while . . . , I used to take that very seriously, if I said something stupid at a meeting or something like that."

Summarizing the messages from our respondents, the increased capacity for emancipated innocence was associated with (1) practice and experience, (2) personal maturity, (3) a redefinition of what constitutes foolish behavior, and (4) less need for prestige coupled with a greater degree of self-confidence.

Attitude Toward Material Assets

In both spiritual and worldly contexts, owning property is described as an obstacle to spiritual or political growth and freedom. Religions describe asceticism as one of the paths to insight and wisdom. Similar advice is given by political revolutionary movements. In a discussion of power and dependence, Blau (1964) argues that revolutionary ideologies frequently include an ambition to reduce materialistic needs, in this way decreasing the power of an adversary offering materialistic goods and keeping the revolutionary spirit alive.

The common denominator of these attitudes is that focusing on material assets has a stagnating, pacifying, and petrifying function. Less focus on material assets, on the other hand, is said to promote both spiritual and revolutionary growth. This thought is also found in some of the folk tales analyzed by Chinen (1989b). The path to wisdom is easier when material needs are transcended.

Quite in line with the theoretical point of departure, a 72-year-old man spontaneously described how his not insignificant fortune restricts him:

> It's tiresome to own. [. . .] one becomes locked up, one isn't free when one owns [. . .] Many say the opposite, but that's wrong. The more you own, the more you have to take care of, to manage, to watch out for. Now I have as much as I'm interested in. I have put up a limit at SEK 500,000 [approximately $75,000]. I don't want more. I was on my way up but I said no and went down.

This man has in no way turned his back on material possessions, but he has realized that owning things limits his freedom and has therefore set a limit. A 57-year-old woman expressed an almost identical view, telling how she has come to experience her art collecting of 20 years as a burden. She argues that the later part of the journey through life should be made with "lighter luggage," having enough for a modern definition of the necessities of life but not more. One should eat and drink well but not stockpile money, said a 79-year-old woman. We might call it a kind of modern asceticism.

The insight expressed in the previous statements is that an economic buffer is good to have but that the volatility of material assets makes saving beyond that meaningless. Many show a tendency to try to reduce the number of "things" they own. "I'm an expert in getting rid of things," said an 80-year-old woman.

Everyday Wisdom

If is often thought that practical, everyday wisdom or common sense increases with age. This was the point of departure when the following theme was introduced: "Some people think that it has become easier and easier to make wise decisions and help others to make decisions. What is your experience of this?"

A number of respondents answered in a way that makes an assumption in our question explicit, namely that it is possible to distinguish between wise and unwise decisions. The respondents often reached the conclusion that it has become more difficult to identify the boundary between wise and unwise.

Given the experience that the boundaries between right and wrong, wise and unwise are transcended, the consequence for everyday wisdom is to refrain from giving advice or helping others to make decisions. The transcendent Eva said that what she had learned above all was to refrain from giving good advice. In a similar vein, an 80-year-old woman said:

> I guess I used to think that I always made good decisions and gave good advice, too. I have been in a situation where I have had to give a lot of advice. [. . .] I had no problems with it. How is it now? I guess I must say that I avoid giving advice. I suppose I have learned that what I think is wise for me can be very unwise for others.

Another way of expressing this new approach is in terms of an increased broadmindedness, tolerance, and humility in response to other people's behavior. Tolerance and acceptance of other people's views have increased. A 78-year-old man said, "I guess I used to have strong views of everything, but I don't today. I understand that it's not . . . , it is not so simple, it depends."

In the case of an 88-year-old woman, broad-mindedness had gone so far that she, with a bit of ironic distance to herself, said that "In the end, I don't see any criminals either."

In summary, in these reports everyday wisdom is expressed by avoiding both giving good advice and helping people make decisions. The origin of this form of everyday wisdom is the transcendence of the boundary between right and wrong accompanied by an increased broad-mindedness and tolerance.

OBSTACLES AND SHORTCUTS ON THE PATH TO GEROTRANSCENDENCE

Since, according to the theory, the development toward gerotranscendence can be obstructed as well as facilitated, it is reasonable to assume various catalysts and obstacles would be described in the interviews. This was also the case. These catalysts and obstacles are described in the following.

MODERN ASCETICISM

One obstacle was identified in the preceding thematic survey: unnecessary material assets. Several respondents said spontaneously that owning too much could be burdensome and binding. Others, elaborating on the same theme, recommended that the later part of the journey through life should be made with "light luggage." In addition, there were descriptions of how this has been achieved by giving away a good deal of property and adopting a simpler life. A 60-year-old woman who did just that said,

I want to own as little property as I can. I have simple china, simple knives and spoons. I want it that way. I don't want it the way it used to be. It's great fun if the kids can use it. [. . .] Some of it is packed up, I don't want to unpack it. I think living simply is nice but I wish I was living out in the country.

This comment reflects a longing not only for simplicity, what we call "modern asceticism," but also for the country life. The interview revealed that the attraction was the refreshing ascetic solitude near nature. This could be a side effect of the current "back to nature" trend, but we could just as well refer to parallels from other time periods and other cultures.

In the Hindu religion, since the ancient Veda culture more than 3000 years ago, there are ideas about how to live in order to achieve purification of the soul and eventual attainment of Nirvana. Tilak (1989) describes how, during the Dharma Sastra period (200 B.C.–200 A.D.), life is explicitly organized into four phases, each with different content and meaning. These phases are (1) the student, (2) the housekeeper, (3) the hermit, and (4) the wanderer. Characteristic of the latter two periods is the giving up of material goods. During the hermit phase, the old man, possibly accompanied by his wife, is expected to give up his house and lands, join other hermits in the woods, and lead a simple life. During the last phase, the wanderer or beggar phase, he has given up all earthly goods and wanders alone from village to village.

Tilak holds that the idea of these phases remains in the normative cultural heritage of Hindus in India. A modern version of the hermit phase, for example, might consist of an old man or woman periodically isolating himself or herself in a room to meditate. This is, thanks to the living cultural heritage, neither misunderstood nor opposed.

POSITIVE SOLITUDE

The modern asceticism just described also contains a prominent element of what we call positive solitude. The need for, and the pleasure of, contemplative solitude is evident in many of our interviews. There are at least two reasons for this. One reason is that solitude is needed in order to achieve and consolidate one's ego-integrity. The other reason is that one has become more selective in terms of activities and social interactions. The 77-year-old man who preferred to read a book or listen to a record expressed part of these two aspects at the same time. Although he experienced social interaction with certain other people as tiresome and meaningless, there was also a new need for the joy and stimulation offered by solitary "activities."

The need and search for a positive solitude is not the same as ultimately choosing loneliness over interaction with others. Rather, the need for positive solitude comes and goes. A 58-year-old woman said, "I need periods of solitude, then it feels good to work things out and maybe change my behavior. And I feel that those periods make me feel well and that I need them. Other people can't understand that perhaps."

This woman eventually touches on a question that is not unessential, namely other people's lack of understanding of the importance of positive solitude. The Swedish language lacks a cognate of the primarily positive English word "solitude." This may be a further reason why the positive need for solitude may be misinterpreted in terms of negative disengagement, depression, apathy, or resignation. Of course, this kind of loneliness exists, too. It is exemplified by Greta, who appears to have stopped in her development toward gerotranscendence. The point is that we probably misinterpret many people's need for a positive solitude.

LIFE CRISES

The theoretical discussion of the concept of transcendence emphasizes the possible role of life crises as catalysts. Life crises may contain the "kinetic energy" that makes the development towards gerotranscendence accelerate.

Our interviews contain several examples in which crises have contributed to an accelerated development toward gerotranscendence. An 80-year-old woman described how the death of a close friend a couple of years ago had changed her and helped her to develop:

> I guess I was a noli me tangere type. This means "don't touch me." [. . .] Now I think that I have come closer to people, I understand people better, I am more open to them, I notice that when I give of myself I get something back. So I have come closer to people than I used to. [. . .] This change was triggered when he died, 2 years ago. When I realized that one must give and not only take.

A 68-year-old man told us in a similar way about how his heart disease and operation opened him up to thoughts that he had not had before. A book that would not have interested him before became the gateway to a process of change:

> I think there is so much in these new things that I have learned that makes things fall into place. You just lose the fear of death, and then there is so much to learn, and there is a lot to be done there [. . .] so I'm in the middle of a process where I have a lot to learn.

The life crisis has changed the direction of life not only through the power of the crisis itself but also by preparing for new thoughts and impressions. In this way, crises can be said to have a double effect.

One way of understanding life crises in this context is that they consist of upheavals that challenge or question the foundations of one's concept of reality. The death of a close relative, for example, undermines ideas of immortality, the notion that "it won't happen to me," and the idea that it is never too late to change. In scientific terminology we would say that crises challenge, question, and undermine basic ontological assumptions, replacing them with new ontological assumptions.

BRIDGES AND LANDINGS

Our respondents gave several examples of what could be called mediating links, bridges to different aspects of gerotranscendence. The transcendent Eva talked about how experiences of nature— swallows flying like arrows over her head, picking nettles for soup—give her life meaning. This can be understood both as part of her gerotranscendence and as a bridge to it. The development toward gerotranscendence is stimulated by small experiences of nature. Also, the 59-year-old man's ability to see himself in the leaves on the trees can be interpreted in the same way.

The transcendent quality of experiences of nature offers a new way of understanding the increased interest in nature and gardening expressed by some older people. Old people's interest in their gardens is often interpreted in other ways, seen as a sort of therapy or a way to fill up their otherwise idle lives.

Apart from experiences of nature, our interview material also contains descriptions of experiences of music and drama as parts of, or bridges to, gerotranscendence. In the section on sources of happiness, a 77-year-old man related how experiences of music had become more important and more emotional for him. This statement can be interpreted in several ways. The man himself said that it was a barrier that had been broken down. In our terminology, we would say that it was the barrier between music and emotion that had been transcended or that music helps in transcending a number of barriers. Music becomes a bridge to a transcendent experience of the whole. In such an interpretation, the increased emotional element stands out as something positive, as an indication that certain barriers have been demolished. Using other frames of reference, the same report could be interpreted as pathological. The increasing emotionality, the softening up, becomes a symptom of a disintegrating personality. The latter interpretation is the most common in the geropsychiatric literature.

If the experiences of nature and music are considered in parallel, however, certain similarities can be seen that clearly indicate their transcendental character. Both cases deal with experiences that appeal more to the emotions than to the intellect. The dimensions of experiences of both nature and music are relatively free. Their limits are set subjectively; they are not limited by predetermined categories. The relative freedom from boundaries, frames, and rules that characterize these experiences can thus become a bridge to new ways of defining existential categories.

DISCUSSION

Drawing on our interviews it must be made clear that the development toward gerotranscendence cannot be regarded as any uniform development that characterizes all aging individuals. We should rather talk about it as a developmental possibility, where the precise form of the gerotranscendence can differ from individual to individual. Also, there are several pathways to gerotranscendence. It may be that "the seed of gerotranscendence" is within us all but needs proper watering to grow. In today's society we probably lack much of the proper watering, which also means the proportion of individuals who reach high degrees of gerotranscendence is quite small.

Nevertheless, in our interviews, mainly based on individuals who may have come further than others, some rather distinct dimensions and aspects of gerotranscendence did arise during the analysis. This does not mean that every subject was characterized by all these aspects. Some of the aspects of gerotranscendence, summarized in Table 10.1, were recognized by most of the informants; some were recognized by just a few.

It should be noted that several of the developmental changes described by our interviewees could be given different interpretations. One set of interpretations originate in traditional gerontological theories; another set of interpretations is rooted in a different paradigm as offered by the theory of gerotranscendence. For example, the decreasing interest in participating in certain social and personal relationship could, from a traditional perspective, be regarded as a negative disengagement, interpreted as part of a social breakdown syndrome. At least among our informants, the meaning of this behavior must be interpreted quite differently, as part of a rather positive developmental change.

TABLE 10.1 Dimensions of Gerotranscendental Development

Cosmic dimension	Self	Social and personal relations
Time and childhood	Self-confrontation	Importance and definitions of social contacts during different phases of life
Earlier generations	Self-centeredness	Social masks
Life and death	Self-transcendence	Emancipated innocence
Mystery in life	Ego-integrity	Attitude toward material assets
Transcendental sources of happiness		Everyday wisdom

In the same vein, the preoccupation with childhood and the "emancipated innocence" could be regarded as a mental breakdown symptom, although our interviews suggest it should be interpreted as parts of a positive transcendence of time and social conventions.

Because our interviews, as well as earlier empirical results by Tornstam (1994), show that these and other aspects of gerotranscendence form individual coherent developmental patterns in which high degrees of life satisfaction and absence of depression and neurotic systems are also parts, the conclusions must be that the "traditional" interpretations have a limited scope. Sometimes the traditional interpretations of behavior such as those mentioned previously may be appropriate; sometimes they may be totally wrong.

Theoretically, gerotranscendence goes beyond related theories, such as Erikson's (1950, 1982) model of personal development. In both cases the process of aging is regarded as a developmental process that at very best, ends with a higher state of maturity—in Erikson's case ego-integrity, in my case gerotranscendence. In Erikson's theory, the ego-integration primarily refers to an integration of the elements in the life that has passed. The individual reaches a fundamental acceptance of the life lived, regardless of how good or bad it might seem from outside. In this way, the ego-integrity described by Erikson becomes more of a backward integration process within the same definition of the world as before. The process of gerotranscendence implies more of a forward or outward direction, including a redefinition of reality. After reading a description of the theory of gerotranscendence, Joan M. Erikson (personal communication, March 15, 1995), wife and coworker to Erik H. Erikson, writes,

> When I got 91 myself, I became aware of the inadequacy of the words "wisdom" and "integrity," feeling that they in no way represented what I was experiencing as an elder. [. . .] So boldly I revised the eighth Stage [. . .] including a Ninth and Tenth Stage, which even attempt to deal with "gerotranscendence."

When our informants tell about an increased broad-mindedness and a tendency to avoid distinguishing between right and wrong, Baltes (1993) would probably argue that this could be understood within the first of his three metacriteria of wisdom. Baltes' criteria are (1) relativism: the development away from ideological positions associated with dogmatism, rightness, and lack of tolerance; (2) life-span contextualism: The defense against the predominance of the present in the conduct and interpretation of life; and (3) management of uncertainty: The development away from the hegemony of determinism and rationality.

These last two criteria are close to aspects of my cosmic dimension of gerotranscendence. Although the aspects within my cosmic dimension of gerotranscendence go beyond our "normal" paradigmatic world, however, Baltes' criteria remain within it. When, for example, Baltes describes relativism as a metacriterion of wisdom, he is only describing a behavior or a mode of thinking, whereas the theory of gerotranscendence interprets this on a new paradigmatic level. The relativism is just as aspect of the general tendency to transcend boundaries and old forms of understanding reality.

ACKNOWLEDGMENTS

This work has been stimulated to a great extent by seminars within the social gerontological group at the Department of Sociology, Uppsala University. The social gerontological group comprises the author; Gunhild Hammarstrom, Ph.D., associate professor; Marianne Winqvist, B.A., certificated psychologist; Peter Oberg, M.SSc.; Fereshteh Ahmadi, Ph.D.; Sandra Torres, M.SSc. The work has been funded by The Swedish Council for Social Research and the Faculty of Social Science, Uppsala University.

REFERENCES

Achenbaum, W.A., & Orwoll, L. (1991). Becoming wise: A psycho-gerontological interpretation of the book of Job. *International Journal of Aging and Human Development, 32*(1), 21–39.

Baltes, P.B. (1993). The aging mind: Potential and limits. *Gerontologist, 33*, 580–594.

Blau, P.M. (1964). *Exchange and power in social life.* New York: John Wiley.

Chapman, M. (1988). Contextuality and directionality of cognitive development. *Human Development, 31*, 92–106.

Chinen, A.B. (1985). Fairy tales and transpersonal development in later life. *Journal of Transpersonal Psychology, 17*, 99–122.

Chinen, A.B. (1986). Elder tales revisited: Forms of transcendence in later life. *Journal of Transpersonal Psychology, 26*, 171–192.

Chinen, A. B. (1989a). From quantitative to qualitative reasoning: A developmental perspective. In L.E. Thomas (Ed.), *Research on adulthood and aging: The human science approach* (pp. 37–61). Albany, NY: State University of New York Press.

Chinen, A.B. (1989b). *In the ever after: Fairy tales and the second half of life.* Wilmette, IL: Chiron Publications.

Clark, M., & Anderson, B.G. (1967). *Culture and aging: An anthropological study of older Americans.* Springfield, IL: Charles C Thomas.

Cumming, E., Newell, D.S., Dean, L.R., & McCaffrey, I. (1960). Disengagement—a tentative theory of aging. *Sociometry, 3*, 23–35.

Cumming, E., & Henry, W.E. (1961). *Growing old: The processes of disengagement*. New York: Basic Books.

Erikson, E.H. (1950). *Childhood and society*. New York: Norton.

Erikson, E.H. (1982). *The life cycle completed: A review*. New York: Norton.

Erikson, E.H. (1986). *Vital involvement in old age*. New York: Norton.

Grotjahn, M. (1982). The day I got old. *Psychiatric Clinics of North America, 5*, 233–234.

Gutmann, D. (1976). Alternatives to disengagement: The old men of the Highland Druze. In J.F. Gubrium (Ed.), *Time, roles and self in old age* (pp. 88–108). New York: Human Sciences Press.

Havens, B.J. (1968). An investigation of activity patterns and adjustment in an aging population. *Gerontologist, 8*, 201–206.

Holliday, S.G., & Chandler, M.J. (1986). *Wisdom: Explorations in adult competence: Contributions to human development, Vol. 17* (J.A. Meecham, Series Editor). Basil: Karger.

Jung, C.G. (1930). Die Lebenswende, In *Lecture, Ges. Werke 8*, Olten: Walter-Verlaq, 1982.

Kaufman, S.R. (1986). *The ageless self: Sources of meaning in late life*, Madison: University of Wisconsin Press.

Kramer, D.A., & Woodruff, D.S. (1986). Relativistic and dialectical thought in three adult age-groups. *Human Development, 29*, 280–290.

Neugarten, B., et al. (1964). *Personality in middle and late life*. New York: Atherton Press.

Peck, R. (1968). Psychological developments in the second half of life. In B.L. Neugarten (Ed.), *Middle age and aging: A reader in social psychology*. Chicago: The University of Chicago Press.

Rosenmayr, L. (1987). Sociological dimensions of gerontology. In M. Bergner (Ed.), *Psychogeriatrics: An international handbook*. New York: Springer Publishing Company.

Rosow, I. (1967). *Social integration of the aged*. New York: Free Press.

Sandemose, A. (1933). *En flykning krysser sitt spor fortelling om en morders barndom*. Oslo: Tiden Norsk Forlag.

Storr, A. (1988). *Solitude*. Glasgow: William Collins Sons.

Tilak, S. (1989). *Religion and aging in the Indian tradition*. Albany, NY: State University of New York Press.

Tornstam, L. (1989). Gero-transcendence; a meta-theoretical reformulation of the disengagement theory. *Aging: Clinical and Experimental Research* (Milano), *1*(1), 55–63.

Tornstam, L. (1994). Gerotranscendence—a theoretical and empirical exploration. In L.E. Thomas & S.A. Eisenhandler (Eds.), *Aging and the religious dimension*. Westport, CT: Auburn.

Afterword

Robert C. Kastenbaum

Some sleep, more fret away their lives.
—Irving Howe

*One of the strange new characteristics of our time is that it is logical to talk about
religion between the covers of a scientific book. In fact, we can't avoid it . . .*
—Ernest Becker

Irving Howe and Ernest Becker are no longer with us, but both the critic and
the philosopher seem to have commented astutely on the mission of this book.
Gerontologists need not labor to justify the study of *Religion, Belief, and Spirituality in Late Life*. Where does it say that we can learn all that we need to know
about long-lived people through the analysis of urinary excretions, physician visits, or short-term memory? Who would like to tell the public that we can contribute
most richly to the study of human aging by leaving out the person? Or by leaving
out what it is at the core of the person—the desires, values, and beliefs that have
guided and perhaps misguided a long life journey?

Scientific theories are stories. Elder narratives are theories. The language, technique, and rules differ, of course, but all are symbolic constructions that attempt
to give shape and meaning to what we observe and experience. Newton, Einstein,
and Hawkins are among the great storytellers. Basha (chapter 5), Lucinda and
Peter (chapter 9), and John Casteel (chapter 8) are provocative theorists. How
churlish it would be to allow the scientists their often-blemished stories and scorn
theories bred in the merciless laboratory of life!

Howe's aphorism has its roots in both his personal observations and his command of literature and history. At the least it reminds us why the spirituality issue
refuses to be evaded: We all know people who have been sleeping or fretting away
their lives, and, from time to time, we may suspect that at least one of them has
our own name. Perhaps, however, Howe's observation goes beyond the shock of
recognition. Perhaps it leads us directly to those most familiar, most clichéd, and

203

yet most unsettling questions: "So, why are we here? Why is anybody here? And what should we be making of our lives between now and whatever or whenever?" Are we here to slumber from one television season to the next? Are we here to play Trivial Pursuit to the max, stirring up the dust of petty irks and complaints every step of the way? How can we be expected to appreciate the gift of a long life if we have slumbered and fretted our way through our earlier years?

The elders whose voices resound throughout this book are mostly realists. They would have invented the decremental theory of aging had it not already existed. They would have wondered why it took mathematicians and physicists so long to come up with the second law of thermodynamics. For good measure, they might have been amused that linguists and social critics would devote their efforts to deconstruction, so puny an endeavor when compared with nature's own mighty program of creation and destruction. That time had done a number on them was beyond doubt.

Not everybody responds to the given in the same way, however. We might conceive ourselves either as innocent victims or as criminal offenders who are being punished by time. We might roll ourselves into fetal balls and view fading reruns in our mental theaters. We might deaden our senses with alcohol and close the shutters of our minds. We might take that number thing into our own hands and shoot or ingest ourselves into the next set of suicide statistics. In a desperate burst of energy, we might become a caricature of our own youth, a fluttering rewind in which neither the focus nor the color are true.

Or—or what?

Several possible answers to the "or what" are sketched by the contributors to this book as well as the elder source people who are represented. On these closing pages it might not be a bad idea to review a few of the alternative visions or theories that offer more positive conceptions of the life of the spirit in aging bodies. This is but one reader's selection; my apologies if I have inadvertently omitted some of your favorites.

THEORIES OF INSPIRITED AGING

Although differing sometimes to the point of contradiction, each of these theories of inspirited aging offers an alternative to bleak despair or regressive narcissism.

CHERISH THIS SMALL MOMENT

We are given King Solomon as a classic exemplar here. In chapter 1, Bertman emphasizes the "all is vanity" theme expressed in Ecclesiastes. It is futile to labor for power or seek for pleasure, even more so to lay up stores of material goods. Even a king could not command time nor convert the shifting sands into permanent monuments. Bertman notes both earlier and later expressions of the vanity theme that, indeed, was pervasive in the cradle lands of our major Western religions. This theme certainly has made itself at home in our own time as well. We must be a grossly materialistic society because we keep saying so ourselves. We are also highly competitive, and not just for survival and other functionalistic purposes. Playing king or queen of the hill occupies much of our energies, even though most of the players realize that being Number One is as transient as yesterday's sports pages.

There are already many drop-outs from the materialistic or ambitious track. Some who have striven and competed for our society's off-the-shelf prizes have opted to smell the coffee or the roses and cherish the small moments. Should we, then, be persuaded by that byword for wisdom, King Solomon? Should we campaign for small pleasures of the moment and against vanity and ambition? Bertman warns us: "If, in late life, we measure the meaning of our years only by the big things we have accomplished, we risk major disappointment . . . pursuing grand designs can be an exercise in futility: they lead us on, only to vanish before our eyes." Instead, we should be "fully present in each moment of time . . . spiritually responsive to the presence of others and to the world around us. . . ."

This vision of inspirited aging leaves open the question of whether we must cultivate a receptive or appreciative type of self throughout the life course or whether we can switch on a kind of spiritual instinct in later life, as Melvin Miller has suggested in his interpretation of Jung's thoughts on midlife transition. One is a little surprised to find that none of the contributors to this book has called on the findings and insights of David Gutmann (1987), whose discussion of mastery styles has much to offer in this regard. This question is consequential because the answer can point either to developing a late-life kind of mastery style from youth onward in order to get it right or to continuing to support aggressive and competitive goal-oriented behavior until the gray hairs start to sprout. Gutmann (1987) also has much to add about possible gender differences in moving from youth to age. Solomon exemplifies passage from active to passive mastery with a dollop of magical mastery for flavoring. By contrast, women who have been nurturant, cooperative, and appreciative throughout most of their lives might only have to keep doing what they've been doing. Both Jung's ideas and Gutmann's data, however, suggest that life may play still another trick on women. A midlife switch to a more direct, assertive, and aggressive mastery style may compensate for their earlier accommodations to male-dominated society, but it may also lead them into a more goal-oriented, or even an explosive old age. One common path to sainthood among men has been to carry on as philandering and power-hungry brutes until weary of that strenuous life and then to transform themselves into a paragon of virtue. Women are usually sainted for qualities shown earlier in their lives. Contributors to this book have made an effort to redress the gender imbalance in studies of wisdom and spirituality, but we are still awaiting systematic examinations of gendered paths to a wise old age with attention to data from the sociobehavioral sciences as well as insights from the humanities.

There are other reasons to hesitate before equating wisdom with immersion in the moment:

- The moment can represent escape from responsibility to indulgence. Many hoist a jug or insert a needle to free themselves from reflection, choice, and obligation. Solomon commandeered young women to embellish his moments without apparent regard for their individual lives. One can hide within the passing moment as deftly as one can bury oneself in ambitions for the future.
- Few would be free to cherish the moment if many did not heed the past and prepare for the future. It is a prime human characteristic to harvest our past experiences for guidance through the present into the future. How can it be the part of wisdom to inhibit our ability to scan the future for both threat and opportunity? How can it be the part of wisdom to flicker in the flame of the moment and forget the lessons of the past?
- Appreciation of the moment often is enhanced and made more treasurable by recognition of its transience. We are breathless in a unique moment because we know, along with Blake, that we cannot "bend to ourselves a joy" or we will "the winged thing destroy."
- The vanity that Solomon decries can, disguised, inhabit the moment. He still seeks his satisfaction, although the "grand design" has contracted to a small space of time. There is an alternative view that was also current in the now-ancient cradle lands of our religions: use our strength and time now to plant a fruiting shade tree for future generations.

In short, "cherish the moment" is excellent advice within the context of a grim pursuit of prizes that we might be better off without. We might well expect a long-lived person to have developed some other guiding principles and purposes, especially if we are to deem that person wise. We might also value the moment as a refreshing temporary getaway from the grind and stress of life. The moment is a great place to visit. I doubt, however, that we can live in and for the moment and call ourselves wise while so many around us, and so many yet to come, face perils we might reduce and need guidance we might provide.

Do Not Go Gently Into That Good Night

One might part company from Solomon and take up the advice a son offered to his dying father: "Rage, rage against the dying of the light." This battle cry has found a large and receptive audience and is in all likelihood the most quoted poem from one of our century's most quoted poets, Dylan Thomas. Anger and resistance are not the most "politically correct" attitudes to take toward aging and death. We have often been tutored to "grow old gracefully" and labor toward the stage of accepting death. There is something within many of us, though, that stirs in resistance.

Thomas (chapter 5) gives us striking examples from one of his recent studies as well as from the gallery of elders earlier presented by Myerhoff (1978). Some of the elderly Jewish immigrants in both samples are described as insistent narrators, inflicting their life stories on all around them. Full of feeling and full of themselves, they were more likely to shout each other down than to listen. Few directed prayers to God, but many kept a direct or implicit dialogue going. It almost seemed as though without God they would not have anybody worth arguing with.

Is there anything remotely approaching wisdom and inspirited aging here? Thomas observes that "the danger of self-centeredness and narcissism . . . is a besetting temptation of old age." This is a temptation that seems to have been greeted with open arms by the elders whose actions and narratives were highlighted by Myerhoff and Thomas.

And yet—And yet we can ourselves feel the urgency and vigor with which these elders attempted to wrest meaning from chaos and value from loss. These people may be fretting, but they are definitely not sleeping away their lives. Our assumptions about wisdom perhaps need to be re-examined. Often we envision a serene state of mind. Not with these anxious, restless, and noisy souls! Moreover, we tend to focus on the finished product, the sagacious perspective, the glowing pearls of wisdom. By contrast, here we encounter the hard-shelled creatures with irritating sand in their craws rather than the luminous jewels. But if we value wisdom, should we not also value those who travel the bumpy, winding, and treacherous road that so often must be traveled? Despite (or because of) their long lives, these immigrant men and women were not themselves finished products. They search. They question. They affirm. They suffer. They persist. If Descartes had the right accent for it, he might have said, "I *kvetch*, therefore I am."

Using a mix of quantitative and qualitative research I once looked into the origins and functions of the saints, the sages, and the sons of bitches (Kastenbaum, 1990; 1994). Two of the observations are relevant here. First, it was noted that society treasures saints and sages but applies a rigorous quota system: We don't want too many of these virtuous people extant at the same time, and perhaps for good reason. Second, it was noted that there is often a strong, if grudging, admiration for those mean and nasty elders who insist on having things their way and on their terms; this attitude seems to speak to a something inside us. (The offensive term, "son of a bitch" is used advisedly with reference to the virile spawn of the once powerful female deities.) It would be a stretch to speak of these people as exemplars of wisdom, but they certainly are inspirited. Who says that the spirit must reveal itself only in ways that are pleasing to the neighbors? Who says that the spirit must be housebroken? For that matter, who says that the devotion to struggle is not itself a stroke of wisdom?

Thomas recognizes a kind of creativity at work among his and Myerhoff's respondents, bringing to bear Benedict Anderson's concept of imagined communities. For example, Basha reports that "Whenever I sit down, I eat with God, my mother, and all the Jews who are doing the same things even if I can't see them." Thomas also is impressed, as I am, by David, who has discarded all the Jewishness he can strip away because of the way God (through the hands of the Nazis) treated his family. "And God killed them alive. Buried them alive. They were covered with ground. Alive." Nevertheless, David has arrived at the equally firm belief that "With God, without God, with kosher, without kosher, a Jew is a Jew." A painful struggle it is, and often painful to observe, but a questing and at times creative process as well. Perhaps, then, the wisdom for at least some of us is to go on going on, asserting, questioning, suffering, and occasionally triumphing every step of the way.

Perhaps we also need to remember how Dylan Thomas dealt with aging and mortality in his own life. Like many other creative artists, Thomas often reflected on death. It would not be too much to say that he was haunted not only by death but also by the inexorable flow of time that washes away youth and seems to leave one stranded in age. Envisioning his father's deathbed scene, he could also envision his own. Father had to set a good example for him, a Beethovian raising of the fist against the hammering of fate's thunder. Thomas could not allow himself to age nor to further resist the forces arrayed against him (knowing full well that these were much of his own doing), however. The brilliant poet and playwright could not even go gentle into that good night; he had to drink himself out of his mind and then out of his body. The deliberative death-by-whiskey suicide of Dylan Thomas might raise the caution flag for the rest of us. Tilting against the windmills of fate has a whiff of heroism but may not take us all the way from a valiantly asserted life through the ordeals of age to a labored exit. Perhaps we should not be too vehement in our insistence that one must rage, rage against the dying of the light. This expectation could place one more burden and stress on vulnerable people. It could also say something about our own persistent fear of the dark.

GEROTRANSCENDENCE: UP, UP, AND AWAY

The more we do something, the more we keep doing it. Same routines, same friends, same conversations, same old. The strength acquired by habits has been recognized through the centuries even before it was subjected to measurement and experiment in more recent times. Other things being equal, the longer we live, the more opportunity we have to convert ourselves into habit habitats. It is also recognized that people differ in their inclination toward stasis, however. There is some reason to believe that hyperhabituation (the tendency to dismiss new information and learning opportunities as though merely a repetition of what we already know) is more a function of person and circumstances than chronological age (Kastenbaum, 1980). Adele at 40 might be mostly repeating herself. Amy at 80 might still be open and adventuring.

Enter the concept of gerotranscendence. The makings of this concept have been around for some time. Tornstam (chapter 10) is among those who have been building a foundation for gerotranscendance as an approach to understanding spirituality in late-life development. He tells us right off that "the very process of living into old age is characterized by a general potential toward gerotranscendence . . . a shift in metaperspective from a materialistic and pragmatic view of the world to a more cosmic and transcendent one, normally accompanied by an increase in life satisfaction." Although it has some kinship with Erikson's (1982) ego-integrity and Cumming and Henry's (1961) disengagement theory, gerotranscendence stands apart for its emphasis on a shift in metaperspective.

This formulation offers a refreshing boldness. It takes a position. Gerotranscendence is a late-developing fruit of time, maturation, and experience. I would think we could regard this time as either aging per se or extended development. In either case, we would see the positive outcome of gerotranscendance as dependent on many years of experience and personal growth. The power of this idea—if I have it right—is that this shift in cosmic perspective does not happen despite but because of aging. It is therefore a claim that is worth systematic investigation. There are two reasonable corollaries: Not everybody will achieve gerotranscendence, and not all who do will come by the same path. In this regard, gerotranscendence has much in common with religious and philosophical beliefs that speak of the evolution of spirit. The Buddhist, for example, believes in the reality of the eighth stage of death—the clear light—but also cautions that not everybody will get that far.

Still and all, I'm not convinced—yet. What's my problem?

First, I would like to see more detail and clarity in the description of gerotranscendent people. Perhaps this is just my problem, but I have not yet seen the core phenomena presented in a vivid, detailed and compelling way. Delineating possible dimensions of gerotranscendence can be useful, but I think we need to see thick descriptions of individuals within their also well-described interpersonal and sociocultural contexts. The available examples of gerotranscendence could be taken as examples of more familiar and less exotic phenomena. There could also be more attention to alternative explanations. Some of the examples given in this volume and elsewhere invite interpretations such as unveiling or disinhibition as distinguished from gerotranscendence.

The distinction made from disengagement theory is not entirely persuasive. It is not just that Greta speaks of herself as "disengaged and disinterested" but that disengagement theory has proposed its own paradigm shift for the aging individual's view of life. It is possible that some shifts that can be regarded as gerotranscendence would also meet the criteria for disengagement. Cumming and Henry's original formulations were by no means superficial, even if many studies and applications of their work have but skimmed the surface. Similarly, Eva's reclamation of childhood might be as much at home with Butler's life review as with gerotranscendence. Furthermore, the gerotranscendence rhetoric at this time does not seem to leave room for contributions from the clinical perspective (e.g., how does depression figure in?). I also wonder if researchers have not been trying a little too hard to extract gerotranscendence from change-oriented interviews with select populations. Perhaps gerotranscendence is so rare and vulnerable a phenomenon that it must be sought in this manner. One would hope, however, that there is enough robustness in this concept to reveal itself without having to be primed.

Why am I being so hard on gerotranscendence? Probably because it is an attractive idea that I would like to accept. In addition to the problems already noted, however, I cannot set aside my experiences with people who have simply hopped, skipped, and jumped to a transcendent view without having taken the trouble to think it through. Gerotranscendence could become a popular quick fix for what ails us about growing old, although this would be far from the intentions of the researchers who are presently developing the concept. I hope to see gerotranscendence come of age, but I do think we have a way to go.

HOW ABOUT SOME MORE THEORIES?

Living in and for the moment, asserting oneself against loss and fate, and transcending the previous limits of self in society are among the salient themes that have emerged in this book. Here is a brief visit to several other approaches that, although mentioned in passing, did not come to the fore. All can claim some degree of familiarity, and all represent attempts to affirm or create meaning in the later adult years.

PERPETUATED YOUTH

This looks to be the simplest solution, if only it would work. We would avoid much of the anxiety and doubt that comes with aging if we managed to stay young. Persuade mirror, mirror on the wall to show us that we are still younger than springtime. Persuade society that we have not lost a step and therefore should remain in the starting line-up. Persuade ourselves (for some the easiest, for others the hardest, job).

To put it in a nutshell, and maybe that's where it belongs, we don't have to become wise or become anything if we stay young.

Not much needs to be said to gerontologists about the gerontophobia we can see around us every day as well as in our studies. The urge to preserve youth or roll back age is itself among our most senior cultural traditions, demonstrated through myths, alchemy, and the latest cosmetic miracles. In examining the case for perpetuated youth (Kastenbaum, 1995), I could not help but notice how tempting it has been to put maturation and wisdom on hold. As with Oscar Wilde's Dorian Gray, for example, one avoids not only stigma and disability but also responsibility to others. I came up with 21 propositions about perpetuated youth. Two of these propositions appear particularly relevant here:

- Generational equity is not possible in a society of Dorians who decline to fulfill productive, reproductive, and other communal obligations (Kastenbaum, 1995, p. 195).
- Age is better suited to the integration of experiences and the evaluation of meanings than youth is (p.223).

So here is a counterwisdom kind of wisdom! Perhaps it is wise to avoid situations that awaken us to responsibility and choice. Perhaps it is wise not to think too much or too often. Perhaps we only vex ourselves and others when we break through the shell of youth and stand, blinking and confused, in a new realm fraught with changes, complexities, and decisions. Here is a brash way of putting it: "Meaning and spirituality are the drugs of age, the consolation prizes—I don't need them; I'm young!"

TIME'S UP—TIME TO GO

We seek meaning and renewal of spirit as we move deeper into age. This observation is offered in various ways by many of the contributors to this book. The journey. The quest.

There is a radical alternative, however, and this perhaps can also be considered a journey, a quest. Why labor to find meaning and value within the ruins of a life? Instead, why not take the hint? If life seems increasingly empty and troubled, maybe that is the way it really is and the way it is really going to continue. Recruited to this alternative may be the judgment that one has had a long life with something of a completed shape. What happens from now on might be just the leftovers, more likely to detract from than to embellish the life already accomplished. Furthermore, it may seem the part of wisdom to avoid both more suffering for oneself and more burden for others. The exit narrative could go something like this: "I'm wise enough to know when it's time to go. I'd like to think that I'm also tough enough to do what's right and at the right time. I know I'm making the best decision in getting out of my own way and opening a place for some young person."

This is not idle talk. The suicide rate among elderly White men is consistently at the top of the list. Society has often expressed the wish to have elders move aside, and health care decision makers have increasingly called for restricting the services available to older people. This view is contested by gerontologists and other age advocates but remains a potent force. If we require the approval of history, there is abundant testimony to the suicide choice by intelligent and responsible people when life circumstances have become unacceptable (e. g., Alvarez, 1972). As for the future, physician-assisted suicide has been receiving such strong public support that favorable laws have been proposed and on occasion enacted, while no jury has yet returned a guilty verdict for Jack Kevorkian.

LIVING IS ITS OWN REWARD

"You're alive! What more do you want?" This might be a rallying cry for those who do not feel obliged or stirred to seek meaning somewhere else. There is a faint resemblance here to the cherish the moment attitude previously explored. More crucial is the difference. Here one does not seek escape from the motion of time or the web of interpersonal relationships. This moment is connected firmly to past and future. One is whom one has become. Moreover, one is still becoming.

The key idea is that one has persisted through time and unique patterns of experiences and relationships. A meaning or value that is superimposed on these patterns is likely to seem superficial if not downright bogus. Wisdom is the art of persisting to persist, in our own patterns, our own lives. There may be episodes of immersion in the moment, resistance and assertion, or illuminating insights. We keep our focus, however, on the person who is continuing to live that one distinctive life within patterns established day by day over the years.

"I just keep on trucking," says one elderly widow. "My home is everything," says another. "I mean, everything is in my home in one way or another, what there was and what's left." Young women attending a university in Chile tended to project future elderly selves in which they move smoothly over the years within the framework of the family constellation. Aging is not seen as threat or discontinuity. "I will be somebody else's grandmother when my turn comes" as one respondent phrased it (Hoagland, 1998). Where society offers stability and coherence it might be the part of wisdom to continue to use all that one has learned and become. There is no terrifying gap to bridge between youth and age, value and disvalue.

The first two of these additional theories of meaning and value have been pretty much excluded from polite gerontological discourse. We think people should grow up, and we think people shouldn't kill themselves. There is more tolerance for the idea that people might find value in continuing to spin out their life patterns. Atchley's (1989) version of continuity theory makes a plausible case for this approach, but even Atchley (1993) is more enthusiastic about the concept of a deeper spiritual development with age.

Am I trying to get at something? Yes, sort of. Our theories of meaning, value, and spiritual development in the later adult years at present are an unanalyzed mix of facts, scholarly conjectures, and sociocultural bias. In addition to what has already been mentioned here, we tend to believe that the wise person will not fear death, a conclusion that has come before rather than after adequate empirical and conceptual investigation. As individuals we are all entitled to our views, but as gerontologists perhaps we should accept more responsibility for seeking the seekers of wisdom without imposing our own rules on them.

A PARTING WORD

Lucinda ("I don't mind having quiet, silence"): Thank you for sharing your sensible, mature, and open-minded quest for meaning. Wouldn't this be a better world to grow up and old in if more of us could say with you: "I don't mind having quiet, silence."

John Casteel: Thank you for reaching first into yourself and then out of yourself to communicate with others who might otherwise have been isolated and lost. There may yet be a publisher for your "too pessimistic" journal.

Gene Thomas: Thank you for inspiriting this book whose multiple perspectives and sense of adventure have removed all reasonable doubt about the wisdom of studying wisdom.

REFERENCES

Alvarez, A. (1972). *The savage God. A study of suicide.* New York: Random House.

Atchley, R. C. (1989). A continuity theory of normal aging. *Gerontologist, 29,* 183–190.

Atchley, R. C. (1993). Spiritual development and wisdom: A Vedantic perspective. In R. Kastenbaum (Ed.), *Encyclopedia of adult development* (pp. 479–482). Phoenix: Oryx Press.

Becker, E. (1962). *The birth and death of meaning.* New York: Free Press.

Cumming, E., & Henry, W. E. (1961). *Growing old: The process of disengagement.* New York: Basic Books.

Erikson, E. (1982). *The life cycle completed: A review.* New York: Norton.

Gutmann, D. (1987). *Reclaimed powers: Toward a new psychology of men and women in later life.* New York: Basic Books.

Hoagland, P. (1998). *A flower from the future: Future elderly selves, a Chilean sample.* Unpublished honors thesis, Department of Communication, Arizona State University.

Howe, I. (1994). *A critic's notebook.* New York: Harcourt Brace.

Kastenbaum, R. (1980). Habituation as a partial model of aging. *International Journal of Aging & Human Development, 13,* 159–170.

Kastenbaum, R. (1990). The age of saints and the saintliness of age. *International Journal of Aging & Human Development, 30,* 95–118.

Kastenbaum, R. (1994). Saints, sages, and sons of bitches. *Journal of Geriatric Psychiatry, 27,* 61–78.

Kastenbaum, R. (1995). *Dorian, graying. Is youth the only thing worth having?* New York: Baywood.

Myerhoff, B. (1978). *Number our days.* New York: Simon & Schuster.

Index